T0291371

Enterprise Risk Management in Today's World, Part A

EMERALD STUDIES IN FINANCE, INSURANCE, AND RISK MANAGEMENT

Series Editor: Simon Grima

Books in this series collect quantitative and qualitative studies in areas relating to finance, insurance, and risk management. Subjects of interest may include banking, accounting, auditing, compliance, sustainability, behaviour, management, and business economics.

In the disruption of political upheaval, new technologies, climate change, and new regulations, it is more important than ever to understand risk in the financial industry. Providing high-quality academic research, this book series provides a platform for authors to explore, analyse and discuss current and new financial models and theories, and engage with innovative research on an international scale.

Previously published:

Uncertainty and Challenges in Contemporary Economic Behaviour
Ercan Özen and Simon Grima

New Challenges for Future Sustainability and Wellbeing
Ercan Özen, Simon Grima and Rebecca Dalli Gonzi

Insurance and Risk Management for Disruptions in Social, Economic and Environmental Systems: Decision and Control Allocations within New Domains of Risk
Simon Grima, Ercan Özen and Rebecca Dalli Gonzi

Public Sector Leadership in Assessing and Addressing Risk
Peter C. Young, Simon Grima and Rebecca Dalli Gonzi

Big Data Analytics in the Insurance Market
Kiran Sood, B. Balamurugan, Simon Grima and Pierpaolo Marano

Big Data: A Game Changer for Insurance Industry
Kiran Sood, Rajesh Kumar Dhanaraj, B. Balamurugan, Simon Grima and R. Uma Maheshwari

The Adoption and Effect of Artificial Intelligence on Human Resources Management, Part A
Pallavi Tyagi, Naveen Chilamkurti, Simon Grima, Kiran Sood and B. Balamurugan

The Adoption and Effect of Artificial Intelligence on Human Resources Management, Part B
Pallavi Tyagi, Naveen Chilamkurti, Simon Grima, Kiran Sood and B. Balamurugan

Contemporary Studies of Risks in Emerging Technology, Part A
Simon Grima, Kiran Sood and Ercan Özen

Contemporary Studies of Risks in Emerging Technology, Part B
Simon Grima, Kiran Sood and Ercan Özen

The Framework for Resilient Industry: A Holistic Approach for Developing Economies
Narinder Kumar, Kiran Sood, Ercan Özen and Simon Grima

VUCA and Other Analytics in Business Resilience, Part A
Deepmala Singh, Kiran Sood, Sandeep Kautish and Simon Grima

VUCA and Other Analytics in Business Resilience, Part B
Deepmala Singh, Kiran Sood, Sandeep Kautish and Simon Grima

Finance Analytics in Business: Perspectives on Enhancing Efficiency and Accuracy
Sanjay Taneja, Pawan Kumar, Kiran Sood, Ercan Özen and Simon Grima

Enterprise Risk Management in Today's World: Enterprise-Wide Risk Management and Strategy, Part A

BY

JEAN-PAUL LOUISOT
JPLA Consultants LLC, France

EDITED BY

SIMON GRIMA
University of Malta, Malta

United Kingdom – North America – Japan – India – Malaysia – China

Emerald Publishing Limited
Emerald Publishing, Floor 5, Northspring, 21-23 Wellington Street, Leeds LS1 4DL.

First edition 2024

Copyright © 2024 Jean-Paul Louisot and Simon Grima.
Published under exclusive licence by Emerald Publishing Limited.

Reprints and permissions service
Contact: www.copyright.com

No part of this book may be reproduced, stored in a retrieval system, transmitted in any form or by any means electronic, mechanical, photocopying, recording or otherwise without either the prior written permission of the publisher or a licence permitting restricted copying issued in the UK by The Copyright Licensing Agency and in the USA by The Copyright Clearance Center. Any opinions expressed in the chapters are those of the authors. Whilst Emerald makes every effort to ensure the quality and accuracy of its content, Emerald makes no representation implied or otherwise, as to the chapters' suitability and application and disclaims any warranties, express or implied, to their use.

British Library Cataloguing in Publication Data
A catalogue record for this book is available from the British Library

ISBN: 978-1-83797-407-8 (Print)
ISBN: 978-1-83797-406-1 (Online)
ISBN: 978-1-83797-408-5 (Epub)

Epigraph

Whenever a theory appears to you as the only possible one, take this as a sign that you have neither understood the theory nor the problem which it was intended to solve.

The old scientific ideal of episteme – of absolutely certain, demonstrable knowledge – has proved to be an idol. The demand for scientific objectivity makes it inevitable that every scientific statement must remain tentative forever.

Karl Popper

You can't depend on your eyes when your imagination is out of focus.

Mark Twain

Our greatest glory is not in ever falling, but in rising every time we fall.

Confucius

The position and momentum of a particle cannot be simultaneously measured with arbitrarily high precision. There is a minimum for the product of the uncertainties of these two measurements. There is likewise a minimum for the product of the uncertainties of the energy and time.

Heisenberg, in *Uncertainty principle paper*, 1927

The world is changing. Networks without a specific branding strategy will be killed I envision a world of narrowly niche services and tightly run companies without room for all the overhead the established networks carry.

Barry Diller, press Tycoon

If a nation expects to be ignorant and free in a state of civilization, it expects what was and never will be. The people cannot be free without information.

Thomas Jefferson letter to Charles Yancy (1816)

Contents

List of Figures and Tables

Figures

Tables

About the Author

Prof Jean-Paul Louisot holds a PhD in Management Sciences (Université PARIS 1 Panthéon Sorbonne – 2014), a mining engineering degree, a Master in Economics, and an MBA from the Kellogg School of Management. Since 1993, he has been teaching and coaching postgraduate students and risk-management professionals. After 9 years at Paris 1 Panthéon-Sorbonne University, and 10 years in postgraduate courses in risk management at the Institut Catholique de Lille, he has participated in the development of the European designation, Rimap, promoted by FERMA.

About the Editor

Professor Simon Grima is the Deputy Dean of the Faculty of Economics, Management and Accountancy, Associate Professor, and the Head of the Department of Insurance and Risk Management. He is also a Professor at the University of Latvia, Faculty of Business, Management and Economics and a Visiting Professor at UNICATT Milan.

Preface: Context for Linking ERM and Strategy

The complexity of the business context, combined with the intricacy and interconnections of risk and objectives – necessitates the organisation implement a strategic approach to business and operational resilience. Indeed, there is a growing focus on resilience exacerbated by the pandemic and ensuing geopolitical upheavals. Resilience is the capacity to recover quickly from difficulties/ruptures; the ability of a business to spring back from any disturbance. This is quite critical and many organisations rightfully merge risk management and business continuity management into what is enterprise risk management (ERM), sometimes defined as a resilience programme.

Any academic studying risk management can only be surprised that at a time when the world is becoming more and more complex and volatile, most MBA programmes are still resting on old scientific principles: they remain founded on Democritus' description of the atom or at best Bohr's. To be specific, management principles are still anchored on classical physics that allows five-year planning exercises. If governments dropped this practice after the fall of the Soviet Union, how is it possible that so many firms are still indulging in it? Could it be that too many managers have failed to recognise that times are no longer such that a deterministic approach to the future is reasonable?

Traditional physics is founded on the principle that similar causes have similar consequences and proportional causes have proportional consequences. This was fundamentally challenged with advances of modern microphysics, which can be summarised in the uncertainty principle, also called the uncertainty relations, set out by Heisenberg. To some extent, it is this research that opened the path to chaos theory, which does not yet seem to have influenced strategic thinking in most organisations, even if some visionaries appear to be inspired by it, consciously or unconsciously.

Of course, the founders of Apple, Google, and other GAFA come to mind. However, there are also leaders of start-ups and small- and medium-sized enterprises (SMEs) that may be visionary in their own right like the founders of Air B&B, Uber, etc. SMEs are at the heart of jobs and value creation not only in developed countries but also in emerging countries.

To summarise, it seems reasonable to assess the strategic processes currently implemented in most organisations as too rigid and sequential; strategy rests still on the idea that the world's evolution is a series of stems that allows controllable processes. Resting on periodic reviews of their internal and external contexts, the leaders of these organisations operate without the continuous scouting of the future that would allow them to decipher low-level noises or sentinel events that facilitate an efficient forecast of future evolutions and anticipation of revolutions so that the organisation's relevance for its stakeholders' networks can be maintained at all times.

Major economic players, including nation states, have now the capacity to develop and implement models that are increasingly powerful and even include learning capabilities thanks to artificial intelligence (AI):

> Our systems learn by themselves from experience; however, we still choose their learning path. But we must always keep in mind that even the more complex games are more accessible to the computers than the general issues confronting the real world.[1]

However, even AI specialists remain cautious when it comes to replacing human brains with machines in complex decision-making. As for Werner Heisenberg, reading his principle makes it clear that he questioned the use of the normal distribution, thus opening the possibility of extreme situations, rupture, or black and grey swans. Risk management professionals prefer the concept of artificially enhanced intelligence.

About quantum physics, Heisenberg stipulated that as the exact position of a particle cannot be known at a given point in time, the future cannot be determined. A specific trajectory does not lend itself to a precise computation, but only a range of possible trajectories can be determined (however, using Erwin Schrödinger's equation, it is possible to assign a probability to each trajectory).

Economists have yet to produce an equivalent of Schrödinger's equation, as the economic world cannot be described with a simple list of drivers. It is complex and necessitates factoring in the human dimension, so interactions are volatile and will need to be approached with fuzzy logic integrations. Would it be reasonable to expect forecasting the future with precision, when even the present eludes the human brain?

For risk management professionals, the good news is that uncertainty and risk must be more and more at the centre of all decision-making, strategic, tactical, or operational; that does not result in the world of decision-making belonging to risk-managers. However, all professionals have understood that the issue of risk has become essential in any decision-making, and they are ready to occupy the field should the existing risk-management professionals not step up to the plate. Competition for the attention of the board for risk issues is open with:

- internal and external auditors with their three lines of defence,
- quality control managers *(whose legitimacy in tackling risk is reinforced by the ISO 9000:2015 which includes a chapter on risks)*,
- security and safety specialists, economic intelligence consultants, and
- continuity managers *(another member of the risk professional community)*!

[1]Denis Hassais, founder of DeepMind.

And the list is still open with resilience management as the newest entry. There is a growing list of risk management in specialised branches, but they can be gathered under one roof as they have common goals and use the same tools. With the proliferation of ISO standards dealing with specific risks, the erection of new silos can be feared.

There is no doubt that risk management has a bright future, especially after the pandemic and the geopolitical unrest, even if it might be shared by many, indeed by all practitioners. As far as the risk manager's function in any organisation is concerned, even adorned with the title of chief risk officer (CRO), a function that is still developing after over two decades of existence while the Chief Information Officer (CIO) is now widespread and involved in cyber-risk management, it will survive in this maelstrom only if the incumbents can acquire the talents and competencies needed to grasp what is at stake and manoeuvre to make it to the front of the pack!

The management of risk is a director's and officer's mission; there is not much debate about it now that the codes of governance worldwide tend to assign them direct responsibility and liability to develop and guide their organisations' policies with a clear understanding of and due consideration to the uncertainties and storms of the future. However, without proper gears and relays at all levels in the organisation and with its main partners, the extended enterprise, even the best-defined policy would have little effect on the well-being of the organisation or society at large.

Managing risk is a core mission for all public and private actors. The survival of all depends on the vigilance of each one. This has a special echo for those individuals who have been trained for special forces or intervention units and those dealing with terrorist attacks!

Furthermore, the generalised explosion of social media, now a key player in all social debates, means that transparency in communication and consultation with key stakeholders has become essential; however, it may interfere with speedy decisions required at the early stages of a rupture when a dramatic strategic change may be called for.

Whatever the situation, any new strategy has a reasonable chance of success only if all those involved embrace the change, not only within the organisation but also beyond, i.e., both internal and external stakeholders. This is the reason why a continuous strategic process must be developed and implemented, provided it is informed by global and integrated risk management and positioned in a change management effort where all can be heard and listened to.

In such a context, the question of democracy in the company, which was at the heart of the debates at the end of the 1960s during the students' upheavals, seems to gain new momentum. However, it is unlikely that there will be a 'one size fits all' route to democracy. Sometimes, it will surge from the base; others, it will result from the will of top management, but success will require both to meet on a common course.

When it comes to change, top management must do it, but all those involved must then embrace it. There is no unique strategy to develop and implement the instruments and processes of resilience, and this is indeed the case for the guidelines proposed in the ISO 31000 standard: it is a toolbox where each artisan must find the most efficient way to use them in each organisation.

In a world evermore complex and volatile, it is not reasonable to build models on deterministic approaches or one man's vision; therefore, ERM becomes a key as it offers an approach in which uncertainty is at the centre of any decision. Furthermore, ERM top-bottom and bottom-up paths ensure that all adhere to permanent change, whereas change is what destabilises human beings in any society, as well as any organisation.

As far as democracy and equality are concerned, nobody (except for a few admirers of Proudhon) wants to stray from capitalism, but many want to see a return to the reduced levels of inequality that prevailed before the late eighties.[2]

Readers looking for simple solutions or checklists will be disappointed. The present book is not a cookbook with recipes but rather a book of questions, on all the challenges that any entrepreneur, director, officer, or elected official must meet if (s)he is to promote resilience and justice for the future in a very uncertain context and to navigate safely through the high seas ahead. ERM does not set aside hazards but aims to optimise risk-taking: enhancing opportunities and curbing threats. ERM is therefore in essence at the core of any strategic exercise.

If climate change is not heavily mentioned, it is because there are already many books offering experts' thoughts on the matter, from the likely causes to the prevention and protection measures that could be implemented, not to mention the Intergovernmental panel on climate change (IPCC) reports.

Furthermore, most of these solutions are beyond the domain of decision and strategy of individual actors, even if individual efforts should not be undervalued. There is also the nagging issue of artificial intelligence, already mentioned. Organisation for Economic Co-operation and Development (OECD) expects AI will become a major threat to humankind within 20 years, but investigations into this scenario seem still at an early stage despite recent developments like chat-GPT. However, all organisations must consider these risks in their strategic process at the horizon of 2030/2050. As with other emerging risks, AI and climate change are sources of threats, but they also offer many opportunities for innovators, including transition risk.

[2]Atkinson, A. B. (2015, May). *Unequality – What can be done?* Harvard University Press. See review. http://www.hup.harvard.edu/catalog.php?isbn=9780674504769&content=reviews

Introduction: Risk-Management in a Pandemic and Post-Pandemic World

> Some risks that we believe are unknown are not. With a bit of foresight and critical thinking, some risks that at first glance may seem unexpected, may in fact be foreseen. Armed with the right set of tools, procedures, and knowledge, we can shed light on the variables that lead to risk, allowing us to manage them. (Daniel Wagner)[1]

Originally written in 2018, this book was revised in the spring of 2023 to be relevant to the 'new reality' generated by the COVID-19 crisis that spilled all over the world followed by the war in Ukraine and the ensuing Economic turmoil. In terms of world governance and strategy, the COVID-19 crisis that developed during the years 2020 and 2021 was an illustration of the very limited anticipation capacity in the international community.

Of course, it is tempting to rewind history to the time when the mad cow disease took the world by surprise; at the time, George-Yves Kevern[2] analysed the crisis using the hyper-space of danger and predicted that one day the world would be confronted with a catastrophic pandemic originating in bush food. However, if the truth must be told, despite his contributions to the World Health Organization (WHO) seminars, his readership was limited to a circle of specialists and followers.

If the truth must be told, even for the organisations that had included pandemics in their risk register, little attention was given to preventing and preparing for a catastrophic event as none had foreseen the velocity and the extent of the event. Speaking about the EBOLA outbreak in Africa in 2014, during a conference still available on YouTube, Bill Gates concluded: 'We were lucky this time'.[3]

---

[1]Director of SIRH D. Wagner & Partner.

[2]See 'The Science of Danger' by George-Yves Kervern, https://www.questia.com/magazine/1G1-16902905/cindynics-the-science-of-danger, and Georges-Yves Kervern, *Éléments fondamentaux des cindyniques*, Economica, Paris, 1995 (ISBN 2-7178-2756-0) (notice BnF n° FRBNF36682872).

[3]Bill Gates: Ebola is an ongoing tragedy. https://www.youtube.com/watch?v=ipE3OIi8j8o

---

Enterprise Risk Management in Today's World, Part A:
Enterprise-Wide Risk Management and Strategy, 1–7
Copyright © 2024 by Jean-Paul Louisot and Simon Grima
Published under exclusive licence by Emerald Publishing Limited
doi:10.1108/978-1-83797-406-120241001

In the course of this conference, Bill Gates predicted that if the world was not readying for it, the disease could cause millions of deaths and result in a catastrophic economic impact. If a new disease could 'spread by air, reaching people who would only experience the first symptoms with delay and still be able to travel by train and air'.

Without rolling back to the last century and the mad cow disease, a NIC[4] report published in 2009[5] on the projected state of the world in 2025 states that: 'If a pandemic occurs, it will occur in a densely populated area, close to humans and animals, as is the case in some markets in China or Southeast Asia, where people live close to livestock'. The only missing element is that the market would be in Wuhan. But NIC experts stated that they envision the emergence of a 'new virulent and highly contagious human respiratory disease'.

The initial daily management of COVID-19, and again for the following waves worldwide, was evidence of the shortfalls of the current world governance: it is not appropriate to react efficiently to such outbursts. Whereas trade globalisation is continuing at an accelerated pace, political fragmentation and local conflicts have prevailed on the international scene. The cold war that was brewing behind the scenes now shows its true face under the raw light of COVID-19 and was further exacerbated by the war in Ukraine. In my opinion, in such a context:

- The mission of the current and future US administrations will be to reinvest in international institutions and to reconnect with America's natural position as a leader in global governance;
- The European Union (EU) will have to be at the forefront of the revitalisation of global governance, as President Macron has attempted in his efforts to revive the G7 and the G20 to deal with the economic and other consequences of the pandemic and more recently trying to promote a specific European voice in the world. The EU must also try to convince the Americans to adopt the geostrategic 'new paradigm' based on transparency and sustainable and equitable development. Hopefully, this might be a by-product of the current geopolitical turmoil.

The combination of these efforts would also offer the possibility of rebuilding the transatlantic relationship while involving countries such as South Korea or Japan, which are part of the 'alliance for multilateralism', led in Europe by Germany and France, and contain China's expansion.

In the United Kingdom, it is clearer after the pandemic that the National Health System (NHS) must still be reengineered from top to bottom and not only in terms of healthcare. Jurgen Klopp, manager of the FC Liverpool, when questioned about the COVID-19 and containment noted: 'If it is a choice between

[4]National Intelligence Council.

[5]Global trends 2025: A transformed world. https://www.files.ethz.ch/isn/94769/2008_11_Global_Trends_2025.pdf

football and the good of society in general, it is not a contest. It is not the case'.[6] The same issues will also have to be reviewed in most EU countries, and some governments have already entered into discussions with stakeholders. In France, could the format of the citizens' convention used to tackle climate change be considered to meet other societal challenges?

In the ISO31000:2018 standard,[7] risk is defined as 'the effect of uncertainty on objectives'. In principle, organisations develop efforts to identify the risks they are confronted with and then analyse and prioritise them. However, the reality has become even more complex with the current COVID pandemic, so risks can no more be approached individually or in nicely labelled silos. Silos do not take into account increasing interdependencies of risks.

Domino Effect

When a risk materialises with the occurrence of an event, more and more often, the organisation endures a domino effect. This means that what starts with only one domino soon cataracts on many other dominos and many other risks. Upon analysis, the recent COVID-19 crisis has started as a health and safety issue in Asia. However, it soon cascaded into a worldwide pandemic, generating additional risks to the economy of many countries. It is therefore not possible anymore to isolate the initial cause, the root cause, from the resulting maze of interconnected risks and objectives.

A Global Impact

The initial health and safety risks in a Chinese province have now expanded into a global issue, and the following factors must be taken into account:

- **Risks on objectives**: With the development of the pandemic, organisations were impacted specifically on their operational objectives. To respond to the situation, they had to revise their objectives. Entities, divisions, departments, processes, projects, and assets: objectives at all levels had to be reassessed taking in the new level of uncertainty generated by the pandemic impacting both old and new objectives. This is the result of the economic and operational impacts of the coronavirus.
- **Risks on operational resilience and continuity**: In the COVID-19 context, organisations are under additional stress and increased exposure in all their processes, from supply to delivery, including production. In many organisations, continuity of operations efforts had been directed only towards information systems, and post-pandemic operations reboot had not even been considered, let alone prepared. Continuity planning in case of a computer virus attack

[6] *Jürgen Klopp's message to supporters*. (n.d.). Liverpool FC. https://www.liverpoolfc.com/news/first-team/390397-jurgen-klopp-message-to-supporters
[7] *ISO 31000:2018*. (n.d.). ISO. https://www.iso.org/standard/65694.html

does not apply when an entire population is contained. Confronted with the loss of personnel, process modifications, and a focus on telecommuting from home, organisations tried to cope while being faced with increased exposure and uncertainty.

- **Cyber-risk:** The extensive use of telecommuting made necessary by confinement has an important impact on computer system safety as the home context is generally less secure than the workplace is. The issues concerning the Internet, the provider, and television programmes in the employees' domicile create many weak points for the safety of the organisation's data and its connections. Furthermore, hackers and organised crime realised that the crisis was providing them an opportunity to infiltrate organisations and steal their data.
- **Third-party risks:** In the case of extended enterprise architecture, which is becoming more common nowadays, half of the staff is not made of traditional salaried persons. Buildings and employees are not enough to define an organisation. Organisations have become a complex network of relationships including suppliers, sub-contractors, salespersons, service providers, brokers, agents, and dealers, not to mention intermediaries. Some situations have been particularly dire with sub-contractors and service providers forced to close down following containment and unable to deliver the promised goods and services. Supply networks have experienced ruptures and cases where deliveries were no longer feasible.
- **Risks to organisation culture and control:** Quick process changes necessary to react to the pandemic have left many organisations without proper control systems. With reduced teams, staffs wear several hats, and that creates an increased risk of segregation of duties conflicts. Employees' attention may be diverted by their worries about the global economy, their own safety and security, and that of their loved ones. Contrary to what some may think, working from home rather than in their offices tends to increase the feeling of insecurity for many.
- **Fraud risks:** At a time when economic uncertainty is exploding with a looming recession, staff is under even more pressure to make ends meet. Employees who were above any suspicion, which did not even conceive of stealing or committing fraud under normal circumstances, might start down a slippery slope due to their economic distress and the uncertainties they are confronted with.
- **Corruption risks:** Procurement networks are stressed and organisations are pressured to reach their objectives; these two factors combine to increase the risk of corruption, passive and active. In addition, customs and import/export services tend to operate at a slower pace in many countries and that could induce some operators to offer bribes in exchange for accelerated customs clearance. It could also be the case for obtaining specific contracts or permits while public administrations are nearly at a standstill.
- **Modern slavery and human rights risks:** Human rights seem to be somewhat flouted in several parts of the world currently. This was already true before the pandemic, but it seems that the situation is exploding now. However, the issue is not limited to civil rights and the treatment of specific groups by authority holders; it is also an open wound in production sites and procurement networks. The COVID-19 has hit particularly hard in some parts of the world.

Factories have lost workers, some are contaminated, and some are even dead. As a result, more children have been put to work, there is an increase in forced labour, and working conditions are deteriorating.

- **Harassment and discrimination risks:** Social unrest has increased even before the pandemic, but with the second wave in Europe, it seems that populations are losing faith in their government and do not see an end to the COVID-19 tunnel. Beyond protestations and fuelling violent actions, the pandemic seems to have exacerbated discrimination and even anger against some ethnic groups especially where even heads of state insist on the 'Chinese origin' of the coronavirus, not only Chinese are targeted but all Asians ....

Men and women working from their homes, not under the usual conditions of an office, have difficulties adapting to their new 'work' environment and giving their attention to the work, especially when children are calling for attention in cramped housing. Interactions through e-mails, text messages, and video conferences tend to become more and more relaxed; some have let down their guard and risk statements that fall into sexual harassment.

And the risk list could be extended to private life risks: compliance issues, with the difficulty of maintaining compliance with all health, safety, and security rules and regulations in the midst of constant changes in operational processes, etc.

However, beyond a better understanding of each risk, it is essential to take into account risk interconnections. Organisations must develop a comprehensive exposure diagnostic taking into account these interactions. One of the risk-management tools available is developing scenarios and brainstorming exercises so that they can envision potential risk development, how another risk can be triggered in a given situation, and what are the potential impacts on objectives.

The COVID-19 pandemic has brought new light on how risks are interconnected in ways that can exacerbate the overall impact, and the geopolitical upheaval that occurred while the world was slowly recovering from the pandemic put an additional accent on the dire reality that managing risk requires a global approach, no risk can be managed alone.

The risk and insurance management community is an important partner both inside organisations and externally to building resilience; risk management professionals have developed a framework that can be incredibly useful when it comes to managing sustainability and related risks. It is clearer and clearer that a robust insurance/reinsurance industry is an essential component of a resilient society.

> Men who take great risks must expect to often bear the heavy consequences. (Nelson Mandela)

Furthermore, the enterprise risk management (ERM) framework provides a paradigm of effective governance and methodologies that may incorporate sustainability into pre-existing processes.

Risk managers have long acknowledged the significance of 'sustainability' and have dedicated several years to addressing this issue, particularly in the realms of responsible corporate practices, climate change, and Environmental, Social, and

Governance (ESG) risks. Risk managers serve as risk coordinators or facilitators within an organisation, gathering information from other risk-related roles to provide a concise and complete perspective to top-level management. The past pandemics such as Severe Acute Respiratory Syndrome (SARS) and Middle East Respiratory Syndrome (MERS) did not affect Europe, so it was not a shock to see that most people were so surprised there. Rigorous governmental lockdowns and lack of mobility were actually a surprise for most as well, as they spread around the globe.

To limit the impact of a disaster and enhance post-crisis recovery, safety, and risk, specialists have designed strategies to strengthen societies' resistance when confronted with hazards. Thanks to increasingly complex and sophisticated modelling probability intervals for the hazard, force and consequential impacts can be evaluated and models gain in precision, thus reducing the level of uncertainty. Armed with this new information, specialists cooperate with leaders, in public and private organisations, to ensure that proper defence tools are put in place to protect society to the best of their understanding.

In the case of flooding, for example, it induced the erection of embankments along rivers, and dams upstream of large cities to monitor high waters, and additionally produce electricity. Furthermore, short of limiting the frequency or force of natural perils, similar strategies have been developed to limit the impacts of earthquakes, volcanic activity, cyclones, tsunamis, etc.

However, the efficiency of such strategies is limited by the fact that it is still difficult to predict where and when the hazard will strike, even when considering the path of past hurricanes. It is exceptional to be able to predict with precision the contact point of any hazard, so many factors are intertwined that it is impossible to have precise forecasts, and therefore, it is a challenge to determine a proper location and scale for protection works. In such situations, to simplify those when no probability law can be assigned, it is necessary to consider new strategies based on the concept of resilience. These strategies do not try only to prevent hazards or reduce impact but prepare to deal with disturbances as they occur to mitigate their consequences and facilitate the organisation's rebound.

Successful countries during the last pandemic like Hong Kong, Taiwan, and South Korea have implemented proper training, capabilities, and capacity to react swiftly, and thus they proved agile in the crisis. Setting priorities is essential, but it is difficult because only so many hospitals can be up and running as they are expensive. Major Asian countries have been living examples for countries of Europe and North America. And from such examples, developed countries could have learned sanitary crisis management. Robust preparation can help avoid dire economic and social measures such as travel restrictions or lockdowns.

If COVID-19 and the pandemic have been the number one risk for everyone for nearly three years, nevertheless, leaders should not forget about the other big risks such as cyber, climate change, supply chain, people and reputation, and even war! The pandemic, the War in Ukraine, and above all growing draught in all parts of the world leading to a global water crisis, will hopefully make it more urgent for all to tackle climate change, the surge of natural catastrophes, geopolitical tensions, and the like. There is definitely a stronger opportunity for risk managers to enter the boardroom if they are not yet invited. The rapid change in the style of working, with widespread home working, has presented a serious information technology (IT) security risk. This is not an overnight project and will promote new ways of working and continuing business.

This evolution will require a big investment in technology and cyber-risk management. Understanding and predicting human behaviour is a major challenge in creating effective cyber and pandemic risk models, and there is a need for creative, but reality-based, imagination to represent forward-looking risk is critical.

One of the main lessons learned from this crisis, and ensuing insurance market restrictions, is that it is primarily up to organisations to develop their risk financing capabilities through retention including captives or provisions, as commercial insurance is less and less relevant to the critical risks that organisations face. Continuing with the sole logic, 'extract, produce, throw away' would lead humanity straight into the wall. In reality, COVID-19 offers an opportunity to launch a new economic model, more robust and more resilient. Circular economy, solace in a gloomy context, may also prove to be the light at the end of the tunnel.

Finally, reframing the current pandemics with the warnings of the past decade, COVID-19 proved more revealing existing endemic problems than generating new ones: Emerging risks are more the exacerbation of existing risks, and COVID-19 is a game changer by revealing interconnections. In a post-pandemic world, nothing could be the same.

Hope is essential, but public vigilance is needed to tackle the many issues ahead to forge a new future. Whatever the 'new normal', circular economy or not, leaders at all levels, individual, organisational, and societal, will have to establish an intimately interwoven strategy and risk-management process to help lift the fog on the future and promote better-informed decisions. Precisely, this book aims to assist leaders in developing robust ERM programmes to strengthen the strategic process and enhance organisations and social resilience.

> If, as a concept, resilience must be based on objective scientific criteria to be highlighted, as a socio-cultural phenomenon, it may be the object of ideologies or fantasies, or policies that attempt to regulate or control the perception of each other in the face of adversity.[8]

[8]See Quelle résilience pour quels modèles de société? *The Conversation.* https://theconversation.com/quelle-resilience-pour-quels-modeles-de-societe-137666

Chapter 1

Risk Management and Uncertainty

Economic leaders who see the world as turbulent, unpredictable, and threatening, and develop a fortress mentality to cope with it, could be tempted to choose isolation strategies, for example, reinforcing control on the internal context of the organisation, thus hoping to limit the impact of external shocks. This implies the implementation of a more rigid discipline, a refocusing on 'core activities', entailing cost-cutting and limitation of 'waste', i.e. lean management. Unfortunately, these strategies tend not to produce the expected results, and revenues decline faster than costs, pulling the organisation into a downward spiral.

In management literature, uncertainties are often seen as limitations in planning and modelling; a Chinese proverb even states: 'Our efforts to uncover the future leave the Gods laughing'. Niels Bohr, already mentioned in the foreword, is known to have said that forecasting was a very difficult exercise, especially when about the future. Nobody needs to be a philosopher, a scientist, or a business leader to understand that, although difficult, planning is essential. Nevertheless, the expected outcomes can never be taken for granted. In the context of personal affairs, planning may relate to a career, an election, the purchase of a home, or even the choice of a lifetime partner. Despite all the efforts put into the project, results may prove disappointing.

Strategic planning has never been easy, but it is becoming more challenging when complexity and volatility, i.e. risk, seem to be increasing exponentially, since the beginning of this century.

There are two main drivers for this evolution of the risk landscape: speed and interconnectedness; they interact to increase the overall level of contextual change. The high-technology environment in which economic, social, and political actors operate produces a real whirlwind of change in which those that do not understand the value of anticipation and timely responses could soon be ousted from their traditional markets, not only by competitors, who are known quantities, but also by substitutes. These are actors popping up with totally innovative solutions to answer the stakeholders' new expectations. In such a situation, any organisation could not only lose market shares but find itself driven out. Furthermore, global interconnectedness means that a trend towards change appearing anywhere on the globe is soon shared by all markets, thus outdating some

Enterprise Risk Management in Today's World, Part A:
Enterprise-Wide Risk Management and Strategy, 9–22
Copyright © 2024 by Jean-Paul Louisot and Simon Grima
Published under exclusive licence by Emerald Publishing Limited
doi:10.1108/978-1-83797-406-120241002

actors, and expelling them even from their traditional strongholds. Under such conditions, no actor should rest assured of his future.

Faced with the constant turmoil and evolution of the environment in which they operate, organisations, public and private, are forced to make significant investments to contain the threats and/or to capitalise on the opportunities they are confronted with. Research demonstrates that these investments are mostly defensive, devoted to compliance, legal and regulatory, or fiduciary responsibility, rather than offensive, geared towards fulfilling[1] the organisation's mission and reaching its strategic objectives. On the contrary, only a proactive approach to risk, both threats and opportunities, will open the way to optimal performance. To this end, each actor should:

- Develop and implement throughout the organisation and its network of major partners a consistent risk-management policy;
- Communicate with all internal and external stakeholders and put in place the control mechanisms to ensure that the policy is effectively implemented;
- Establish diagnostic procedures (identification, analysis, and evaluation) for all its exposures and contain them through a systematic and proactive approach;
- Define metrics to measure policy results and set objectives to monitor and track results, curb threats, and enhance opportunities, thus creating value;
- Integrate strategic planning, *management* of risk, and change management so that at all times, the organisation maintains optimal performance through efficient strategy and ever-adapting implementation.

Enterprise-wide risk management (ERM) brings numerous benefits beyond those of the traditional risk management (TRM). At any point in time, it would be possible to confront and compare TRM and ERM using different perspectives; however, whereas it is simple to identify TRM centred on accidental risks and insurance buying, ERM continues to evolve into an ever more strategic tool, while the missions of a risk-management professional are still a work in progress. Some organisations have been engaged in ERM programmes for some time, especially in the financial sectors, and they have chosen to stress the evolution of this function by renaming the risk manager and giving them a new title; chief risk officer (CRO) signals the entrance of risk management into the C-suite. In this book, the acronym 'CRO' will be used to qualify the head of risk management in an organisation, and risk-management professionals will refer to the members of the risk-management team, both at headquarters and in operational units.

The ERM approach is essential for the organisation to fulfil its mission and to enhance its overall performance; ERM offers a framework to integrate risk, both threats and opportunities, as early as possible into the development of a fluid strategy; a systematic proactive risk-management effort means anticipating and taking

---

[1] An organisation's mission is its 'raison d'être', the object of its existence. Therefore, the 'mission statement' must be reviewed periodically to reflect the evolution in its context and validate its relevance in meeting its partners' and other stakeholders' expectations.

into account contextual developments that allow the organisation to improve its long-term resilience through a continuous validation of the relevance of its mission for its main stakeholders. Indeed, ERM rests on a global and integrated management of the uncertainties that an organisation is confronted with to leverage them to ensure that they benefit the organisation's strategic goals and objectives.

Curbing threats and enhancing opportunities, while taking a portfolio approach making the best of covariance and correlation between sources of uncertainties, is what will allow the organisation to reach the optimal performance for a given level of risk. At the end of the day, ERM not only preserves value, but creates value, for the investors, of course, but also for society through the optimisation of risk-taking.

The traditional approach to risk management was limited to the downside of risk, the threats, and essentially operational risks with a silo approach aligned with insurance lines. In an ERM programme, the organisation also manages speculative risks in an integrated framework that allows it to navigate the best route among uncertainties thanks to enlightened decision-makers at all levels, strategic, tactical, and operational; they rely on timely information to monitor and anticipate stakeholders' expectations. Communication and consultation with major stakeholders must be maintained at all levels and are enhanced by top-down and bottom-up data harvested at the closest possible level and processed through a business analytics system that delivers relevant information to decision-makers.

1.1. Survey of the Literature on Managing Uncertainty

The fundamental question academics and practitioners are trying to answer is how to develop a sound strategy in a highly volatile business environment.

Some executives seek to shape the future with high-stakes bets; some would even call them a wager. More risk-averse executives hedge their bets by embarking on a portfolio of smaller investments. Also, some executives choose flexibility that allows the company to adapt quickly to a changing environment. However, agility comes at a price and may seem to hurt day-to-day efficiency.

Finally taking a back-seat strategy, waiting for the future to unfold, or gathering more information may prove extremely costly as competitors or substitutes may rush into the window of opportunity thus offered to them.

Uncertainty/volatility is the currently prevailing rule and is probably there to remain for the foreseeable future, thus executives are confronted with a three-way decision: betting big, hedging, or waiting to see. In such an environment, the traditional strategic-planning processes cannot provide much insight. This traditional approach rests on the analysis of the future with enough precision to quantify future cash flows paving the way to discounted cash flow (DCF) analysis.

In such a case, a post-optimal analysis would allow one to play around with key variables while maintaining the objective of developing a strategy based on the 'most likely scenario'. But using central tendencies to make decisions can prove dangerous when the dispersion of the probability distribution is such that huge variations from the 'expected' are 'uncomfortably possible'.

In the present volatile world, traditional strategic-planning models developed for much more stable conditions can prove extremely dangerous.

The first pitfall is that traditional models might bring executives to a black-and-white vision of the future, either the world is « certain » and lends itself to modelling based on precise predictions, or unpredictable in the sense of the 'unknown-unknowns', i.e. no planning is possible. In such an organisation's culture, managers may choose to bury their heads in the sand and underestimate uncertainty to justify their strategies. However, uncertainty/risk is fundamentally neutral; systematically underestimating uncertainty may lead both to failure to curb threats or to enhance opportunities.

Risk-averse managers may take refuge in not making critical strategic decisions, settling with lean management solutions entailing reengineering, quality management, and cost-cutting programmes. Even if these can prove useful, they do not guarantee long-term resilience, which requires remaining relevant to critical stakeholders, meeting their future expectations, and catering to their needs.

Making strategic decisions in volatile situations requires new approaches based on concerted efforts to develop a range of possible scenarios with the help of open brainstorming sessions including critical internal as well as external stakeholders. Top management must develop a long-term vision and forge the future rather than experience it.

1.2. Managing Uncertainty Through a Continuous Strategic Process

The section title is borrowed from a lecture delivered by Dr Kathy Pearson to an audience of graduate students of the *Executive Master's in Technology Management* of the University of Pennsylvania, cosponsored by the Wharton School and Penn School of Engineering. The full title of the conference was: 'Managing Uncertainty Through a Strategic Approach While Disciplining the Thinking Process in a Complex and Volatile Environment'. This is interesting coming from a quantitative academic, as it illustrates the speaker's view of the limits of an all-out quantitative approach.

Moreover, Dr Pearson, who manages a consulting firm, coaching and teaching seminars for executives in all branches, has specialised in healthcare organisations. In that capacity, she was invited to provide advice for strategic decisions including the Royal Bank of Scotland, which came to her after it was engulfed in a governance issue in the United Kingdom.[2]

Dr Pearson did not mince her words when she illustrated what caused the financial crisis that started in 2008. Her core message was: 'To rely on mathematical models, is not reliable'. However, she also reminded the audience that those who developed the models stressed that they were valid only under strict conditions, and that practitioners never bothered to verify as long as the models seemed to bring in record returns. Forgetting the models' limits and constraints was all the

[2]See article on the Walker's report in the United Kingdom – *Harvard Business Review*, No. 155, 18 December 2009.

easier for the decision-makers to forget that their compensation packages, which were directly linked to their short-term results, were increasing exponentially!

In her practice as a consultant, she often meets business leaders who complain that making decisions is more difficult now than at the end of the 20th century. Likely that most of them can hardly compare as they were not in a position to make strategic decisions two decades ago, unless in the context of their MBA classes. But to find adequate solutions, it is essential to understand the root causes of the present situation, be it reality or perception. Short of a Decalogue, here are the nine principal causes identified:

1. **Rising uncertainty and complexity**: This situation combined with insufficient relevant data makes it difficult to develop reliable mathematical models that would decide for us. This contradicts the Organisation for Economic Co-operation and Development's (OECD's) fear that artificial intelligence may lead to the end of humanity. On the other hand, it is aligned with what Bertrand Robert calls the 'rise of the absurd' and the occurrence of rupture in a chaotic system.
2. **Overflow of information**: In contradiction to what is stated in the preceding comment, leaders are overburdened with information, but not all of it is relevant. The key to success is to find ways to sort out what is relevant and unbiased. This is illustrated in a comment by General Powell, former chair of the Joint Chief of Staff of the US Armed Forces and Secretary of State of the United States. An 'informed decision' can be made only if at least 40% of available information is gathered; on the other hand, if the commander waits for 70% before deciding, the field is paralysed and victory is offered to the enemy.
3. **Acceleration of technological breakthrough**: Most actors immediately think that this relates to computer and information systems, but its acceleration encompasses many other fields like nanotechnology and biotechnology, to name but the most visible.
4. **Exhaustion or depletion of resources**: Beyond the fossil fuels that have been at the centre of most recent controversies and economic wars, at the macroeconomic level, other 'natural' resources are scarce: many minerals that are needed in new technologies for example. However, when looking at the horizon for 2040–2050, not only will developed countries still have the problem of human resources due to low birth rates, but China will be held back by the consequences of the many years of the 'one-child policy', thus giving India an edge. At the microeconomic level, the leaders of organisations engaged in activities calling for the use of sensitive raw materials complain they have to do more with less to smooth out their quarterly results, even when oil prices remain low.
5. **Conflicting objectives**: As is evidenced by the explosion of social media 'scandals', companies have to take into account the expectations of a growing number of 'key' stakeholders if they hope to protect the major asset that the trust and confidence of the public and private actors in their markets constitute, i.e. their reputation. Therefore, decision-makers have to arbitrate

between conflicting expectations, and these are often painful and require tactful communication.

6. **Lack of precedents**: As mentioned earlier, as the world is going through a maelstrom of developments, it is often impossible to refer to past situations to assess what the future may hold; feedback from prior experience can be used with utmost caution. Therefore, it would be better to develop a model to develop 'experience anticipation'. Of course, many use creative approaches, like scenario development. However, these are still biased by the team members' experience, only the hyperspace of dangers, proposed within the cindynic approach allows the anticipation of rupture situations long before they develop, thus facilitating the posting of sentinels to allow their timely de-escalation.
7. **Higher stakes**: 'Winner takes all' tends to be the new norm: no place to be second, even if they 'try harder'. The main consequence is that there is no room for errors of judgement; you must be right the first time; the price to pay is too steep, and there may never be a second chance.
8. **Globalisation**: The major issue resulting from globalisation for economic actors is that they are but a knot in a complex web of relations that do not lend themselves to tight management, hence the rise of interest for procurement and logistic risk management. Furthermore, the reality is far from a 'procurement chain', as in a linear dependency where upstream and downstream partners are identified and contracted with. The network may even prove to be a cloud, at the borders of which the actors cannot even be visualised. The interdependencies of an organisation can no more be apprehended in their entirety, as the consequences of the 2011 Tsunami in Japan were made all too clear.
9. **Accelerated leaders' turnover**: Most leaders seem to be on a merry-go-round except for the two years following the financial crisis and a pause during the COVID-19 pandemic; then most top managers remained on their mission as reason and ethics requested. Since the beginning of the century, the turnover rate at all organisational levels has dramatically risen, especially in emerging countries like China. The move is particularly significant among executives, a fact which causes issues with strategic consistency and sourcing needed competencies. This induces one to short-term vision rather than long-term performance.

However, the causes for the downfall of companies listed above are not new, and companies go through a life cycle. But it is worthwhile trying to understand the fundamental causes behind leading companies' disappearance from the landscape. Some of the reasons that have been corroborated by a recent study conducted at the Cass School of Management are the following:

- Disproportionate arrogance and conceit;
- Insufficient attention to weak signals;
- Lack of vision and/or risk-taking;
- Entrapment in past/outdated *business models*;
- Discontinuous strategic decision process (batch process);
- Being mired in the short term and getting cold feet when it comes to risks.

For readers, already familiar with the cindynic approach, this list is closely aligned with the 10 empirical systemic cindynic deficits (SCD) identified by Georges-Yves Kervern[3] thanks to the concept of hyperspace of danger he developed in the early 1990s. It is probably significant that his long career in historical French companies (which have since disappeared), at a level where he could observe first-hand the decision-makers at work, provided the elements that fed this conceptual development.

However, many academics at the time took exception to the concept of resilience, probably due to specific reference to the metallurgical understanding of the term, i.e. returning to an initial state; the concept of entropy would be better applied to a system in constant evolution; therefore, there is no turning back, and resilience would mean a withdrawal, an inward looking that could prove fateful. In the fields of sociology and psychology, resilience has come to define the capacity to survive and thrive through dire conditions, even chaos. Without entering into a discussion with the proponents of the 'Green Philosophy'[4] that fights the idea, when applied to an organisation, the concept of resilience has come to signify a continuous adaptation to a complex and evolving environment.

Therefore, an organisation must reinvent itself at all times to remain relevant to stakeholders' expectations, as EXXON and IBM have learned to do. Resilience is not inward-looking, on the contrary, it requires the development of a positive answer to the stress brought about by the developments, and even more so, by the ruptures that the internal and external contexts of the organisation have been experiencing since the beginning of the century.

At the same time, another debate is opened, which is still a field of research, if not an issue for practitioners: what are the areas of convergence and divergence between the expectations (of stakeholders), trends (in the environment), and uncertainties (real or perceived). As a mathematician addressing a mostly philistine audience did she mean to oppose a probabilistic future that lends itself to modelling thanks to sufficient relevant data, on one hand, and the wider domain of domesticated intuition through the use of influence diagrams (Bayesian networks) for example? It is most likely.

However, beyond the non-probabilistic domain, one must keep in mind the concept forged by Bertrand Robert,[5] which he called 'the rise of the absurd'. This domain of the 'unknown-unknown' calls for the establishment of sentinels for the implementation of strategies and tactics.

One of the major hurdles on the pathway to a sustainable economy, which was stressed by several speakers during a RIMS ERM Summit,[6] is the economic

---

[3]Georges-Yves, K. (1994). *Latest advances in Cindynics.* Éditions Economica.

[4]See Atlantic, R. S. (2011, April 1). *Green philosophy – How to think seriously about the planet.* Main Edition.

[5]Bertrand Robert, managing director of Argillos, specialised in crisis management coaching and support.

[6]See article in French: Conduire l'ERM vers de nouveaux sommets! *RiskAssur-hebdo*, No. 1. https://www.riskassur-hebdo.com/

reality: top management's compensation rests heavily on short-term results, and individual objectives, which are the keys to bonuses, which do not bring 'sound decisions' into the equation. There are three conditions for a sustainable result:

- **Taking into account uncertainty:** that presupposes being beyond the comfort zone of « comfortable » trends, based on models and data, to envision black swans, or long tails like in the stress test for financial institutions;
- **Robust decision -process**: this implies that it is consistent, rational, and considers the contradictory interests and expectations of all stakeholders;
- **Efficient implementation:** this is the level at which risk owners are found and at which models and disciplined management serve the engineering science.

A 'continuum of the fog of the future' must reflect the different levels of uncertainties, i.e. how thick is the fog, and Kathy Pearson proposes a five-level scale:

1. Certainty (trends);
2. Risk;
3. Uncertainty;
4. Ambiguity;
5. Chaos.

The classic modelling tools address the issues of the traditional approach to risk, i.e. limited to insurable risks; it falls within the domain where there is a quantifiable probabilistic uncertainty and an actuarial model that fits the situation. This quantification bias has led futurologists and scientists alike to assume that uncertainty only results from insufficient information. This seems to underlie the definition of risk in the ISO 31000:2018,[7] but the assumption is qualified when it calls for complete and timely information. The initial posture implies that if more was invested in seeking information somehow, the future might become certain. This philosophical postulate is dangerous as it seems to go against the reality of the limitations of the human brain and the complexity of situations. Furthermore, it does not seem to take into account the new findings of quantum sciences.

An important feature of the environment in which organisations operate today is ambiguity, whereupon another set of tools must be called upon including a process through Bayesian network and sentinel networks (low signals) to anticipate events. These tools influence the evolution of any organisation so that strategic goals and objectives are updated to reflect at all times the new realities through a continuous strategic process.

This is why any organisation must learn to control its growth while taming uncertainty. It falls to all in leadership positions, top management, government heads, and religious and spiritual leaders, to find the appropriate balance between learning and performance. It would be extremely naive to fail to acknowledge that all organisations, be they not for profit or state, are managed to reach defined

[7]ISO 31000:2018. (n.d.). ISO. https://www.iso.org/standard/65694.html

goals, to obtain results, including the re-election of the head of state. However, there is always a balance to find depending on the time horizon chosen to measure the results: short, medium, or long term.

The current difficulties and tensions in the world, pandemic, geopolitical unrest, climate change, etc., are mostly linked with the definition of the horizon, especially when using the qualification 'sustainable', which has a different meaning, for different stakeholders.

A summary allowing for comparing and contrasting the two paths, learning and performance, to be reconciled according to the four identified attributes is provided in Table 1.1.

In 1997, a Belgian specialist, Arie de Geus, wrote a book[8] in which he identified four essential attributes for survival:

- **Personality**: sharing values deeply rooted in the organisation's collective conscience;
- **Frugality**: being attentive to spending and limiting to absolute necessity (lean management);
- **Tolerance**: leaving room for staff of all levels to experiment but within a defined frame;
- **Openness**: listening and watching the outside context in which the organisation operates.

There is a common trait of humankind that many research tests have confirmed and that is that we tend to see what we expect to see. The Black Swan story seems to have its origin in the following: apparently, European explorers in Australia when they first arrived had difficulty in finding food, especially meat. In those days, in Europe, swans were considered game and hunted, but they were white. The explorers nearly died of hunger next to flocks of swans, as they were black, they did not recognise them as edible ... They did not see them as food! This illustrates that, in a changing environment, it is essential to deploy economic intelligence tools that allow us to analyse all events without a priori or biases and thus gain a 360° vision.

Table 1.1. Balancing Learning Process and Performance.

	Learning Process	**Performance**
Structure	Fluid	Procedural
Reward	Innovation (trials)	Results (short term)
Tradition	Open to experimentation	Respect for tradition
Focus	Centrifugal – outward looking	Centripetal – inward looking

[8]de Geus Arie. (1997). *The living company*. Harvard Business Review Press.

Therefore, diversity is essential in any decision-making panel; but at the same time, decision-makers like to stay comfortably among their peers of the same social background, similar academic curriculum, and uniform partnerships; in the same way, audit firms tend to recruit a standard model junior in whom the partners see themselves some 20 or 30 years prior. In France, the mould is called 'Grandes Ecoles', in the United Kingdom 'Oxbridge' or Russell Group, and Ivy League Universities in the United States.

On the contrary, when executive committees are staffed with an individual from very different organisational paths, they tend to be confrontational, as each member appreciates a situation from his/her point of view or silo competence; efforts from all are required to come to a consensus decision when differing opinions have been polished like stones in a river.

Each member comes to the room with his/her baggage, and jargon, and cannot listen to the others to agree on a common language or a common set of values; whereas this cultural melting pot is a key to forming an effective team that would prove essential not only in a time of a crisis but every day to contrast and combine differing visions as described above.

These sociologically and culturally homogeneous executive teams reinforce some natural biases that skew decision-making processes, i.e.:[9]

- **Loss aversion**: change is seen as threatening to their authority and only the downside of risks are seen, the threats, leading to total indecision as to an acceptable level of risk;
- **Over-self-confidence**: the differing visions are eliminated at the door, and the members are too certain of their competencies and of information leading to two differing pitfalls, over-optimism when looking at perceived opportunities, and over-pessimism when looking at perceived threats;
- **Sunk costs impact**: this could translate literally into throwing money into a sinkhole, like continuing to finance a project objectively doomed rather than admitting past errors or accepting the consequences of drastic changes in the environment and trying to find a more valuable use of future investment, assign a new objective for the 'sunk costs';
- **Gregarious instinct**: follow the leader without daring an original idea, shying away from outside-the-box thinking. This is where consanguinity between the board and the executive team can be seriously dangerous;
- **Emotional accounting**: lacking objectivity when assessing an investment and relying on the trust of the proposed leader, losing track of quantified evidence;
- **Fixation on the past**: projection into the future the past successes of the organisation without due consideration of the changes in the internal and external context, new competition, and new stakeholders' expectations, which are the keys to the success or failure of a proposed initiative. This could be called the rear mirror syndrome as if driving a car without looking ahead could lead one safely home;

---

[9]Adapted from Jules, G., & Tony, E. (2012). Seven sources of drift in decision making. In *Uncommon sense, common nonsense* (p. 36). Profile Books Ltd.

- **False (fake) consensus**: accepting silence as approval and not forcing a debate around the table so that each member of the decision-making body can address his or her specific point of view, thus leaving aside part of the information that could have been brought to the table. As mentioned earlier, encouraging dissent is essential for long-term resilience, even in the boardroom or in the C-suite.

Is survival then imaginable in the current context, or could it be 'mission impossible'? Survival is possible, so long as the organisation can adapt to changes and anticipate them to participate in forging the future. However, the organisation's leadership must find a way to follow three fundamental tenets; based on scientific reasoning, Georges-Yves Kervern[10] would call postulates, in order to avoid being caught in a rut. That will require:

- Experimenting with new frameworks and structures;
- Establishing 'peripheral vision' based on operational managers input;
- Organising and regulating dissent and creative dissonances.

Finally, the central message is stronger as it is shared by hard sciences specialists: in any decision, one must keep in mind that uncertainty cannot be eliminated, especially in a situation of ambiguity or chaos. It can only be tamed through control based on dynamic monitoring, and continuous adjustment of strategy and tactics, thanks to an 'intelligent' implementation by operational managers and risk owners, who are trained in listening to low-level noises to report down-up.

One of the keys to efficient ERM, i.e. mature, is precisely the provision of experience feedback in any situation that deviates from the 'expected'. This is the only way that the organisation can learn from its past errors and not repeat them in the future. Error is always part of the human experience and any project, due to human fallibility. Ineptitude, on the other hand, is much deeper; it is a counter-productive attitude that becomes inherent to the organisation's culture if leadership is not attentive to fighting it, which means it *must* encourage productive dissent. The ultimate mistake of top management would be to discipline any honest one-time mistake while tolerating sneaky incompetence.

To be clear, experience feedback exercises aim to correct errors, not to look for, let alone punish, guilty individuals; these exercises constitute one of the value creation tools associated with ERM; if well carried out, they will uncover the root causes of an unwanted situation and also the incompetence sources that might transmute a simple error into a major catastrophe.

All these elements emphasise the importance of ERM, i.e. the integration of risk management as early as the development stage of any strategy, and its continuous adjustment at any stage of the implementation with the continuous challenging of the underlying hypothesis by ever-unfolding reality. The game is to detect as early as possible the drivers of change even before that change occurs. This presents a particular challenge at a time when external and internal contexts are the siege by a constant maelstrom of contradictory forces.

---

[10]Bertrand Robert, managing director of Argillos, specialised in crisis management coaching and support.

This is the reason why the presence of a high-level risk-management professional, a CRO, in the executive committee, such as Sir David Walker,[11] is required for governance purposes; he/she will bring to the table a transversal vision that will transcend the silos, even amid the executive team, and contribute to the promotion of a shared language of common sense. The CRO's mission is not only to temper the hasty executives but also to inform the directors on the reality of risks, accepted or sustained, i.e. core risks and ancillary risks, so that they are in a position to fulfil their mission as 'flame keepers'.

At the end of this development on managing uncertainty, it is tempting to borrow a conclusion of Charles Darwin's, in which he claimed that in the evolution of the species, 'it is not the most powerful, nor the brightest that survives, but the most adaptable'. This conclusion applies not only to individual organisations but also to whole societies, and why not primarily to risk-management professionals, today and tomorrow?

1.3. Decision-Making in an Uncertain Future[12]

This title might be an oxymoron to the extent that any decision concerning future developments is always made, in essence, in a fog of uncertainty. Even the most prominent leaders can make abysmal decisions. They might result only from a lack of luck or calendar mistakes. However, many research studies have identified cognitive and behavioural biases to explain most of them. Of course, techniques have been developed to get rid of biases in the decision-making process, but it proves difficult to apply when it is the leader's prejudices that are at stake. Below is a list of slippery situations where action is required.

Experience shows that prejudices interfering with the decision-making process belong to two categories, confirmation and complacency, or over-self-confidence:

- **Confirmation prejudice:** defines an unconscious trend to give more credit to information that confirms our beliefs, hypotheses, and recent experiences over those that could challenge them;
- **Complacency prejudice:** defines a natural trend among leaders to overestimate their competencies, and in the illusion that they will always be able to control the consequences of their decisions.

Combining their misreading of the context and their overvaluation of their powers or control can lead to catastrophic outcomes. Two illustrations come to mind: Kodak was so sure of its technical superiority that it could not imagine a substitute, and Blockbuster rejected the takeover offers by Netflix and soon regretted it. And these are only the most symbolic situations.

---

[11]See article on the Walker report, *RiskAssur-hebdo*, No. 155, 18 December 2009, Annex 1 or webarchive.nationalarchives.gov.uk/+/http:/www…uk/d/walker_review_261109.pdf.

[12]Philip, M., Olivier, S., & Torsten, W. (2015, April). Are you ready to decide? Before doing so, executives should ask themselves two sets of questions. *McKinsey Quarterly*.

Could it be that the situation cannot be redressed? Luckily, as mentioned earlier, there exist efficient methods to rid the decision processes of the prejudices that taint them. More precisely, to clear the room of prejudices, the presence of a risk-management advisor at the decision table is one of the essential components. If only in asking at the appropriate moment the key question 'What would happen if?' the risk-management professional aims at discovering other points of view, commanding further analysis. Executives or directors are confronted with further uncertainties, risks, potential threats, and/or opportunities that might have been left aside in the absence of a systematic risk assessment process. That may prove an efficient means to address the overconfidence issue. This may also encourage a dissenting opinion in the group to be voiced and listened to. If all goes well, this will dwindle and contribute to the establishment of a listening culture, and away from a one-leader culture, provided top management is really open to it.

Projecting into the future with different alternatives puts the decision and the future in perspective, allowing both for less favourable, and sometimes more favourable outcomes, but in all cases, outcomes not envisioned in the first instance. If the organisation's culture does not allow staff to be frank and candid, it might prove useful to hire a consultant to play the 'king's jester' and dare say when the king is naked. In all cases, the issue is to envision what could go significantly differently than anticipated and become aware of the early signs of things going in a different direction from those envisioned when the decision was made.

Another solution would consist of setting up a *brainstorming* session to widen the range of hypotheses underlying a project and some even suggest creating war games to allow each to change sides and imagine the competitors' positions; however, these methods can consume considerable time and resources. At any rate, top management should be the one to decide that such a move is needed, whereas he/she may be not introspective enough to analyse his/her prejudices, which will bias his/her decision-making process at a crucial time when a strategic move must be made, curbed, or even reversed.

When middle management makes an ordinary 'honest' mistake, e.g. measuring or calculating key drivers, they can learn from their mistakes and make sure they are not repeated. But when prejudices combined with a totalitarian culture leads them to cover up their mistakes and find sideways dodges, then there will be no impetus for them to correct their ways or even acknowledge their error, until someone and/or some process brings them to reassess the situation.

Then, there must be a way to make sure that leaders can verify whether they are falling victim to their prejudices or those of their immediate advisors. Because they are unlikely to easily spot their prejudices or those of their advisors with similar backgrounds, the first improvement is to make sure that the proposal was developed through a robust and objective development process, even before giving attention to the proposal itself. Two main questions can validate the process:

1. 'Did the process include different perspectives and points of view?' This requires gathering a diverse group of individuals from the inside and/or the outside and making sure that all the main stakeholders' networks are represented, which means sometimes empowering panels and using social media

to investigate the situation. The number of persons involved is a good indicator of how robust the process is, to the extent that they are really a diverse group. This may indicate that the initial solutions were submitted to the test of contradiction rather than adopted through a wishy-washy consensus.

2. 'Were all possible negative outcomes taken into account?' That supposes that all elements and drivers in the internal and external context of the organisation are properly considered; this means identifying all issues at the organisation level, at the branch level, and at the macroeconomic level without forgetting about social and cultural issues or political trends. Have they all been integrated into the threats and opportunities analysis?

The issue of propaedeutics is essential here: are executives and middle managers sufficiently trained for the development of a fruitful intercultural dialogue based on mutual understanding and respect? The questions asked in the meetings and panels must be sufficiently open and relevant to the decision to be made. This will allow transcription of all the responses and remarks in a matrix to be used as a decision-support tool. The decision-makers should consider a dual strategy to generate new perspectives and new visions of the risk. The use of the proposed process is aligned with a mature ERM programme as it assures that all uncertainties and their root causes are properly identified and considered; supplied with this widely open information, the directors and executives are less likely to let themselves fall into biased decisions. It is the best protection against hazardous decisions that could lead to disaster until such time that the board of directors reflects enough social and cultural diversity within their ranks.

Chapter 2

Managing Strategic Risk or Strategic Management of Risk

A new acronym for risk management (RM) has been developed in the first decade of this century: SRM for strategic risk management. However, this might be only the result of a flawed implementation of enterprise risk management (ERM) in the early years of the 21st century. This is due in part to the lack of necessary tools for truly global and integrated RM. The fourth industrial revolution and developments such as the cloud, big data, and artificial intelligence bring new capacities.

The need to develop a portfolio approach, break the silos of all the functions, and find a common language emerged when the root causes of the 2008/2010 financial crisis were uncovered and highlighted with the swirl of disruptive events since 2020. ERM has been rapidly developing for over a decade with RM extending beyond its original scope, as it combines qualitative and quantitative approaches.

These developments are made possible by a robust data model design and access to big data. They open the way to business analytics and the possibility of mining risk information, both internal and external. Thus, it is possible to predict and optimise actions, using the new capacity of artificial intelligence to 'intelligently predict'. This is why it is important to revisit risk perception and risk appetite, the history of RM, and the open issues on ethics, sustainable development, and governance (ESG).

2.1. Risk Perception and Risk Appetite

Even before the explosion of social media, professionals commonly explained that when it comes to risk, perception is reality. But then, how much more is it the case when the rumour spreads at light speed? There is no time to call on scientists to come and explain the situation in objective and scientific terms to calm down the stakeholders fired up by 'popular wisdom' the sources of which are not and cannot be verified.

Enterprise Risk Management in Today's World, Part A: Enterprise-Wide Risk Management and Strategy, 23–35
Copyright © 2024 by Jean-Paul Louisot and Simon Grima
Published under exclusive licence by Emerald Publishing Limited
doi:10.1108/978-1-83797-406-120241003

However, what is true for the population at large is likely to be true also of those in positions to make decisions. There is abundant literature on this subject that readers can turn to, but here below is an expert from a recent book.[1]

> It is interesting that reasoning by analogy is a constant and a predominant logic with all deciders in the survey. We are convinced that systematic experience feedbacks are needed over administrative simulations where critical issues are brushed over. The systematic process aims to familiarise individuals with situations for which they have no reference in their experience and yet can develop benchmarks on which to base their attitude in unusual situations in the future. This can be efficient only if they are exposed to a sample large enough to provide reference relevant to reason by analogy.
>
> However, too much information may hinder the thinking process in pre-crisis situations, disturbances that might develop into crises if not curbed rapidly. By the same token experience, feedback allow decision-makers to pose the problem in a way that will uncover solutions, while questioning their thinking through the entire process, taking account of the depth, or absence thereof, of their understanding and knowledge of the issue at hand. But, it must always be kept in mind that in a pre-crisis situation, decisions are made under pressure: time is of the essence. This constraint of a timeline to be met is evidenced by research.
>
> Nevertheless, it is surprising to note that decision-makers do not seem to be bothered by this bias in the process and that they accept it as a postulate and understand they have to take it into account as one more variable but they are no longer afraid of it. It would be presumptuous to try and explain how any decision-maker reasons, it is nevertheless important to identify the indicators on which their modes of reasoning are likely to be developed.

There are many projects conducted in the scope of RM for which the underlying substance is a risk even if it does not appear in the title: economic intelligence, metrics, quantification (relevant to risk), decision-making with limited information, conducting feedback loops, etc. However, there is one major issue that still baffles many decision-making entities (e.g. directors, top management, and elected officials) in their efforts to deliver corporate governance; the underlying issue is risk appetite and risk tolerance, they are the two sides of the same coin, intertwined and often mistaken. As these concepts are essential to the topic of this book, it makes sense to go a little deeper into their meaning.

[1]Louisot, J.-P. (2023). *Comprendre et mettre en œuvre le diagnostic des risques* (Chapter 2, p. 27). AFNOR Éditions.

They are easy to define at the corporate level:

- Appetite – Level of risk required to reach the organisation's objective;
- Tolerance – Level of risk that the organisation can bear without jeopardising its resilience.

But the big challenge is to allocate to each entity in a group/organisation the amount that it can take without exceeding the global organisation set boundaries.

Therefore, generalising the concept of risk appetite/tolerance is not enough, it is necessary to dig further and look at the three major levels of decision traditionally reported: strategic, tactical, and operational.[2]

1. Strategic level

At this level, the organisation should investigate its ability to manage specific risks associated with its portfolio of projects, especially when it could provide competitive advantages in the private sector or enhance its capacity at fulfilling its missions in the public sector. If opportunities to be pursued must be identified, threats to curb will be defined with precision.

The selection of risks to embrace or to accept must be done with consideration of the organisation's performance, and culture but also of ethical and behavioural issues that may influence the organisation's actors as well as stakeholders' expectations.

It is also at that level that the organisation's leadership must select efficient control as they must balance control against initiatives. Setting excessively strict controls to reduce anxiety might abort all initiatives needed to remain relevant in a constantly changing environment. It is important to keep in mind that top management may be isolated in their « tower » and, therefore, less likely than operational managers to be aware of developments and necessary adjustments. The main difficulty lies in finding the right balance between control and initiative aligned with an organisation's culture and history.

At the strategic level, the central consideration for private organisations is value creation for owners and/or stakeholders; it is usually measured by the present value of long-term future cash flows. A model could be derived for public entities provided the value of the services provided to stakeholders and society could be reasonably quantified and then compared with the costs incurred to deliver them. The second issue for public entities is to find an appropriate rate to discount the cash flows: how to define a public equivalent to the cost of capital? The level of risk of alternative solutions or projects must also be factored in. However, the issue of 'risk premiums' is key in financial planning but beyond the scope of the risk manager.

---

[2]For this development on risk appetite, ideas have been borrowed from a document published by the Institute of Risk Management (IRM), in May 2011: 'Risk Appetite and Risk Tolerance'.

ERM's main mission is to support the organisation's strategic objectives; this is why it is important to use the same metrics when considering the different consequences by which to assess risk and make sure to develop *a* business impact analysis (BIA) for each of the alternatives. Despite the ISO 31000 main principle, RM professionals still debate the relative importance of value preservation versus value creation, but ERM should focus on net long-term value creation and resilience.

2. Tactical level

The main difficulty in many organisations is the implementation of their strategy. Even the best-defined, and regularly revisited, strategy cannot withstand defective implementation. And one of the steps in the implementation process is to allocate risk appetite at the tactical level for each entity within the organisation; it must be consistent with the global appetite to ensure global alignment or risk uncoupling the strategy as defined by the board and its implementation. This is why it is essential to set controls that assure the decision-makers of the implementation alignment.

The risk appetite policy is effective only if efforts and resources allocated to risk control are sufficient. For a high level of risk accepted, the control system must be specific and reliable, without becoming too finicky. For example, a sizable investment to develop new information technology (IT) solutions is ripe with uncertainties concerning the budget, the timetable, and the final improvements or breakthroughs. Specific controls are needed to ensure successful completion, but at no time should controls of the existing system be lowered as it might provide an entry point for a cyber-attack or ransomware. The consolidation of control must not prematurely engulf expected benefits but provide the leaders the assurance they exert proper governance.

3. Operational level

When it comes to detailed processes and procedures that are needed for the manufacturing of goods or the delivery of services in a consistent fashion through time and space, it is clear that the risk appetite must be kept at a very low level, correcting human errors before they have dire consequences for clients or customers, limiting controls that could slow down the processes, and setting up systematic experience feedback to avoid any repetition of error or omission. This is where RM and quality are intertwined as the present version of the quality standard ISO 9000:2015 rightly acknowledges.

When it comes to implementing a project, when strategic and tactical risks have been properly addressed, operational risks for the follow-up and completion of the project are similar to those for current operations. This is even more the case today as the volatility of the context has transformed many 'current operations' into projects to adjust to new circumstances at all times. For projects as well as ongoing operations, foremen and supervisors must be responsible and accountable for daily risks but have the authority to correct deviations before they turn into ruptures.

Thus, at the operational level, most of the RM resources are devoted to curbing threats, without leaving room for opportunities that should have been included in the strategy; however, middle management can see operational opportunities that should be reported to their line managers. This is possible only if line managers and all 'associates' are trained to identify risks early and to react appropriately to emerging risks. This supposes that they understand and work according to an ERM framework implemented where they can open their concerns to their chain of command. This is what is meant by a framework, the culture throughout the organisation must reflect the values and expectations of top management.

In a for-profit enterprise, this means that all members of the operational plant management team should be trained to act as sole entrepreneurs trying to optimise his/her performance. However, at the same time, each must be fully aware of where is the red line, the boundary of their autonomy beyond which the chain of command should be advised before acting. Under all circumstances, there should be an entry in the daily operational journal so that incidents can be analysed if need be (in the same fashion that 'undesirable' events are reported in healthcare organisations).

As a control over strategic resources, it is at the tactical level that the results of the organisation's RM are monitored and measured through a set of key indicators (*Key Risk Indicators*, KRI; *Key Performance Indicators*, KPI). It is important to note that a widely used indicator, the 'direct cost of risk' measured as the annual average cost of risk, is the result of the multiplication of frequency/probability by severity/impact. However, this indicator provides only a 'long-term' average, which may be very different from yearly experience, especially when the probability distribution is heavily skewed, with a 'fat tail'.

Most organisations are now familiar with the use of dashboards and the monitoring of performance indices; the issue at hand with risk is that internal and external auditors, as well as internal control, must get to grips with the specificity of RM: the time horizon for risk is not annual, let alone quarterly, except maybe for frequency risks; the horizon is decennial or centennial, possibly even longer for most severe risks. The difficulty is to envision such long time spans when they extend far beyond the director's and officer's terms in office and even the human life expectancy. Family businesses often outperform publicly traded companies, as they work for the benefit of future generations and also should prove more resilient.

As regulatory and level context worldwide requires, risk governance is the officers' and directors' responsibility, and they must develop a risk strategy for the organisation including risk appetite and tolerance; therefore, they should at all times keep in mind the following 10 recommendations:

1. Directors are, directly, individually, and collectively, responsible for risk attitude within the organisation and the setting of risk appetite. This can be achieved within the scope of the risk appetite established for the organisation through a collection of criteria that provide information to the directors; thus, they are in a position to determine the nature and the extent of significant risks they deem acceptable for the organisation. But they are also responsible for risk monitoring to get the assurance that all actors within the organisation make decisions and act on those decisions within the limits of

the risk appetite they have defined, including the staff in charge of making sure that major partners operate within the same framework.

2. The risk appetite statement is one of the strategy drivers at the highest level. It should be designed to develop plans for the implementation of the strategy; it is also a tool for the development of appropriate tactics and change planning. While the board cannot delegate all its responsibilities concerning RM, neither can it follow daily operations; therefore, a 'risk committee' consisting of both executive and non-executive directors can be set up to prepare the work, develop the statement to be approved by a full meeting of the board, and then to monitor the implementation of the statement at all levels by risk owners.
3. Top management and line management at all levels have the responsibility of making decisions and implementing them within the limits defined in the risk appetite statement. Their mission is to make sure that all those reporting to them understand the limits of their action and act accordingly within the scope of their responsibility and authority. Foremost, they must be fully aware and vigilant when the limits set in the risk metrics are on the verge of being reached or even exceeded.
4. When developing the risk appetite statement, the size, nature of activities, and complexity of the organisation, as well as the context in which it operates must be part of the process. When it comes to deciding on which risks are acceptable, the following must be considered by the directors:
   - Nature and extent of the risk confronting the organisation;
   - Extent and classes of risk they deem the organisation can bear;
   - The likelihood that the risk will eventually materialise;
   - The organisation's capacity to reduce the risk probability and its impact, should it happen;
   - The cost of installing and/or using the reduction measured, compared to their efficiency *(cost-benefit analysis but including CSR[3] consequences, ethical considerations, and overall reputation impact).*
5. The risk appetite statement must be contextualised in the RM framework. It is particularly important during the exposure diagnostic (risk assessment) phase as, once identified, risks must be prioritised. Therefore, the organisation, the risk owner, must quantify risks based on their impact, probability, and velocity. The impact or severity and the likelihood, probability, or frequency are familiar to all dealing with risk. More recently, another dimension of risk, velocity, has become a key factor in a volatile world. It aims to measure the time left for the organisation to react between the moment when the likelihood of the risk happening increases suddenly and the threat materialises in the organisation.

   Risk evaluation is the last step in risk assessment. The organisation reviews the finding of the risk analysis, in light of the risk reduction measures already in place, and compares the 'residual risk' with the criteria defined by the board and resulting from the risk appetite/tolerance statement. Linking

[3]Corporate social responsibility.

the criteria to the statement assists the directors in assessing the situation and measuring the impact of the alternatives they must decide on following a presentation by the risk committee. The definition of a common taxonomy and a common language, avoiding professional jargon, will help risk consolidation to facilitate global portfolio decisions, assuring consistency throughout the organisation, and even in the relations with economic partners. This allows the aggregation of risk and identification of the existing correlations leading to a single simple matrix, combining all information for more efficient decision-making, while keeping in sight the stakeholders' expectations, and strategic objectives, thus enhancing the chance of success in reaching the desired outcomes. *However, RM practitioners must keep in mind that correlations and co-variances do not necessarily imply causal relationships.*

6. Identification of acceptable risks: each organisation must define a specific approach and establish an appropriate process. As mentioned above, the procedures will rest on the risk appetite statement from which acceptable risk criteria are derived. For this to happen, the risk appetite statement must be the result of a sequence of iterative steps: beginning with establishing a diagnostic of the current situation, i.e., a systematic listing of the organisation's exposures resulting from the current strategic choices. At this stage, the directors may have provided only a global risk appetite relating to the financial situation of the company, and the first list will provide a guide for splitting the overall appetite into limits for the operational managers, at least at the level of the major entities within the organisation.

   Thus, the RM professional can collate and aggregate information from operational risk owners; this will through time constitute the internal data bank on risk that will feed further modelling. This will facilitate interaction with the risk committee to develop a more substantial and specific risk appetite statement that operational managers can understand and implement within their risk portfolio.

   Iterations are needed for the directors to revisit their statement in light of the changes in the internal context (*new talents, new capacities, financial resources, etc.*) and external context (*major shareholders, leadership, legal and regulatory context, competitors and substitutes, as well as cultural and societal shifts*).

7. An organisation's set of criteria must remain consistent and reflect a chosen taxonomy; however, they do not have to be uniformly applied to all risks as some risk categories could be more acceptable than others. For example, in a highly competitive environment, failing to meet customers' expectations or contractual obligations may be a non-starter, whereas in the case of an innovative start-up, customers may be game to accept occasional non-quality in exchange for constant innovation. When the criteria are developed within the scope of 'residual risk', it is essential that the main reduction measures and control mechanisms that are behind the mitigated level are identified and their effective implementation verified regularly, and that their cost, maintenance, and use be updated. This is how both effectiveness and economic efficiency can be tested.

8. When determining the nature and extent of any risk it is ready to accept, an organisation must consider the following:
   - The global present exposure of the organisation in light of its capacity to assume a given risk; and
   - Whether the authorisation mechanisms are in place to make sure that the maximum tolerance level defined by the directors is never exceeded.
9. For the development of the risk appetite statement, as for the risk criteria derived from it, the organisation must cater to the three levels of risk (strategic, tactical, and operational), and any global appetite will have to be split with due consideration for the interactions between risks. Nevertheless, there is no 'one size fits all', and each board will have to do their homework regarding the size, branch, and complexity of the organisation.

   Most of the chosen risks, the risks for which the organisation can be rewarded (risk premium), are to be tackled at the strategic level. Most of the tactical and operational risks are suffered, or ancillary, and most of the time, the goal will be to curb them, as they are not in themselves value creators. However, curbing them not only preserves value but may create value if 'good risk management' is compensated by economic partners who value it in their effort to manage their procurement risks. There again, it would be necessary to distinguish between different types of organisations, public, healthcare, industrial, commercial, and even financial institutions.

   In the case of financial institutions, speculative risk-taking is their core business; nevertheless, they must take risks that create long-term value for their shareholders and/or their clients when they manage funds for them while complying with all laws and regulations that apply in the territories in which they operate.

Risk appetite is a key driver for organisations' strategy, whereas the risk criteria are guides for planning strategy implementation and tactical moves. Criteria are also key in the decision process regarding projects and/or investments and when setting limits for risk owners so that they are not corseted and have room to manoeuvre and react to local evolution while being monitored so as not to put in jeopardy the overall organisation strategy if they took unruly courses of actions *(this opens the debate between responsibility and authority for risk owners at the operational level)*.

2.2. A Short History of RM

Whereas spectacular events took place at the end of the 20th century fuelling a 'fear of the year two thousand' as a repeat of the millennium scare 10 centuries ago. However, the first two decades of the 21st century have not experienced any slowdown in the pace of catastrophes be they generated by a technological failure or a natural event and sometimes combining both like the 2011 Tsunami in Japan. The social and cultural environment has also known several disturbances, from the Arab Springtime to the Creation of a temporary Islamic State, ISIS, in the Middle East with its procession of terrorist attacks in the Western world and Africa.

Traditional investigative media, despite the efforts to discredit them, remain at the forefront of the denunciation of globalisation and weaknesses of the world socio-economic system, while questioning sustainability. Relationships between the many actors in the situation are becoming more and more complex and their interdependencies are more and more daunting. All these tensions are even exacerbated by the growing influence of social media, which is not vetted for truth as the traditional media pieces are. This global situation is so complex that traditional cause-and-effect approaches cannot provide an understanding; it may be time to use chaos theory to try and make sense of the maze of information.

The last millennium closed with the Year 2000 Bug. Nothing seemed to have happened on 1 January 2000, at 00:00, and some concluded that the fears had only been fuelled by consultants' eagerness to draw some income from the confusion. For RM professionals, it was only an illustration of one of the paradoxes of the trade: the catastrophe was avoided thanks to heavy investments in risk reduction, and the efforts were so efficient that the success seemed to erase even the need for proactive RM! Twenty-three years later, the Bug's threat is dwarfed by the level of disturbance in cyber-security that cyber-attacks, ransomware, etc. seem to bring all over the world.

In France, the irony is that the emergency and crisis management procedures set up for the Bug, activated as early as 20 December, 2000, proved key in remediating the effects of the two storms, with hurricane-speed winds, that struck the French Territory on Christmas Eve.

The third millennium started like a fireworks display beginning with the terrorist attacks in the United States, soon followed by the AZF explosion in Toulouse (France), ENRON's collapse, the Tsunami in 2004 in the South-East, with the financial crisis of 2008–2010 crowning the first decade. The next decade was not left behind as every week a new incident seemed to take place, relayed worldwide with social media providing direct phone footage that makes it so real for everybody connected. And how could we qualify the first three years of this decade with the pandemic and the war in Ukraine, and their consequences? The 'rise of the absurd', with no reference to Ionesco, is generating disturbances and ruptures of a level never experienced before. To lead their organisations to a safe haven amid the chaos, leaders and elected officials have to learn to keep a cool head and a clear mind to sail through a crisis.

In such a volatile context, the traditional vision of RM, centred on the purchase of insurance covers, to protect mostly physical assets and liabilities, has become obsolete. It is replaced, probably not fast enough, by a global and dynamic vision with a 360° periscope so that the interdependencies linked to the network of partners are kept in mind at all times that the stakeholders' expectations and trust (reputation) are given due consideration, i.e., their risk fears, real or perceived.

This is why some professionals and academics suggested a new framework for managing risks under the name of SRM; they intended to stress the interaction between RM and strategy required to optimise the efficiency of the organisation and its resilience. The term 'organisation' is a generic term for all types of human endeavours, individuals and collective, from the mom-and-pop shop to healthcare facilities, and the policies of a nation.

Many governments have developed silo RM policies, be it only for their sovereign duties for the security of their citizens, both internal (police) and external (armies); however, few have already integrated all the facets of risk, both threats and opportunities, into a global approach to risk at the highest level of government, president or prime minister. Only a global policy on risk will allow embedding the complexity and fluidity of the world context to ensure the societal resilience that their citizens have come to expect!

However, both academics and RM professionals have concluded that the principles underlying RM, the framework, and the process are the same for any level of management as soon as the risk owner has the responsibility and the authority to manage them as they are found in the international ISO 31000 standard. At the same time, the tailoring of the core concepts to the specificity of a given organisation will reflect the openness and complexity of their internal and external complex. When it comes to local authorities or states, the issue is to control the uncertainties in a system where many independent actors must be on board to implement the societal management of risk needed to ensure the current and future well-being of the populations, i.e. sustainable development!

2.3. ESG

When looking back to the events of the last half-century, it appears that the fall of the USSR, i.e., the apparent erasure of the communist alternative, has prompted the mushrooming of ethics courses in the management curriculum around the world. It did not bring the 'end of history' predicted by some, but it drew politicians as well as entrepreneurs to take in the citizens' new expectations in terms of sustainable development, environment, governance, and more generally the fulfilment of commitments and transparency. They adapted their discourse but not necessarily their course of action.

Since then, there have been several instances where ethical concerns have been compromised at best, brushed away at worst. Ethics cannot be only a concept, a flag to be waived in front of the crowds. It must become a practical tool in the managers' toolkit, in the private as well as in the public sector. Put simply, ethics must be translated into actions, let the actions speak for themselves. This is why we prefer to refer to 'ethical acts'.

If all actions could be classified in a binary fashion as black and white, life would be simple. But if the principles underlying ethics are universal, the implementation is linked to cultural and social contexts. Therefore, they are constantly changing through space and through time. This means that ethical actions are evolving and that organisations' objectives must be reassessed regularly for 'ethical compliance' and even adapted to affiliates in a very different political environment, without compromising the organisations' fundamental values. To summarise, there may not be 50 shades of grey, but the shade assessment varies depending on who does the evaluation.

When making decisions, ethical acts will align with important verbs: 'can' and 'must'. It should be at the heart of any decision and reflect the key question of making sense and giving meaning to all actions. The interrogation can be summarised in a question that a journalist could ask to write a piece: *Where are we going, why, whom for, and how?*

Ethics in action is the questioning of an old proverb: 'NO: the ends do not justify *any* means longer'. Although there are still many illustrations to the contrary, it is becoming clearer and clearer that the ends (financial optimisation) cannot justify any means (the negation of the universal human conditions and the disrespect of basic and/or fundamental rules of life in society).

The election cycles in Europe alone illustrate how poorly citizens react to large publicly traded companies displaying record profits and dividends when at the same time they embark on massive redundancy plans blamed on lean management of the competition. This is all the more resented since the beneficiaries are often pension funds in the United States or Canada.

After the fall of the Berlin Wall and the subsequent dismantling of the USSR, the neoliberal economic system was left without competition and managed to impose its rules worldwide under the name of globalisation. There is no limit to the expansion of the 'Market' that would recreate the world in the image of developed countries. But the reality is not so rosy. Possibly, for the first time in the history of humanity, humans are not at the centre of the universe, with the end goal of happiness and self-accomplishment: wealth is dematerialised, reputation is the key to success for an organisation; but even more than that, the intangible economy seems to be developing its markets that defy human logic with self-feeding mechanisms that have nothing to do anymore with the real economy.

Even after the explosion of several bubbles at the beginning of the century and the financial crisis triggered by the 'Subprime', economic actors seem to have recouped and continue business as usual, except that the population is still suffering, and specialists have begun warning about a new crash. In the meantime, the US stock index is over 33,826,[4] so all is well, until reality hits home again!

Confronted with growing questioning from citizens, some governments have understood that the legal and regulatory environment must make room for the expectations of sustainability and transparency. In the European Union, after the eighth directive on governance has become law in all member states, several new directives are following including The Corporate Sustainability Reporting Directive (CSRD) that entered into force on 5 January 2023. In France, the principle of precaution became part of the constitution during the Chirac presidency (1995–2007).

But these initiatives will not be enough unless all actors, individual and collective, internalise the goals of these regulations and develop an integrated and global approach to manage risk for a portfolio performance perspective. Some academics/consultants, like Felix Kloman, use the concept of the 'holistic approach'. In the French-speaking part of the world, the concept of 'Cindynic sciences' is gaining traction, and may even spread further as a presentation is included in ISO-IEC 31010:2019. The foundations of Cindynics, or sciences of danger, were

---

[4]As of 28 April 2023.

developed in the last two decades of the 20th century by Georges-Yves Kervern, who structured his developments on the published works on systemic approach by Nobel Prize Winner Herbert A. Simon.

With the recent development of risk conscience in the population, it has become essential that all engage in RM, and that goes beyond the organisation itself when it concerns a public space, local or national: all the citizens must adhere to the project. Therefore, beyond perception, there is a need to meet the challenge of risk illiteracy. When the United States had barely been established, Benjamin Franklin saw the future of democracy through the education of the citizens so that they could read, write, and understand risk. It is as an heir to this tradition that Professor Gerd Gigerenzer, of the Max Planck Institute for Human Development in Berlin, spoke at a conference[5] in 2011 and condemned risk illiteracy, a defect of all modern societies, in particular when confronted with the challenge of technology. When looking back at this opinion, one can see that the developments since then have justified his fears when all are involved in some aspects of cyber-security.

What is at stake is that all should understand statistics and their pitfalls, so that all citizens can be statistically savvy and avoid falling into traps set by statistical sorcerer's apprentices, which bias the presentation of arbitration between threats and opportunities to make sure the solution adopted is to their advantage.

As an illustration, when the results of recent local elections in France were published, a party leader noted that the party had increased his presence by '200%' when in fact they had gained two seats, against zero before, when the total number of elected is over 4,000. The increase may seem impressive, but the party leader was wrong: it was an infinite increase from 0 to 2!

When it comes to financial decisions, it has been pointed out that, presented with normal distributions when the phenomena really fell under fat-tailed probability distribution, directors were misled when they made decisions concerning the threat that these extremely volatile products represented for their institutions, and especially the potential dent on equity in the 'worst scenario case'.

The importance of statistics and data processing have become even more important with the advent of big data and the development of internal risk data banks that facilitate the modelling of 'predictive' solutions. Therefore, it is even more crucial that business leaders, today and tomorrow become truly 'statistically literate' whatever their background. Many universities have realised the importance of this issue and have taken the initiative to address it.[6]

Ethics, governance, and sustainability rest on transparency of information so that all involved can effectively have their voices heard in the decision. Therefore, university programmes may not be enough, and following Benjamin Franklin's steps, governments should consider an introduction to statistics as part of basic

---

[5]IRM Forum, Liverpool, March 2011.

[6]Among others, see a very interesting course proposed online by the University of Washington 'Calling Bullshit in the Age of Big Data'. https://www.youtube.com/watch?v=8RHDMERs3Ho&list=PLPnZfvKID1Sje5jWxt-4CSZD7bUI4gSPS&index=11

civic education: citizens' enlightened choice, both in elections and in their professional lives, supposes that they can ask the right questions and read the figures without being fooled by 'those who know'.

Sound governance means navigating through troubled times, including storms and hurricanes, as they are the situations where results can be gained if they learn to maintain at all times the time-varying equilibrium thanks to constant adjustments and even bold policy changes when it comes to that. But this will necessitate being more innovative and staying away from the old deterministic models that were taught until recently in the school of management still locked in the time of the 'Thirty Glorious Years' that followed World War 2.

Chapter 3

The Fundamentals in Risk Management

The importance of the involvement of all staff, and even stakeholders, in the « new » risk management (RM) approach is a recurring theme in RM literature and practices in the 21st century. More precisely, what is known now under the acronym ERM (*enterprise-wide risk management*) is based on the underlying assumption that all actors in the economic, political, and social life, the risk owners, do indeed take ownership of the risks that fall within their sphere of activity, wherever their consequences are felt within or beyond the organisation. In an ERM context, RM is at the heart of the mission of all staff, and primarily in all chains of command from foremen and supervisors, all the way up to the chief executive officer (CEO). All must understand that RM is a key performance tool for their performance, and bonus, as well as the organisation's overall efficiency. However, this will work only if the proper resources are allocated to the training of staff to bring them the needed RM competencies to graft RM on the existing organisational culture.

3.1. RM Strategy: Setting Objectives for the Management of Risk

Within an ERM project, the RM strategy is directly linked to the organisational strategy, speaking of a stand-alone RM strategy would be improper, but rather there is an RM component underlying the overall strategy. This stresses that RM's mission is to support strategic goals, questioning them when they are established and monitoring them during the implementation stage at the tactical and operational levels. What is often called 'risk-management strategy' is really the framework within the management system and the process all risk owners are required to follow to ensure consistency of the approach to risk throughout the organisation. The foundation of ERM rests on establishing an exposure diagnostic (called risk assessment in the ISO 31000 standard) consisting of identification, analysis, and evaluation. The process or method chosen must include a regular updating of the diagnostic to reflect the changes in the context and monitoring of the results of the risk treatment methods implemented. The size of the 'organisation' is of little importance, whether it is a project (project RM) or a global organisation with complex and diversified activities.

Enterprise Risk Management in Today's World, Part A: Enterprise-Wide Risk Management and Strategy, 37–48
Copyright © 2024 by Jean-Paul Louisot and Simon Grima
Published under exclusive licence by Emerald Publishing Limited
doi:10.1108/978-1-83797-406-120241004

The implementation of a consistent risk diagnostic process at all levels in the organisation is the pillar of risk culture. It is the first step in understanding risk and building an internal database on risk called a risk register. No risk-taking optimisation is possible without the necessary information. The ultimate goal of RM is to protect persons and all assets including reputation, the ultimate intangible asset and key to both survival and value creation. The RM committee, already mentioned, will be revisited later for a detailed review of its missions; it does not have to interfere directly with the diagnostic process other than setting up the process and allocating resources and, in liaison with the compensation committee, making sure that the bonuses are linked to a battery of RM effort indicators. However, the risk committee should address the issue of the risk directly linked to the directors (capacity/experience and diversity of the members, conflict of interest, quality of the decision-making process, information provided). Each director must be assessed in terms of risks (threats and opportunities) as these may impact a strategy review and/or strike a significant blow to the organisation's reputation.

At the academic level, RM is one of the branches of management sciences that developed a set of methods and tools to optimise organisations' performance under uncertainty, i.e. considering for all decisions and actions the risks involved, threats, as well as opportunities. All human endeavours are confronted with risk as they unfold in a rapidly evolving context. Any organisation is assigned or assigns itself a mission that it will fulfil through a strategic path, which aims to reach specific goals and objectives: profit, growth, market share, customer satisfaction, public service, delivering on electoral promises (for elected officials), etc. To reach these goals, there is a prerequisite that is in fact the mission of RM in society: survival to *any event that might happen and cause losses, including loss of reputation (threats), while leaving enough room to size up new possibilities, the opportunities.*

Within the 'new' RM, the core mission of the risk manager is twofold. On the one hand, he/she must make sure that top management is well informed on major risks to make enlightened decisions and, on the other hand, to provide the assurance that all other risks are managed. Therefore, the coaching of staff and the facilitation of RM throughout the organisation are key to leading the ERM programme to maturity, and this can be achieved only if all risk owners are educated so that they can manage daily risks while reading the early signs of rupture to buy time for a proactive action from top management: remaining on the lookout to *transmute potentially destructive ruptures into* 'creative ruptures', i.e. systematically look for opportunities behind threats.

This is why the RM process calls for analysing the internal and external context as a prerequisite to any RM action; this is part of the strategy process to ensure that sustainable goals and objectives can be defined and refined at the tactical and operational levels. Considering uncertainty, monitoring the evolution of the context, including through low-level noises and sentinel events, will ensure that the organisation remains relevant through the vicissitudes of the times. Furthermore, the RM's missions include making sure that the directors act according to the ethics and values of the organisation and stay on course in matters of corporate social responsibility (CSR). This will include a systematic critical review of all projections and scenarios by the combination of information generated internally and proposed by external sources (big data).

3.2. The RM Process Revisited

As mentioned, the establishment of the context is a prerequisite shared with the strategic development process, and it leads to a first iteration of the strategic objectives that could still be revised in light of a detailed diagnostic of exposures that confront the organisation for the implementation of the strategy. At this stage, a RM process in three steps will constitute the first line of defence (Fig. 3.1).

Step 1 – Exposures diagnostic (risk assessment): It consists of a systematic listing of all exposures that might prevent the organisation from reaching its strategic objectives; the outcomes are defining a risk profile of all activities and entities in the organisation, drawing a risk matrix to help decision-makers, and developing a risk register for risk monitoring and audit. The diagnostic consists of three steps:

- **Identify** the resources that may be 'at risk' and the uncertain events that could disturb their level and/or quality available to the organisation;
- **Analyse** qualify or quantify (likelihood, consequences, velocity, etc.) the impact on the objectives in the absence of any treatment (gross risk);
- **Evaluate** the impact of the existing treatment/mitigating measures that are effective (residual risk) and compare it with the risk criteria established, which should reflect the risk appetite/tolerance of the organisation.

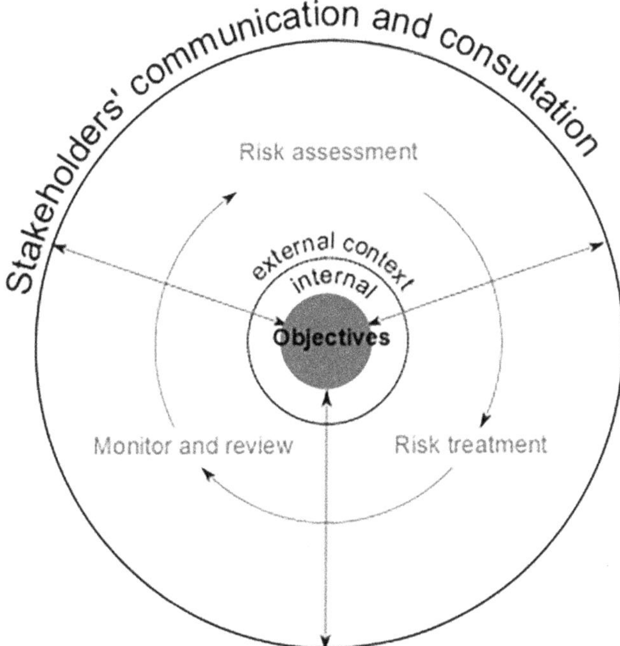

Fig. 3.1. RM Process Circle. *Source*: © J.P. Louisot.

Step 2 – Risk treatment: When it comes to risk reduction, all possible tools must be considered, beyond the traditional prevention and protection of tangible assets, all functions must be brought into the picture: marketing, manufacturing, procurement, legal, information technology (IT), etc. The goal is to set up physical, procedural, and managerial instruments to mitigate risks to keep them within acceptable limits (risk indicators or risk criteria). For risk financing, a global portfolio approach is needed so that interactions between risks are recognised and the aggregate need for exceptional financing is quantified at the headquarters' level; risk financing is a component of the overall organisation's finance strategy with the two traditional objectives or constraints: optimising return while protecting liquidity, i.e. solvency. The process is the following:

- **Map** the risk treatments available to reduce the exposures (some brainstorming may prove useful to 'think outside the box'.
- **Develop and get adhesion** of the risk reduction plan by each risk owner aligned with the RM guidelines derived from the risk statement, but final approval may be top management's decision depending on the investment level and/or impact of the flow of future revenues.
- **Implement** the risk reduction measures; the implementation is a mission of the risk owner with follow-up by the chain of command and audit (see Step 3).

Step 3 – Audit of the RM programme (monitor and review): The feedback loop to verify if the RM programme is still relevant and efficient. Top management and directors are now responsible for risk governance in the broad ERM approach; therefore, this step is now quite critical. Self-assessment by the risk owners is the first step in monitoring the RM programme as they are close to risk sources and best suited to scout changes within the scope of their mission. However, third-party control is necessary to provide top management with reasonable assurance that all risks are managed. This task falls in the internal auditors' field. Internal audit operations include RM, as recommended by the Institute of Internal Auditors (IIA). As internal audit is performed at all entity levels and production units, when it comes to risks, RM professionals should be at hand to assist with their specific competencies.

However, this cooperation between RM and internal audit might end up with auditors taking over the risk function; indeed, IIA suggests that the auditing process should rest primarily on 'major risks' but stop short of laying down who should define them. There is a trend to combine both functions in a single team, including sometimes internal control. This ensures that all three functions are represented in the executive team; the solution can prove unavoidable as there are always a limited number of C-suite members. In such a situation, the best solution is for each of the three teams to report directly to the department head and be separated as their missions and competencies are different and complementary: it is difficult to be both police and advisor. Furthermore, a risk manager without imagination would be useless, and an auditor with imagination can prove dangerous!

Indeed, RM professionals must dare to ask the questions that no one else would: emerging risks cannot be identified without thinking outside the box, and it is even more real for the 'unexpected risks'. Furthermore, the extended field of risks has called for new risk reduction tools that must be devised specifically; this is especially true when it comes to recent evolutions around continuity at the operational level and new risk financing mechanisms at the strategic level. Both require the risk manager to always be on the alert for new risks, new mitigations, and new financing so that he/she can provide relevant information and advice to the chain of command, from operational managers to the board, and top management, including the chief financial officer (CFO).

Finally, the RM process can be seen as a circle (see Fig. 3.1). However, professionals must be aware of the risk of a vicious circle and make sure it becomes a virtuous circle, like a Deming wheel of continuous improvement. The feedback from internal and external sources at each turn of the wheel is a way to fine-tune the control mechanisms and integrate new risks into the equation. This circular representation of the RM process is aligned with the process proposed in the ISO 31000 standard but allows for a better understanding of the iterative nature of the process and the role of communication and consultation with stakeholders as the ultimate reputation protection and link with CSR.

3.3. The Role and Importance of Business Intelligence

Reliable data on risk are essential to RM and projecting alternatives into the future for decision-making purposes; data are needed to allow the development of predictive models and algorithms. The first generation was known as risk management information system (RMIS), and they were often limited to gathering loss data about risk and claims, with little possibility to extract information except for frequency and impact of insurable risks. They have progressively migrated from simple Excel spreadsheets to interactive databases, and they have been integrated into internal databases across departments and entities and include all sorts of events, even incidents with no tangible consequence. With the absence of an integrated data model, functional silos could not talk with each other; the newer portfolio approach has brought with it the need to integrate all silos through federated risk taxonomy.

Today, integrated internal data can be combined with external data (big data), and using clouds has reached interaction and extraction capabilities at such a level that they are called 'risk intelligence', by analogy with artificial intelligence or economic intelligence. This data approach has allowed unifying different types of storytelling under one common story. This evolution changes the three lines of defence with an integrated second line of defence (data) and a third (audit and control) to serve the fundamental first line (operational – risk owners).

This makes the use of predictive models simple and pervasive, allowing at the operational level continuous monitoring triggered based on events or metrics and thresholds (rather than a pre-set timetable) that integrate RM in the global management of any organisation.

Business intelligence system (BIS) is also known as analytics. A 'BIS' is a set of techniques and tools that convert raw internal and external data into useful information through data mining. Thus, top management may make their decisions on reliable information about the organisation's performance and assess strategic alternatives that it can embark on. Therefore, it is an essential tool for leaders to make enlightened decisions and monitor their implementation.

Therefore, the choice, development, and implementation of BIS or business analytics system, represent a key business project as it will serve as the organisation's search head or the periscope/sonar to detect what is happening outside if you visualise any organisation as a submarine navigating in murky waters. Strict project management must be applied to the development of the BIS to the extent that the future agility of the organisation will rest on it. As with any project, there are risks associated with the BIS project, both threats and opportunities. Among the threats would be reliance on colourful, well-documented reports full of exhibits that really do not provide any meaningful information for decision-making or monitoring and/or worse that induce wrong decisions due to the biases they bring to the discussion. As a guide to decision-making analysis, the following '5 steps' rule is suggested:

1. **Partner's choice (service providers):** Although they have developed substantially in the last 15 years, especially around the governance, risk, compliance (GRC) movement and now offer solutions combining internal and external data, there is still a need for tailored solutions even if only with specific settings. The internal IT specialists must make sure that whatever is purchased can be hooked onto the existing systems. At any time, the capacity of dialogue with the system and the nesting of robust algorithms will prove essential in times of crisis as scenarios and hypotheses must be tested to provide real-time information to decision-makers who must act quickly. Sound reliable services are essential for such a key service provider.
2. **Specifications** (needs analysis): The future users must do their homework, and the initial step will be to create the organisation's risk profile, like an Internet profile, to initiate the dialogue with prospective partners to finalise the specs and make sure that all needed functionalities will be operational in due course. Due to the strategic impact of exposure, the dialogue cannot be extended to an open field of potential partners. It is essential that information extraction from the system be straightforward and presented in an unbiased fashion (beware of rumours). Furthermore, with the rapid evolution of technology, the system must be adaptable to new developments, as well as to the new needs of the organisation. Of course, the systems must tell the history, while being capable of drawing the future. Again, in the long run, the BIS must be a performance enhancer, a value creation tool, through the lifting of the fog of the future, to help decision-makers not only to choose but also to monitor and adapt the decision to anticipated developments thanks to system projections.
3. **Contract** (establishing contractual terms and conditions): The BIS is at the heart of the organisation and its analysis capacity. Therefore, it is a critical investment for the future development of the organisation. The contractual terms and conditions must ensure that the service provider is committed to continuous upgrading so that the organisation's future needs can be met as technological development permits. Furthermore, the integration of new developments to existing systems must be seamless, and the overall BIS must

have the capacity to integrate future development in analytics, such as new forecast and modelling tools; this must be contractually stated, but the commitment is only as good as the partner is *(see Point 1, partner's choice).*

The service provider must provide advice on new developments and bring reactivity when the situation becomes 'hazardous'. Without being an expert on crisis and/or continuity management, the service provider must be able to offer new information quickly and test new hypotheses to assist decision-makers in times of disturbance. This capacity must be stated in the contract, but it will have to be tested in 'quiet times' through exercises. Beware of fees that could be added for specific activities not included in the specifications *(see Point 2, specifications).*

4. **Compromise** (trade-offs on required capabilities): Stability through time and reliability of the chosen solution is an important component of the overall quality, and keep in mind that choosing one solution means giving up others. Compromise may have to be sought to prefer durability over unnecessary sophistication. More and more, the system will have to be compatible with laptops and tablets and that may require selecting which applications are needed on these devices, including sometimes staff who own devices (BYOD policy), which should be reserved for higher capacity in the office; this might prove an essential component of cyber-security. Again, let us state that stability and security must be preferred over sophistication when the latter does not offer necessary applications. With integrated solutions, it should be possible to reconcile both requirements consistently to collect internal data and make use of external data, so that each level of management, operational, tactical, and strategic has access to the information necessary to make their decisions. This is critical in times of major disturbance and to monitor implementation of the plans needed under such circumstances. In the end, all management levels should have access to data on a need-to-know basis.
5. **Brain** (true intelligence): With the advent of artificial intelligence that accompanies the development of business analytics, the long-held disregard for BIS from top management should be vanishing; however, the baby-boomers and Generation X, who are still at the helm of many organisations, were not born with IT, and some of them still view it as a super report printing machine. However, that will change, and Gen Y and the Millenniums take command.

   BIS, implicit in the name, are becoming more and more 'intelligent' and can integrate statistical capacity (including covariance and correlation), algorithms, and media analysis (including social media) so that they can really produce information that will provide a holistic vision of the organisation and the context in which it operates. They now have predictive capacities under different sets of circumstances/scenarios that provide decision-makers with insights into complex systems and underlying (root) causes of past or potential events, decipher trends, and establish weak signals and sentinels so that operational managers in the shop can send a warning to top management long before the events occur. This is true for both threats and opportunities and provides the organisation with a competitive advantage.

3.4. Local Authorities' Specificity: From RM to Good Governance

It makes sense for all risk managers to understand how local authorities manage their risks as they are always significant stakeholders for all plants and activities developed on their territories, especially when it comes to the security and safety of residents, their long-term well-being, and sustainable development. Therefore, whereas governments are part of the 'stakeholders' communication and consultation' for top management, operational managers must pay attention to local policies (city, county, etc.) when developing their RM programmes and contingency planning. This way all managers involved in strategic issues must pay special attention to the expectations and requirements of all elected officials and civil servants and their approach to RM for territories over which they have authority and responsibility.

What is new for all organisations is more important for local authorities: purchasing insurance cover is only a caricature of a RM policy. At the same time, they work with tight budgets while they need to contain local taxes; therefore, insurance purchase plays an important role when developing a long-term stable financial strategy, including risk financing. At the same time, local authorities must develop a global approach to risks, not so much by compliance with law and regulation but to fulfil citizens' expectations, their prime stakeholders. Only a mature ERM programme can lead to societal resilience, but it takes years to implement such a programme that may prove the key for their re-election!

Furthermore, local officials have to investigate the RM practices of their service providers (water, sewage, garbage disposal, electricity, etc.). But the safety of their territory requires that they communicate with industrial and commercial organisations which have activities on their territory. Regarding potential pollution risks that spread over several territories, cooperation with neighbouring authorities may prove essential.

Beyond insurance cover, officials can cooperate with their insurers those that are specialised can assist in risk assessment and treatment at least for buildings and equipment, and the main liabilities, as well as personal responsibilities elected officials, may incur. This cooperation will help them get the essential cover, at the best 'price'; and insurers can assist in the design of efficient continuity plans to ensure the 'continuity of public service' at least in case some buildings and/or equipment are temporarily unavailable.

Engaging in ERM is not a choice anymore for elected officials; public opinion pressure, citizens' expectations relayed by the public, social media, and investigative journalism make global management of risk a core mission of a city, departmental/county council, etc. The scope of the ERM project must encompass the authority's assets, the security and safety of inhabitants, and all physical persons and legal entities whose threats and opportunities landscape is impacted by their decisions.

The explosion of RM during the last quarter of a century means that ERM is spreading and changing the scope and methods of RM. At the turn of the century, risk professionals were focused on accidental risks and insurance coverage. It is now a shared responsibility of all elected officials and civil servants in which the mayor for cities, or the chairperson for other entities have a direct responsibility and their re-election is on the line. The additional challenge in territorial entities is that they are open areas where everyone, whether residents or temporary visitors, shares the same need for risk management (RM), making the city or county leadership responsible. For private organisations, 'risk management culture' must be instilled in all their associates; for a territory, all persons and entities even those with no direct link with the entity must be convinced to adhere to RM policies developed by officials. Furthermore, interactions with neighbouring territories may include cross-border entities.

If RM belongs to all, some might conclude that risk professionals are not needed any longer; on the contrary, more and better educated are needed as risk owners need to be assisted even when their risk maturity is such that it becomes a second nature. The local council renewed at least in part each election cycle needs regular refresher training; local authorities need a 'risk-management reference' possibly even more than private entities. Furthermore, many mayors and council chairpersons when questioned about risk translate right away insurance, and few have the global vision to think of a community risk profile. However, the mission of RM in synergy with public relations and communication/consultation has a direct impact on the voters' perception of the quality of the overall management and impacts the next election cycle. Thus, it is essential that RM activities are directly supervised by a close associate of the mayor and are monitored by a council committee where both majority and opposition serve. This ensures both transparency and continuity should the majority party lose the next election. The RM professional must be perceived as unbiased and 'above parties', and the selection and appointment process should result from a non-partisan process and ensure that all elected officials are trusted by the stakeholders.

There is little doubt that managing risks in local authorities is a daunting task. Developing and implementing ERM programmes for such open systems requires patience and perseverance, hence the need for political savvy from elected officials and support from leadership.

However, if the right resources are allocated to secure a robust political strategy and the development of the entity, then elected officials should win the next elections: voters will see the progress made during their term and a new term should consecrate the risk manager role in reaching the objective and the best performance even in turbulent times. Then, all stakeholders will understand that a risk culture resting on recognised competencies and talents is the best ground for 'sound governance', with all interests being given due consideration.

The issue is not new: in an article published in the French daily *Le Monde* as early as 27 May 1981, Jacques Ellul, sociologist, anarchist, and theologian, went against mainstream thinking at a time when the socialist party had gained power in France for the first time in a quarter of a century and all left-leaning economists thought that the government should invest massively to boost the economy. Ellul wrote: 'Nothing in the fundamental trends of our society would be modified'. And he completed his thought further that sustaining the economic growth 'would constitute a major folly' since 'the quality of life is in total contradiction with the increase of the industrial output and the industrialisation of agriculture'.

Probably few people read this article then or now, except for a handful of academics gathered to celebrate the 100th anniversary of his birth in two symposia.[1] However, his 'quiet voice' as well as other radical thinkers of the time is now heard in social media and in executive suites through CSR efforts, but they are still somewhat buried under the deafening noise of the neo-capitalistic economic model.

There are signs of changing times as more and more leaders understand the value of sustainability. In spite of the disappointing results of the Rio+20,[2] the Paris Agreement on climate change has brought about new hopes, even if the following COPs have been disappointing, including COP27 in 2022 in Egypt. However, even in the United States, states and cities have implemented policies that move in the right direction, in spite of the posture of the federal government during the Trump presidency. Local authorities, close to the citizens, have seized on the importance of communicating and consulting with the public.

A well-designed and correctly implemented strategy will allow elected officials to gain or regain the trust of the electorate only if they are provided with adequate unbiased information and kept in the loop with their feedback collated and analysed. It will require elected officials and civil servants to keep fully informed of the evolution of their expectations in terms of sustainability, starting by clarifying what the concept means in practical terms. However, the GIEC[3] has become quite alarming in its reports.

Sustainability means borrowing from the resources of nature to progress now without impairing the future. Therefore, societal resilience is at the core of any public policy; resilience is the ultimate goal of RM, as well as the path to political success:

- **Diagnostic and risk aggregation are essential**: risk assessment cannot be limited to identifying individual exposures, it is essential to give due consideration to the impact beyond the authority's assets and revenues to the well-being of those around and envision the interactions between risk (correlations and causality) in a portfolio approach;
- **Potential extreme events (black swans) must be considered**: risk universe is by and large a collection of 'fat-tailed probability distribution' events, and they should never be reduced to normal distributions, which would erase the 'bumps on the road'; this implies crisis readiness.
- **Quantitative tools are needed, but qualitative tools and judgement should not be neglected**: when presented with models, and the result of algorithms, the decision-makers must always keep in mind the limits of modelling and quantification, and the heavy assumptions underlying them, implicit and explicit, let alone a

[1]EHESS in Paris, on 30 May 2012, and University of Bordeaux, on 7 and 8 June 2012.
[2]The initiative is continuing to develop in a specific organisation the Insurance Development Forum (IDF) that brings together at the initiative of the International Insurance Society (IIS) several economic actors (insurers, public entities and officials, and international organisations like the World Bank or the UN development programme) to create the world resilience conditions over the 2025/2030 horizon.
[3]GIEC – sixth assessment report. https://www.ipcc.ch/assessment-report/ar6/

future that reflects the past. Therefore, experts' opinions *(including Bayesian influence networks)* and qualitative approaches should be used, including when relevant, plain common sense, and town hall meeting deliberations.
- **Risk appetite/tolerance must be defined**: The nature of ERM makes it a strategic activity, it must be in a position to offer cost/benefits analyses to the decision-makers, but in such a way that they may be understood and accepted by citizens and opinion leaders. This cannot be done unless there is a clear definition of risk appetite *(see above in Section 2.1)* which must be accepted by the citizens. The additional difficulty in the context of a territory is that the elected officials cannot assume that they have a delegation to make such decisions unless their electoral manifesto is clear and then again, it is unlikely to be detailed enough to serve as a risk appetite statement.
- **Risk culture must be rooted in the city/county**: Civil servants and elected officials must make sure all risks are managed at the proper level, but that includes educating the public to be risk sensitive, to do what they can at their level to manage risk and warn authorities when they perceive things that seem 'not normal' and that is tricky. So that 'witch hunts' be avoided, risk awareness cannot become fear of change.

As an illustration of the point of view of local authorities, a *Long-Term Sustainability Strategic Planning*[4] (SSP) developed in the city of San Francisco, states:

> Sustainable City is a dedicated initiative to achieve the long-term sustainability of San Francisco's built and natural environment. It includes city-wide and neighbourhood-scale efforts addressing classically environmental sustainability categories: climate protection, energy, water, waste and materials, air quality, ecology and resilience.

The Department of Utilities of the city has established a dedicated team to ensure that all initiatives are coordinated and offers two recommendations to public entities that would like to follow the same path:

- Identify all stakeholders' networks before embarking on the project and ensure that their concerns and expectations are given due consideration in decision-making processes to maintain sustainability;
- Map all risks that might practically derail the organisation's core missions so that strategic action is more efficient.

Each local authority is a knot in a complex and open web of relationships with stakeholders of various origins and purposes including elected officials, civil servants, citizens, supervisory authorities, suppliers, and service providers, without leaving aside the adjoining authorities. Some are not for profit, others are profit-seeking, and this must be acknowledged. The authority is linked in some cases

---

[4]https://sfplanning.org/project/sustainable-city

with contracts, in others only by 'proximity of exposures'. In all its relations, the authority must receive and provide the assurance that all risks shared are managed globally, systematically, and efficiently whoever the risk owner is. Indeed, one of the issues is to make sure that all identified risks are assigned to a risk owner. One of the sources of advice to all authorities in matters of ERM is the *Orange Book*[5] from the United Kingdom which states that 'risk assurance' is an integral part of the relationship of the authority with all its stakeholders.

With Julia Graham,[6] former Chair of Federation of European Risk Management Associations (FERMA) and CEO of Airmic, echoing the *Orange Book*, the RM bible for local authorities in the United Kingdom, the right conclusion might be that risk managers must act as scouts scanning the future: 'On top of all the issues, it is essential to remain awakened to the permanent evolutions of the world around us, to keep on the alert to anticipate the changes and anticipate to remain agile and develop appropriate response'.

[5]*The Orange Book: Management of risk – Principles and concepts.* (2004, October). HM Treasury. www.hm-treasury.gov.uk/d/orange_book.pdf

[6]Her address to the AIRMIC conference in Liverpool, 13 June 2012.

Chapter 4

ERM: An Efficient Approach to the Management of Uncertainties

In a global and volatile world, all actors, private as well as public, need to integrate uncertainties in their daily decisions and actions and be aware that a systematic and exhaustive approach will require consideration of all sources of uncertainty, i.e. risk, be they exogenous (outside of their control) or endogenous (under their direct control). The best way to find the right answers and embrace change while optimising management to leverage uncertainties is to set up an enterprise risk management (ERM) programme; ERM is wider in scope and deeper in integration into the management system than traditional risk management (TRM).

As mentioned earlier, TRM that developed initially in the second half of the 20th century focused on accidental risks and insurance solutions for the financing of residual risks and essentially on insurance-provided solutions to mitigate risk, i.e. reduce the initial risk. Risks included in this approach were mostly fire and related perils, machinery breakdown, theft, and other human acts of hostility. Therefore, the typical risk manager's profile was a middle management technical staff person in charge of insurance purchasing, managing claims, and choosing the appropriate traditional methods of risk mitigation.

The first wave of ERM at the end of the 20th century, while looking at the overall risk portfolio of the organisation and engaging the risk owners in a dialogue, remained somewhat focused on assisting in achieving goals and objectives as defined in the organisation's strategy. More recently, the second generation of ERM is bringing new insight into the future due to the breakthrough in risk modelling and under the pressure resulting from accelerated evolution in the world, both economically and socially; it is therefore legitimately part of the strategic process as it offers improved:

- Decision-making in a volatile world, and
- Communication/consultation on risk.

Enterprise Risk Management in Today's World, Part A: Enterprise-Wide Risk Management and Strategy, 49–66
Copyright © 2024 by Jean-Paul Louisot and Simon Grima
Published under exclusive licence by Emerald Publishing Limited
doi:10.1108/978-1-83797-406-120241005

4.1. Improving the Decision-Making Process

Whatever the activity or nature of an organisation, for-profit industrial and commercial, service provider, not-for-profit charitable centre, local authorities, or non-governmental organisation (NGO), the leadership is confronted with challenges that will consist in balancing contradictory interests on their path to fulfilling the organisation's mission, reach its goals and objectives. In a rapidly changing world, the ERM approach provides the organisation with a systematic method to explore new opportunities for growth and economic efficiency, while containing the threats within the context of a rigorous analysis of its internal and external context. However, to be successful, it will have to allocate its limited resources to critical risks, sometimes called headline risks or killer risks, as they are at the core of value creation, through seizing opportunities or curbing threats, thus ensuring long-term resilience.

Headline risks[1]*:*
Thorough risk assessments are frequently carried out, either in a comprehensive manner or through several evaluations in various areas of an organisation, project, or programme. While specificity might be useful for tactical judgements and specialised treatment planning, it is frequently excessive and not conducive to supporting strategic decision-making.

A headline risk serves the purpose of succinctly summarising potential events and their resulting effects by condensing a significant quantity of information. The development of risk identification may occur through two approaches: a bottom-up approach, which involves analysing a group of specific hazards that have similar characteristics, or a top-down approach, which involves identifying risks that originate from organisational-level or external sources (such as big data) that may not be evident at lower levels.

The advantages of utilising headline risks encompass:
The summary provides a comprehensive overview of the significant risks faced by the company, enabling informed strategic decision-making and instilling confidence in the management of corporate risk treatment.

Streamlining a vast and somewhat disorganised array of hazards produces a more controllable inventory, emphasising recurring patterns that impact several areas of the company and enabling more lucid decision-making.

Consolidation has the ability to identify systemic or common-cause hazards that may otherwise go unnoticed due to their individually moderate or low levels of risk. This enables these risks to be handled in a comprehensive manner.

Managers get more confidence in decision-making by obtaining a comprehensive awareness of hazards at a higher level.

[1]Headline risks: Seeing the big picture – Dale Cooper/The Risk Doctor Partnership – August 2017.

Utilising headline risks can be especially advantageous in the following scenarios:

- Risk assessments are commonly conducted for specific business units within an enterprise or for particular projects within a programme or portfolio. A business must also comprehend the impact of uncertainty on its entirety; however, individual risk registers may not always be the most suitable approach for this purpose.
- An initial risk assessment may require a high level of specificity in order to facilitate in-depth study of hazards, formulation of treatment strategies, or compliance with regulatory standards. Nevertheless, senior managers may struggle to obtain a comprehensive top-level comprehension of the primary areas of uncertainty due to an excessive amount of detailed information.

Questionnaires are occasionally employed with a corporate team to get their first perspectives on hazards and possibilities, which are then utilised as input for a risk assessment session. This motivates individuals to consider uncertainty prior to engaging in a workshop, and the combined potential risks serve as a solid foundation for evaluation, enabling a swift and effective process of identifying hazards.

In order to create a compilation of potential concerns that might attract attention and cause concern:

- Identify significant/perilous risks while disregarding minor or insignificant risks.
- Consolidate moderate or low hazards that occur in several locations (e.g. owing to shared causes). Incorporate them as potential hazards that might affect the entire system or necessitate intervention from external sources for specific business sectors or initiatives.

Identifying the optimal collection of headline hazards is seldom possible, and there is no straightforward method to generate them. To develop a good high-level list, a significant amount of discernment is required, taking into account the particular causes, controls, and effects outlined in the risk register. However, the endeavour is worthwhile as a concise collection of potential hazards is simpler to comprehend and encourages enhanced and well-informed decision-making, resulting in more efficient risk management (RM) at all levels.

An organisation's ERM team needs proper resources to identify, analyse, and prioritise risk and develop appropriate responses. But its main function is not only to assist decision-making at the headquarters only but also at the operational level to speed decision and response process when something happens 'out of the ordinary'. Therefore, their overall mission is rather to support and coach all risk owners to empower them to make and execute swift decisions, but at the same time, they must present a global vision thanks to risk aggregation at the corporate level.

Understanding interactions between risk, knowing threats and opportunities with strategic impact, together with the assurance, or comfort, that minor risks are taken care of at the appropriate levels, clear the minds of strategic decision-makers to make informed strategic decisions, take the right level of risks to fulfil the organisation's mission, and manage the portfolio of projects needed to achieve its goals and objectives. In summary, the main benefits of ERM are the following:

- Improved performance – increased long-term profitability (economic efficiency);
- Reduced volatility (including fat tails);
- Improved capacity to achieve strategic objectives;
- Strengthened accountability of leaders.

4.1.1. Improving Performance (Maximising Profits or Economic Efficiency)

ERM approach improves profitability or economic efficiency (for not-for-profit entities) not only because of the preparation for a proper response when the threat becomes a reality but also because of the joint management of threats and opportunities and the impact of risk covariance on the global result; it allows for taking on of more risk within the same risk appetite. Practically, ERM is not only concerned with stress testing, i.e. situation of cash levels, and the risk of bankruptcy, at different levels of confidence. ERM is also about assessing the feasibility of different opportunities, with a rational decision process that can include several levels of confidence so that decision-makers at the strategic level can validate their risk appetite/tolerance and make sure the tactical and operational levels stay in line with their choices.

Thus, strategic, tactical, and operational decisions are now made with better information but also with a visualisation of the impact on low-level decisions entailed by high-level decisions. Thus, top-down consistency is ensured while bottom-up information flow will provide feedback for the adjustments needed when the future turns into reality. In other terms, the consistency is maintained through time throughout the implementation, and not only at the initial stage. This provides a virtuous decision cycle thanks to implementation adjustment to the best course all the way, maintaining performance at the highest level.

Since the 1980s financial analysts and economic media have been looking at the financial health of listed companies with a much shorter period as the fund managers were looking at short-term opportunities rather than long-term investment. It was then that quarterly results started being monitored both internally and externally. This time conflicts with the risk horizon that should encompass decades, centuries, and even millennia. Adopting an ERM framework should drive organisation's leaders to look at the middle- and long-term results while keeping an eye on the volatility that might impair the financial community trust if the quarterly results are too uncertain. This means that they should set on a long-term path to optimise performance and yet not lose track of the volatility issue to retain stockholders' trust.

This will be possible through continuous monitoring of the context and the performance to detect deviations that could bring problems, which means devising metrics with acceptable levels and alerts when the unacceptable limit is 'on sight'. Thus, at all times, resources can be diverted to achieve optimal allocation. Even many natural events or unexpected threats and opportunities may lead to initial ripples that are warning signals, sentinel events, or low-level signals, that operational managers must learn to read as early as possible to react appropriately. Even if an unfolding event cannot be stopped, at least reading early signals will buy time for the organisation to prepare itself to face the disturbance at the appropriate level and with the lowest possible impact on resources.

Of course, one of the elements of the context that requires closer monitoring is what some authors call 'the extended organisation', i.e. the network of partners that the organisation relies on to produce and deliver goods and/or services to their ultimate customer. It is sometimes called procurement or logistic network RM; it is a key element for ERM efforts to achieve organisational resilience.

In terms of risk-linked decision-making, one illustration would be a manufacturing firm that markets a very profitable specialty that induces a large number of product liability claims; the issue is whether to discontinue the production of this product or not or to identify ways to modify it to remedy the claims it generates. To reach a rational decision, the firm's leadership must consider a large number of variables; one of which is whether the department in charge of the production brings in a return on assets far exceeding the rest of the firm. Then, the case is to evaluate if the 'premium' on the return justifies the risk taken. To conclude, the impact on all the business (business impact analysis [BIA]) should be carefully analysed, for example:

- Could the level of claims for the product impact negatively the reputation of other departments or the organisation as a whole?
- Is it possible to improve the product design, the quality control process, or the channel of distribution?

Only this systemic and integrated approach to risk, introduced by the ERM, could allow for optimising the firm's allocation of resources for maximum economic efficiency.

4.1.2. Reducing Volatility

Volatility has already been mentioned, and it is important to review the issue from the perspective of funding an organisation. Any organisation has to manage short-term cash flows to avoid shortfalls that could lead to bankruptcy or receivership, but long-term financial stability is also a key to finding long-term financing to fund development and investments. Part of this takes care of exceptional funding for 'unexpected losses' as well as « unexpected uses of funds ». To include this component of RM, organisations must implement a methodology tailored specifically to consider an array of variables including changes in the internal and external context, technological breakthroughs, competitive pressure, and legal and regulatory environment.

For instance, Red Cross' finances depend heavily on public donations essential to fulfil its missions. Therefore, the Red Cross must manage its reputation to enhance the trust and confidence of donors, which results in making sure most of the money donated is used to help those in need, and as little of it is diverted for the NGO's overheads. Therefore, the Red Cross must adhere to a conservative investment policy and act as a prudent steward of its resources. Conversely, a for-profit public company engaged in drug development must accept that developing new molecules is a risky business and the shareholders expect high returns produced only through heavy investment, even 'co-opetition' in R&D occasionally.

When an organisation is contemplating a new investment, the funds necessary for their completion need to be secured; financing may come from existing sources or require specific financing. In this process, it is not enough to finance plant and equipment, the working capital induced must also be covered by long-term sources. In his planning, the organisation's treasurer must see through good times and bad times; cash flows generated by all of the organisation's activities are combined, taking into account their correlation. Activities depend on different market conditions and considering the ups and downs is part of managing 'speculative risks'.

Back to the Red Cross, the organisation may expect donations to depend on economic conditions; should the volume of donations drop substantially, the Red Cross may have to revise its range or level of services to the community, without compromising on quality. However, it must assess the conditions of its rescue operations to be able to fulfil its core mission and come efficiently to the rescue of catastrophe victims without risking its reputation; if the Red Cross proved unable to provide the response expected by the public during a disaster, social media might trigger a downward spiral!

Another illustration is the case of a national chain of bargain clothes stores whose strategy rests on low prices that it can offer thanks to low labour costs in foreign countries where it sources its manufacturing. The initial cost/benefit analysis considered all direct and indirect costs, including operational, political, and exchange risks, but the chain's top management left aside the impact of child labour, acceptable in manufacturing countries. When a national investigative channel takes up the topic with a vivid broadcast, the story becomes viral on social media and Internet sales drop dramatically as well as traffic in its outlet.

In such an event, the chain's cash flows get a double hit due to lower sales and higher public relations costs to try and redress its image. If the chain has several activities, these could suffer also through a domino effect, and even fashion designers might choose to dissociate their name from the brand. Assuming the company survives the issue, it might have to adopt a low profile and forfeit opportunities that pop up during the event. Soon the company may be confronted with higher costs for clothes to improve work conditions for manufacturing employees, and the issue of child labour may still be pending.

With a mature ERM programme, the chain could identify threats linked to child labour and even change it into an opportunity by offering older children salaries, work conditions, and free schooling to have a different story to tell before television started this investigation; this is a case where corporate social responsibility (CSR) is part of sound RM. Such a move would have contained its cash-flow volatility.

When an organisation's ERM programme reaches a high degree of maturity, top management can have a global assessment of its investments' portfolio and better control the aggregated cash flows. Should the organisation look only at the downside of risk, those to be eliminated or transferred, then it will not be in a position to optimise risk-taking; it will over-evaluate the downside and be limited in its initiatives by the stated risk tolerance, whereas optimal risk-taking can be reached only if interactions between threats and opportunities are considered simultaneously. Then, the organisation may consider risky operations like mergers and acquisitions, development of new products, expansion in new markets, etc.

4.1.3. Enhancing the Capacity to Meet Strategic Goals and Objectives

Thanks to the ERM programme extended to all aspects of an organisation, all the risk owners, top and middle management, are engaged in the strategic exercise of their organisations. Therefore, all competencies are mobilised to bring input into the strategic process. The ERM process calls for a systemic identification of all factors in the internal and external contexts that can influence the strategic objectives: drivers as well as retarders. Thus, the probability of reaching, or even exceeding, ambitious goals is enhanced.

Major factors to be considered when developing strategic goals include:

- Understanding the competitive landscape;
- Analysing substitute products or services (to fulfil the same public needs); and
- Defining the network of partners (upstream and downstream).

The partners' network has become the core of the 'extended firm' with the globalisation of economic exchanges which accelerates the spreading of any tear in the economic fabric to all the extended family.

Concerning the upstream flows in the procurement process, the organisation must manage its suppliers and sub-contractors to ensure reliable flows of raw material, spare parts, or subassemblies, while optimising costs. However, the trend towards a limited number of partners and the just-in-time approach had made organisations vulnerable, all the more so when suppliers are in foreign countries, generating a procession of risks to be considered. These trimmed 'supply chains' and zero inventories have provided a competitive advantage through reduced cost and the need for working capital, but they should be reconsidered given the current geopolitical turmoil, as a source of disturbances.

What would happen if a sole supplier were to go through a difficult time? This question must be extended to all sources of difficulty the supplier may have to face which may include raw material supply disruption, cash shortage, energy downtime, or lack of proper labour skills, not to mention political or social unrest, especially in foreign countries. This illustrates how auditing major partners' RM practices, as part of a global ERM programme, reinforces the chances of meeting operational goals as it mitigates discontinuity risk.

A global and integrated approach to RM strengthens relationships with partners and helps develop contingency planning in the procurement network.

These illustrations prove that an ERM programme with its systematic and integrated approach to exposure diagnostic and risk treatment will contribute to mitigating bumps in results and enhance the chances of reaching objectives, even exceeding them.

4.1.4. Strengthening the Leaders' and All Managers' Accountability

Whereas ERM means that risk owners manage their risk, at the same time, it calls for the establishment of an executive position to coordinate risk efforts at the top level, sometimes, with the title *Chief Risk Officer* (CRO); his/her role is one of coordinator and facilitator, as well as internal consultant. It must be defined within the framework of a successful ERM implementation, i.e. risk-owner empowerment; then, risks are managed as close as possible to their 'point of entry', so long as their impact does not exceed the risk owners' vision and authority. This is why a risk culture must be instilled in the organisation; actually, a better vision is to graft RM competencies onto the existing organisational culture.

However, this operational RM does not reduce the overall responsibility that falls on the board and top management for « risk governance », a concept forged originally in the King[2] reports in South Africa. But each department head must implement risk governance at the tactical level, the CFO for finances, the CIO for information technology (IT), the Chief Marketing Officer (CMO) for commercial, etc.; whereas each must take care of his/her domain, they have to communicate risk in everyday language and RM methods facilitated by the CRO. Each member of the executive team owns the risk at this level, but middle managers reporting to them must own the operational level risks. Therefore, middle management plays a key role in the success of an ERM programme.

Middle managers may retain the ownership of risks, for which they are accountable to their hierarchy. However, they may find it more efficient to delegate the ownership to local managers, and even plant supervisors provided they are coached and trained to take on risk and have sufficient vision to analyse the impact of risks on their operations and beyond. Within the approach suggested in this book, the granularity level is called 'risk centre'; it is a generic term but each organisation has its structure (service, department, business unit), its risk glossary to be shared by all in the organisation, and its level of 'granularity' to best suit their processes. For example, banks who operate under the Basel 3 agreement must consider 'processes' even when they are shared between different risk owners, one of whom must become the 'lead'.

The generalised delegation of the management of risk to risk owners at the operational level has considerably modified the job description for risk managers (CRO) but at the same time changed the ideal profile for the job. Communication and pedagogical skills as well as a strategic vision have become essential talents for a successful CRO. The person must gain the trust and confidence of top and middle management as well as all employees. An ERM programme can only be efficient if all concerned, all risk owners and their staff, join in the project. Otherwise, the ERM project will be delayed or doomed.

---

[2]King IV – Steering point – A summary of the King IV report on Corporate Governance™ for South Africa, 2016. https://www.pwc.co.za/en/publications/king4.html

Delegation of actual management of risk to risk owners drastically changes the mission and the profile of the headquarters' *RM* team whose leader has to become a facilitator and a coach as well as a trusted advisor to the board and the C-suite; a role that differs markedly from the technical TRM mission.

At the same time, the introduction of RM substantially modifies the risk owners' missions and processes, and they must see what benefits they will ultimately gain from these new, and sometimes, daunting responsibilities. Middle management needs to support the ERM programme, accept these new responsibilities, and have the competencies to embrace them. It is a real evolution in their priorities; therefore, change management and pedagogy are new skills necessary for an efficient risk manager.

What happened at the Société Générale (now branded as SG), French Bank, at the end of 2007 illustrates the importance of middle management: a 'rogue trader' did not stay within his mission. The trader in charge of a portfolio of 'vanilla' products, i.e. low-yielding financial products, engaged in operations far beyond his mandate and started trading on derivative markets and cumulated a loss of more than €5 billion before he was stopped in his tracks. His unaccounted-for transactions degenerated into a diverging spiral that led to a major loss, one of the largest frauds in a bank, at least among those that were publicised. Since then, other events around the world made clear that SG is not the only financial institution whose faulty RM processes proved costly.

There remains hope that a mature ERM programme would have prevented the occurrence of such events. However, it must be noted that the bank, and the other banks worldwide, had already engaged in a robust RM programme about operational risks as recommended by the Basel 2 agreement, now Basel 3.

To summarise the issue of accountability, directors and officers are enabled by ERM and can comply with their mandate regarding communication and consultation with stakeholders, as part of the risk governance; while delegating the tactical and operational responsibility to middle management, they get the assurance that all risks are identified and managed to allow them to concentrate their attention on their core mission: risks that impact the strategy and resilience of the organisation.

4.2. Improving Communication on Risk

There is a growing body of laws and regulations, especially in the Western world that requests organisations to communicate on risk, their RM efforts, and financial issues, of course, so that shareholders can make decisions on the level of risk they are willing to accept; the annual report is an essential communication medium with shareholders. All stakeholders are interested in an array of risks that have an impact on their well-being: among others, environmental risks and technological risks (those that are the subject of the 'Loi Bachelot' in France and the Reach directive in the European Union [EU]). Transparency is not enough, strong communication relies on relevant information and listening for two-way communication.

ERM can flourish only if it is built on information systems that break the silos and facilitate organisation-wide information flows crossing all internal barriers.

The concept of silo in the information world is a reference to the access to it, limited to the staff of a particular department, whereas the system is sealed for outsiders. In some cases, the vocabulary used would be enough of a barrier as some companies using local jargon are like a Tower of Babel. However, the need for trans-functional access to information should not become a source of information hazard; this is why the principle of a need-to-know basis is essential, i.e. each staff member has access to all the information required for the mission and processes of the job but not more: 'need to know for the service needs'.

The need for information extends beyond the C-suite: for the ERM to be efficient, communication and consultation must be at all levels, both internally and externally. In line with the previous paragraph, the need for information at the operational level is dictated by the risk owners' ability to assess their risks, the risks within their sphere of responsibility, and specifically those that might deviate the course towards strategic goals, i.e. those that have an impact on the overall organisation's strategy. This is why risk information must be collected from the entire extended organisation, including its major economic partners and be organised consistently thanks to a common taxonomy relevant to all activities, frameworks, and processes. No ERM efforts would be efficient without these databank capabilities.

This improvement towards an organisational integrated information structure, with the setting of low-level noises and sentinel events, will limit the probability of the organisation's leadership being caught out by an unexpected disturbance. Events that will be anticipated thanks to this risk radar might have escaped the common-sense vigilance of the TRM framework. Therefore, response time and the quality of the response for events 'feared' or 'hoped for', in the case of opportunities, will be improved substantially, thus facilitating a timely and transparent interaction with stakeholders.

Finally, communication on risk must reach external stakeholders, and it must demonstrate that the ethical values held by the organisation are indeed reflected in its RM efforts. ERM loses its soul and reason if it is not conducted with the underlying ethical philosophy of the organisation; it must be nested in all decision-making processes at the strategic, tactical, and operational levels.

Sound communication on risk, both conditions and deliverables of ERM, is also the key to all internal and external significant stakeholders rallying around the organisation so that its 'social licence to operate' is protected and strengthened.

4.3. The Managerial Consensus and the Risk Committee

ERM contributes to the consensus within and around the managing team to the extent that all staff is in a position to understand that all risks, threats, and opportunities are considered in all decision-making processes; the ultimate goal is to achieve performance excellence through edging uncertainties. Delegating risk-taking optimisation within a defined mandate thanks to a risk appetite statement provides the board with 'reasonable assurance' to the extent that operational managers are informed properly and have a good understanding of their situation, make appropriate decisions based on a robust knowledge of risk impacts, and have authority to effectively implement their decisions. ERM procedures, including managers' decision process to implement RM risk treatment at their level, ensure consensus around top management and the chosen path more than any hierarchical directive would: all staff are real actors of the change rather than pieces on a checkerboard.

Therefore, the integration of RM in the management system at all levels creates consistent decision-making at the core of managerial consensus. But the consensus depends on the board of directors and top management's capacity to develop underlying reasoning for their risk initiative and readiness to allocate the resources needed for the ERM programme to be successful. But as for any project, the board must monitor the results to track the progress; it is extremely important since ERM is a multi-annual project, and past experiences call for a seven-year effort to reach maturity. Therefore, performance indicators are needed; they should include such factors as RM quality, total cost of risk, risk reduction, continuity, and reputation. These indicators must be used in the managers' 'bonus formula' so that they take seriously the issue and visualise how ERM success enhances their performance.

Managerial consensus will be strengthened and formalised by setting up risk committees at different levels. At the board level, it will contribute to the alignment of RM and strategy and enhance information flows to the various committees that participate in the life of the organisation, even when risk is not at the core of their mission like the compensation committee, the audit committee, environment committees, etc. The visibility of a dedicated committee will enhance the risk-taking posture of the board, and it is advisable not to combine audit and risk in the same committee.

When it comes to risk committees at lower levels in the chain of command, they are set up and organised based on the organisation's specific needs. A former Risk and Insurance Management Society (RIMS) president stressing the variety of risk committees mentioned the 'many flavours', as if in an ice-cream parlour. The executive risk committee and the operational committees' missions and membership depend on several factors: the organisation's size, the legal and regulatory environment, and the expectations of the board of directors, etc.

Even though the various committees have different objectives and characteristics, a written mission statement for each should ensure smooth operation and cooperation. Allocating adequate resources and appointing wise members is a recipe for success.

1. **Level 1 – The risk committee of the board of directors**: The committee consists of a limited number of directors, with some RM background at least for the chair, and in principle non-executive members, to be independent of the executive team and thus bring to the table an external view from persons informed as an insider on strategic issues. The committee's mission is to prepare RM statements then discussed and approved by the board and to monitor their implementation throughout the year and between two reports to the full board (at least semi-annually and whenever a new development calls for one). Boards need to approve risk strategy, risk appetite statement, and risk criteria.

This committee is established at the beginning of the ERM project but is fully operational when the risk maturity of the organisation feeds it with the needed information and projection to be integrated efficiently into the strategic process to improve the chances of success. The CRO should attend as a resource person. The committee's main responsibilities typically include the following:

- Control the structure of RM within the organisation *(as part of their management system);*
- Integrate risk and strategy to jointly optimise their interaction *(with due consideration for the organisation's risk appetite)*;
- Monitor RM and the evolution of risk exposures;
- Inform and advise the board of directors on issues concerning strategic impact risks;
- Approve internal rules for the operational risk committee; and
- Support and supervise the *risk manager.*

2. **Level 2 – The executive risk committee at the C-suite level**: The membership depends on the size of the organisation and of the executive team itself. For a small- and medium-sized enterprise (SME), top management should participate in the committee (when there is no board, like for limited companies SARL in France, for example, the missions of the board committee would apply to this one). For a larger company with an executive of 8 or 10 members, the committee would be typically limited to 3 or 4, including the CRO and the CFO, and may be their immediate second in command.

   The main mission of the committee is to review the risk strategy and those risks that have a cross-cutting impact on the organisation that might not be within the control of the operational risk owner or when the risk owner does not have the information and/or vision to develop a *Global Business Impact Analysis*. Thus, its major responsibilities are aligned with those of the board committee, and the CRO acts as a liaison between the two.
3. **Level 3 – The operational risk committee**: At the operational level, there may be several committees assigned to different areas of activity depending on the complexity of the organisation. Each committee is made up of senior and middle managers in charge of the area concerned and usually risk owners themselves. Their role is essentially limited to operational risks; however, some of these may have strategic impacts that should be passed on to the high-level committees through the office of the CRO. A member of the RM team should attend as a resource person. Its main responsibilities are the following:
   - Coach and assist risk owners during the exposure identification phase throughout the organisation;
   - Consolidate risk control/reduction programmes to optimise the cost/benefit ratio, including continuity issues;
   - Bring insights into the risk-financing strategy through the development of post-event exceptional cash needs based on implementing continuity (and/or crisis) plans.

The type of risk committee that best suits any organisation depends on its governance structure. If the organisation tackles risk at the strategic level, the Level 1 committee is a must. As the current regulatory evolutions are increasingly laying the burden of risks on the directors, individually and collectively, it seems essential to set up a board risk committee. In an organisation with no board and a limited executive team, a single 'Level 3' committee might prove enough. In any case, all risks must be identified and managed, but the low-level committees should clear the table for top management to turn its attention to strategic risks; this requires that directors have the assurance that low-impact risks are managed and monitored at the operational level; a robust risk prioritisation in place should imply that boards are immediately notified of any 'unusual' change. The RM team is the usual channel for both top-down and bottom-up information.

In many organisations, there is still only one committee dealing both with audit and risk. It is not an acceptable solution anymore, as the risk mission is essential when resilience has reached such a major role in stakeholders' concerns. Some might object that audit procedures recommended by the Institute of Internal Auditors (IIA) call for focusing on major risks, but that does not mean taking over the RM process and/or formally developing and endorsing an RM strategy; audit should only control the proper implementation of RM policies. Furthermore, the board's risk committee is a regulatory compliance issue for financial institutions and is necessary for capital-intensive industries such as utilities, energy producers, and all organisations involved in speculative markets that are volatile and subject to emerging risks. When it comes to technological innovations and cyber-security, all organisations are confronted with them, and the board should get directly involved in those risks given the dire consequences they may have on resilience.

These are the main missions of the board's risk committee of the board: prioritising the risk registers to bring to the attention of the directors only those that would have strategic implications, when it comes to selecting investments, getting out of an activity, and mergers and acquisitions deals. The committee should also inform the directors of their evaluation of the C-suite job in dealing with these risks. But the mission can be performed only if directors sitting on the board have sufficient RM acumen to be able to forge their opinions on these issues and not only rely on the chief executive officer's (CEO's) opinion. They must have the competencies, skills, and expertise to bring effective advice to the board.

The board has to assess the current situation in terms of risk governance, satisfactory or not, and decide if they need to be better informed to make enlightened decisions, in terms of risks, and overall strategic issues. To gain a better understanding of the situation, and of stakeholders' expectations, the board may decide to contract an external consultant to gain an objective evaluation and be advised on possible improvements.

As mentioned above, grafting *RM* competencies to the existing organisational culture is the cornerstone for the successful implementation of ERM. Staff, including the risk owners, get actively involved in the ERM project only if they understand that their efforts serve an efficient performance tool, not only for the organisation but also for each of them individually; successful ERM will improve their career prospects within a successful organisation. The ERM development is not a one-person project, and the risk committees are natural relays of the CRO action so that information flows are continuous and transcend the silos that would limit RM results; thus, RM is enabled to become proactive and create value and avoid being limited to a defensive role limited to balance sheet protection thanks to the purchase of insurance cover.

Each committee has a specific role, and they are designed to complement each other, avoiding overlaps or discontinuities, but they all are confronted with a similar challenge. As all committee members are engaged in multiple activities, the question is whether they take sufficient time and effort to tackle risk issues seriously with a time horizon extending far beyond their professional life, while understanding what events could abruptly block the horizon tomorrow.

The selection of committee members is crucial for its efficiency. Those that have the maturity to project their vision beyond their life will help in optimising long-term risk-taking and reaching performance excellence, setting ambitious objectives, and even exceeding them if they help in bringing to the organisation the agility needed to preserve its relevancy as a key knot in its partners' network in a rapidly changing world; then, the organisation acts as a responsible economic actor and citizen.

4.4. The Definition and Function of Key Risk Indicators (KRIs)

Dashboards are necessary to monitor progress, and the issue of designing risk indicators (KRI) must find practical answers and bring to mind performance indicators (*key performance indicator* [KPI]) with which top management is much more familiar.

The role of a KRI is to provide metrics to monitor the evolutions of risk/threat levels and help in detecting low-level signals so that the organisation can at any moment gain an awareness of its risk panorama and avoid crises or diffuse them to the greatest extent possible. Independently, or in conjunction with other data on the context, such as loss history, risk evaluation, and open risk issues, the KRI brings in a better understanding of fracture lines in the business or the strengths and weaknesses (SW) in the management of risk, opportunities and threats (OT), in the organisation. Readers might recognise the acronym SWOT used in strategy development. KRIs are metrics that are needed to understand the risk-profile evolution and its major components. However, the current evolutions of the internal and external context (SWOT) requires looking at KRIs not only from an internal perspective but also from an external perspective, i.e. they must measure stakeholders' perception of risk and RM efforts of the organisation.

The protection of the organisation against operational risks, as well as the management of its reputation, presupposes the periodic review of the KRIs. The review should be a mission of the board's risk committee so that they are aligned with the strategic evolving objectives while considering the contextual evolutions. This review process requires risk information given to the directors and top management to be relevant, on time, and accurate so that KRIs enhance decision-making. Nevertheless, assessing risks individually is not enough; decision-makers must understand how they relate to objectives *(see further the five lines of assurance)*. This means gaining insight into root causes and the chain of causality that links KPIs and KRIs. As many complex situations are beyond the human brain's capacity, the relevant information is available only when a business analytics system is sufficiently integrated to produce KPIs projection based on KRIs hypotheses.

To qualify as KRIs, the metrics must be measurable, whether the quantification is in percentage, numbers, or financial sums. They must lend themselves to projections and allow trend forecasting so that the organisation's path between the threats and the opportunities can be readable. They must provide information regarding the objectives and targets so that they can efficiently act as a catalyst for decision-making. They are so important that they must be developed with care and tested in an activity before implementation in the entire organisation; they must also be reviewed periodically and also when events dictate after a feedback exercise when the organisation has been surprised. Developing efficient KRIs and mandating risk owners to monitor them as a self-evaluating tool supposes that objectives are linked to the KRIs so that risk owners' interest is maintained.

Strategic initiatives must be translated into KRIs resting on vital metrics and enabling tracking through time. Thus, KRIs are part of monitoring the implementation of strategic initiatives and strengthening their chances of success, as well as mitigating the threat of disturbances, ensuring the highest level of continuity.

The intrinsic link between KPIs and KRIs is a measure of performance in light of potential uncertainties to manage them for optimal results. Some organisations tend to blend the two, whereas it is appropriate to keep in mind the differences. KPIs illustrate the level of performance reached at any point in time; they reflect the past to assess the path already travelled towards success. On the contrary, KRIs project a light into the future. They help anticipate, and avoid or mitigate difficulties and should provide early warning signs to avoid being caught off guard. Finally, the timeline is not the same; KPIs are usually measured quarterly, whereas KRIs, even if monitored regularly, should be reviewed every time something 'exceptional' happens, and the time horizon is anything between a year and a century; so KRIs are milestones on a long road.

The challenge of developing KRIs is that they should rest on root causes when it would be so much easier to remain at the 'immediate' cause level. The connection with KPIs is not always as straightforward as the above explanation might make it: the devil is in the details. Then, the significant levels that will trigger action must be set. There are numerous challenges to meet before a battery of KRI can be implemented throughout the organisation. There is no one-size-fits-all, ready-to-use set of KRI. However, some recommendations may help an organisation embarking on the 'KRI journey':

- Prioritise the strategic objectives and the risk, both the downside and upside; that influence them and define KRIs for the main causes identified;
- Make sure KRI values are recorded automatically in the data bank to make sure it remains up to date;

- Link KRI and KPI to enhance risk forecasting;
- Set alert/action thresholds so that action and thinking are synchronised so that it is appropriate and on time.

4.5. Stakeholders' Involvement and Consent

ERM's ultimate line of defence is to enter a continued dialogue with the organisation's internal and external stakeholders. The expression of the RM guidelines (ISO 31000:2018) 'communication and consultation' refers to two-way communication. Risk communication is not a public relations exercise to 'inform' but more a listening exercise to understand stakeholders' expectations; this supposes establishing listening posts and communication channels. Some professionals use the word 'cooperation' but that seems difficult to organise as different stakeholders may have conflicting views and getting them together in a consensus might prove explosive.

The issue of staff involvement has been addressed earlier but with a focus on risk owners. The support of the line of command is essential, but 'in an organisation risk management is everyone's business'; therefore, all staff must be on board. For all associates to support the project, they must see what they have to gain through sound RM extended to their tasks, wherever it is – on the shop floor or in the offices. This will require training specifically designed to address their concerns and show how they are addressed: safety, health issues, continuity of employment, etc. However, they must be able to measure the evolution by themselves; a typical KRI for a construction site could be days without an accident, the number of injured since the beginning of the project, etc. RM must be driven home as a daily concern, the ultimate effect on the resilience and performance of the organisation must be translated in terms of salary raises, job opportunities, etc. For managers, it may include bonus packages, career opportunities, etc. This micro-approach to managing risk ultimately translates into overall economic performance, and that is one way that ERM creates value.

An ERM programme will also prove attractive for external stakeholders insofar as it gives due consideration to their concerns *(see the contrast between TRM and ERM – Table 4.1)*. Through global protection and enhancement of the organisation's assets, tangible and intangible, ERM reassures its economic partners of its resilience and the continuity of their relations, and the neighbours and society appreciate its concern for safety and the environment. In one word, ERM is the cornerstone of stakeholders' trust and confidence, the foundation of its major asset, reputation.

Managing reputation is an important part of strategic management in an organisation, and it has become even more crucial with instant communication through the Internet. Furthermore, reputation has become the main asset of many organisations, and it would be useful to put a value on reputation. However, it is very difficult to develop a reliable model. Some have suggested referring to market capitalisation for listed companies: deduct the fixed asset and quantifiable intangible asset values and the result provides an estimate for reputation value.

Table 4.1. Contrasting TRM and ERM – Stakeholders' Involvement.

Risk Categories	TRM	ERM
Operational risk	YES	YES
Financial risk	NO	YES
Strategic risk	Limited to operational strategy	YES
Integration with strategy	Only operational – *technical RM*	On all aspects of the organisation
Performance metrics	Activity and result indicators	Metrics designed for specific risks or contingencies
Organisational penetration	Limited Integration: risks are approached in silos and the operational responsibilities are assigned to delegates in the departments or assumed byte *risk manager*	Systematic integration: risk owners at all levels with RM mission in all job descriptions, global approach, breaking the silos
Result	Minimise, mitigate, or eliminate the risk	Optimising risk-taking

With such a valuation model, the volatility of stock prices directly hits the value of reputation. However, it shows that reputation can represent between 60% and 80% of the total asset value. This is an additional benefit of ERM as it aims to strengthen relationships with stakeholders; hence, managing risks to reputation is a principal output (see Section 6.6). Looking at long-term resilience means using metrics not solely based on short-term financial results.

A crisis is the ultimate stress test for reputation. Crises are characterised by a sudden development, like an avalanche that might wipe out all in its path. Therefore, managing a crisis means reacting promptly and adequately as soon as the first symptoms of a potential rupture situation are detected. This cannot be spontaneous and supposes to be prepared by forging the mind that can function under stress. Rupture can come from different and complex causes, natural events, technological mishaps, human errors, and sometimes a combination of all three like the consequences of the 2011 Tsunami in Japan.

These bundles of multiple causes are such that preventing the event before it starts may prove impossible. That is why training decision-makers on making decisions under stress and with limited information is a key to preparing for a crisis. Of course, communication, including social media, is a crucial element to maintain trust; trust built before any crisis helps keep contact with stakeholders in hectic times. Prioritising stakeholders and communication channels must be established ahead of time so that all options are carefully weighted.

In times of disturbances, the internal communication team should be assisted by external consultants, specialised in crisis communication. By standing back from the event, this assistance will bring serenity to the 'crisis team' if they understand the culture and stakeholders' fears and concerns, which means that they must be selected beforehand and training sessions with them organised to make sure the team will be seamless when the crisis threatens. Their understanding of the situation and their search engine ready to hit keywords will help uncover negative blogs and find the proper action to stop and/or engage them.

Whatever the quality of the RM programmes, a surprise is still possible, and this is why each organisation must assess the level of risk it is willing to take to reach its strategic objectives; the issue of risk appetite/tolerance has already been addressed and it is pervasive in all RM activities. However, when setting the appropriate level, boards must keep in mind the long-term impact on stakeholders' trust and confidence, their involvement in the RM activity will help manage the aftermath of a crisis.

Chapter 5

Improving Risk Management Processes Through ERM

For enterprise risk management (ERM) to contribute to the organisation's overall performance, it must be fully integrated into the *management system of the organisation*; including ERM in the strategy development process is the cornerstone of this integration. ERM was first developed in financial institutions, as it fits organisations that rely on risk to develop their business. However, it has gained traction in all companies that handle a portfolio of projects to optimise their return on assets. However, ERM is not useful only for for-profit organisations, of all sizes, including small- and medium-sized enterprises (SMEs), but also for public entities and healthcare establishments, even nongovernmental organisations (NGOs) that aim to optimise their performance. Regional and local authorities and even nations would benefit from ERM in their search for management excellence and societal resilience.

ERM brings to organisations' leaderships a serenity that allows them to tackle uncertainties that their organisations are confronted with confidence and make strategic decisions in a reduced-stress environment. Thus, they are best equipped to enhance opportunities and curb threats. However, the ERM positive performance impact supposes the organisation fully comply with laws and regulations that their activities and locations call for, including those linked with the management of risk; risks with a potential impact on the environment, and the quality of life of all citizens, are clearly at the top of the agenda call for a liaison with corporate social responsibility (CSR) issues.

5.1. Improving Strategic Decision-Making Processes

The main benefit of ERM in the strategic process is to bring high-quality information concerning the uncertain context the organisation has to navigate; this information helps the organisation adapt to change, i.e. its survival agility. So, ERM enlightens directors' and officers' decisions, which improves their organisation's resilience and assists them in delivering their responsibility of stating and monitoring the risk management (RM) strategy and making sure it remains relevant through changes in the context and stakeholders' expectations, thus avoiding future failure.

Enterprise Risk Management in Today's World, Part A:
Enterprise-Wide Risk Management and Strategy, 67–76
Copyright © 2024 by Jean-Paul Louisot and Simon Grima
Published under exclusive licence by Emerald Publishing Limited
doi:10.1108/978-1-83797-406-120241006

Strategy development is a process through which an organisation's leadership (executive committee, supervisory board, board of directors, etc.) develops, amends, or refines a strategy that reflects its vision of the future. The fundamental reason why the process has to be revisited regularly is that no *business model* is eternal as the context in which an organisation operates is constantly changing: new technology, information revolution, shifting markets, and consumer expectations. Formalising the puzzle of uncertainties and combining them in a readable projection is the main output of an ERM programme; thus, the ERM programme improves the strategic planning process in various ways that create long-term value:

- ERM allows curbing threats and specifically envisioning and preparing the proper response to catastrophic threats;
- ERM facilitates enhancing opportunities and incorporating them into the *business model* or in inventing new models for a successful future;
- ERM offers a tool to reduce the volatility of an outcome around the desired target, thus improving the overall organisation's performance.

To summarise, integrating ERM into the strategic process contributes to the success of the organisation, its performance, and its long-term resilience.

Business model consolidates the fundamental aspects of an organisation including vision, missions, strategies, infrastructure, policies, offers, and processes.

5.2. Integrating ERM into the Strategy Development Process

The ERM framework calls for the organisation to implement an RM process including establishing internal and external contexts, developing an exposure diagnostic (risk assessment), choosing the best treatment for critical risk (exceeding risk appetite), and then proceeding with self-evaluation and audit (monitor and review). But the ultimate 'line of defence' is the continuous process of 'communication and consultation' with all stakeholders, internal and external. Integrating the ERM programme into the strategic process enhances the capacity of the organisation to efficiently manage the risks with which it is confronted (see how JPLA_Consultants proposed methods are aligned with ISO 31000 – Table 5.1). The integration requires the organisation to:

1. Develop objectives and criteria for the ERM (*while establishing the internal and external context and assessing organisational objectives*).
2. Identify exposure (the *first step in the exposure diagnostic or risk assessment*).
3. Analyse, evaluate, and prioritise 'critical' exposures to address the major issues (the *second and third steps in the exposure diagnostic – risk assessment*).
4. Treat critical exposures, with special attention to the high-priority risks (*risk treatment*).
5. Audit critical exposures *(monitor and review)*.

Table 5.1. Alignment of JPLA_Consultants Method with ISO 31000 Process.

Communication and Consultation with Internal and External Stakeholders				
Establish the internal and external context	Exposures Diagnostic (Risk Assessment).			JPLA consultants Risk treatment Identify and select reduction methods
	JPLA consultants Risk identification	JPLA consultants Risk analysis	JPLA consultants Risk evaluation	
		JPLA consultants Audit Monitor and review	YES/NO depending on whether residual risk is acceptable	

Notes: The ERM process, proposed by ISO 31000, and described above, is reflected in the RM process in three steps developed by JPLA_Consultants; diagnostic (identification analysis, evaluation), treatment (list the reduction methods and select the optimal solution), and audit (monitor and review).

However, JPLA_Consultants elaborate on three points over the ISO 31000:

1. Establishing the internal and external context implies a direct link with strategy development (SWOT);
2. Communication and consultation with stakeholders is a continuous link throughout the process, which serves as the external 'line of defence';
3. ERM makes clear the decision to be made at the evaluation stage, i.e., whether residual risks are in line with the risk appetite/tolerance defined by the board. If it is acceptable, the controls in place are kept and the process continues directly with monitor and review. If it is not acceptable, a different risk treatment must be designed and implemented.

Usually, exposure identification results in a long list of risks that could have consequences for the organisation. This is why risks must be prioritised based on their potential impact on the organisation's capacity to reach its strategic objectives, and under some circumstances at least survive; in other terms, their degree of criticality. The core mission of ERM is therefore to screen through the diagnostic process the risks that are critical to the organisation. However, what is critical must be defined by a battery of risk criteria relevant for the organisation, thus reflecting its risk appetite/tolerance determined during the establishment of the internal and external context.

For example, a local authority may have zero tolerance for terrorist attacks impacting its population and equipment. Therefore, it will have to upgrade the resistance of structures to explosions, car attacks, etc., while, all the time, increasing its intelligence efforts in cooperation with national police. A company relying on raw materials purchased on a speculative market may consider that price volatility would constitute too much of a burden on its margins and choose to buy futures to hedge against price fluctuations (thus forfeiting possible gains to avoid possible losses).

Through time, new risks emerge while others fade away. This is why the organisation engaging in an ERM programme must ensure that the process is iterative so that the critical risks list can be updated regularly to review the positive and/or negative impacts so that the priorities assigned remain relevant.

5.3. Developing ERM Objectives (Establish Internal and External Context)

The first step in the integration of the ERM process into the strategic process is to make sure that ERM objectives are aligned with strategic objectives and reflected in the *business model*, but this means that risks are considered in the strategy development process. In principle, the board of directors and the executive team develop, and regularly review, the vision, the mission, and the strategic objectives and their consequence on the financial forecasts in the short term (cash position), the middle term (uses and sources of funds at a three to five-year horizon), and the long term (need for capitals to feed growth – investing and working capital). ERM objectives must be set and updated precisely when the board is reviewing the long-term objectives.

Examples of objectives for RM relevant to an ERM programme

- Identify opportunities and threats that could have a significant impact on the strategic objectives;
- Forecast and reduce the volatility of the expected result;
- Identify and anticipate emerging risks;
- Improve the organisation's resilience and ensure its sustainable development;
- Ensure consistency of risk-taking through space and time;
- Optimise risk-taking for the organisation, within the limits of the risk appetite and risk tolerance defined by the board;
- Reduce the volatility of financial results (within limits acceptable to the financial community);
- Improve RM competencies throughout the organisation (and with its major economic partners);
- Promote a proactive attitude to RM;
- Bring together stakeholders to develop a common consensus on RM;
- Develop operational managers' responsibility and authority in the managing of their risks, and include RM in their bonus equation;
- Set up consistent procedures so that risks are included in decision-making processes at all levels;
- Improve the quality of hygiene and safety for all staff, partners, and society at large;
- Develop and implement the most efficient risk reduction tools to limit losses;
- Strengthen the trust and confidence of internal and external stakeholders;
- Develop and maintain better information for the instances of governance;
- Develop transparent and relevant risk communication and consultation mechanisms;

- Ensure compliance with all laws and regulations at the local, national, and international levels; and
- Develop an interdisciplinary risk conscience integrating local socio-cultural differences.

An organisation's ERM objectives must give due consideration to several factors:

- The organisation's risk appetite and risk tolerance;
- The motivations underlying the decision to invest in the development of an ERM programme;
- The organisation's expressed needs in terms of ERM output and the structure of its ERM programme;
- The scale of the ERM project and its rhythm of advance to full maturity;
- The leadership expectation for the ERM to improve the chances of reaching or exceeding the strategic objectives; and
- The ERM understanding developed by the organisation.

These fundamental choices will dictate the decisions to be made through time to establish the ERM programme and set up the internal structures and processes that will support the three steps, diagnostic, treatment, audit, and provide the elements to audit and/or coach the main partners on risk to improve the reliability of the procurement network.

5.4. Analysing and Evaluating Risks to Prioritise Critical Risks (Exposure Diagnostic or Risk Assessment)

The board of directors and executive committee must focus their attention on the uncertainties that are linked to the fundamental hypotheses behind the strategy, i.e., threats and opportunities that could create havoc in the 'usual way of doing business' and jeopardise the mission and objectives of the organisation. They may result from drastic changes in the external and/or internal context in which the organisation operates that could result in hugely different levels of resources than those assumed when developing the strategy. Major areas of concern include, but are not limited to, the following:

- Competition evolution;
- Demography and consumer attitudes and expectations;
- Technological breakthrough;
- Current state and perspective of the economy;
- Political decisions and legal and regulatory atmosphere; and
- Organisation's capacity to comply with all rules and regulations.

An effective approach to identify and quantify the potential consequences for the organisation, and its partners' network, should these events happen, is to ask the question: 'What would happen if …?'

As an illustration, here is a list of situations where the question should be asked to develop possible worst-case scenarios.

What would be the consequences for the organisation if…:

- Current exchange rates (especially for major currencies like US Dollars, Euros, Sterling, Yuan, Yen, etc.), which provide a competitive advantage were substantially modified?
- Frost in Florida would destroy our Floridian competitors' crops?
- Confrontation with an emerging new competitor who initiates a price war?
- Compliance with a new regulation would add 12 or 18 months to our new product's development time?
- Technological breakthrough will make our N° 1 product obsolete overnight (the question of substitute rather than competitor)?
- Consumers request for 'greener' products than our current line?
- Limited resources (competencies and production capacities, etc.) mobilised for the launch of a new product?

Risks with potential impact on strategy are sometimes called 'critical risks', and they must be considered carefully, especially if they are likely to have interactions that could trigger a catastrophic cumulative effect and derail the organisation; they put at risk not only success but even survival. Some risks may have a 'delayed impact', time expanded, to include middle- and long-term consequences, as the short-term assessment might be deceptive. They must be singled out as the diagnostic must expand into a longer time horizon!

Once risks to strategy (critical risks) have been identified, they must be prioritised according to their criticality to select an optimal allocation of resources for further investigation and mitigation. There are many methods to quantify the criticality of a risk, but all rest on the measure of the probability of the event to occur and the impact on the level of resources of the organisation when they occur; however, they should also assess the impact on the capacity of the organisation to achieve its objectives, as well as the potential consequences for the 'main' stakeholders. This overall approach is now called *Business Impact Analysis* (BIA); although the difference will be addressed further; the BIA consists only of conducting the diagnostic to its end, i.e. including contingent loss of revenue.

As mentioned earlier, most traditional metrics include the probability of occurrence (frequency or likelihood) and the consequences (impact or severity). However, if this is reasonable for the high frequency-low severity risks where the 'expected loss' provides an acceptable assessment of the annual cost of a given risk, it falls short of bringing useful information for the more catastrophic risk (low frequency-high severity); for these, the annual volatility of 'cost of losses' requires expansion of the study to other variables: volatility (fat tails providing a non-negligible chance of a catastrophic loss or 'black swan') and velocity (the speed of the event to strike and cause damage).

For each of the critical risks identified, it is important to identify triggers and warning signals that will allow the anticipation of an impact with an alert when the chance of the event taking place, the level of threat, is suddenly increased. The latest cognitive science discoveries dictate the list of critical risks to be monitored at the risk committee level be limited to no more than seven. However, the list should be revised regularly, at least each quarter, or when a drastic change in the context takes place, including events requiring a continuity plan or crisis management to be implemented.

5.5. Treating Critical Risk Integrating Priorities (Risk Treatment)

The answers to the 'what if?' questions mentioned above are part of the diagnostic process (risk assessment) and represent what is also known as a scenario analysis. It provides the elements needed to develop the risk treatments adequate for identified risks. Depending on the probability or likelihood (low, medium, high), the organisation is in a position to start the needed action to enhance opportunities or curb threats.

Practically, the risk treatment tools can be classified into five categories as follows:

- **Suppression/avoidance**: stop the activity or find alternative processes that eliminate the root cause of the risk and thus its consequences;
- **Acceptance**: live with the risk while setting up early warning and mitigating methods to be implemented only when the risk becomes reality;
- **Transfer/share**: assign the responsibility for managing the risk (risk-ownership) to a third party or share it with him/her. For risk reduction, outsource it to a supplier or a sub-contractor. For risk financing, purchase insurance coverage or include a contractual clause to transfer the risk – to a non-insurer;
- **Reduction**: set up methods to reduce the probability of occurrence of the risk (prevention) or the consequences (protection) so that it will be kept below the risk appetite/tolerance of the organisation;
- **Optimisation/exploitation**: develop actions to maximise positive consequences and reap profits, including in the case of threats if managed more efficiently than competitors (gain competitive advantage).

5.6. Monitoring Critical Risk (Monitoring and Review)

Critical or killer risks must be reviewed periodically to discern and validate the trends, warning signals, and trigger events updated when the diagnostic phase (risk assessment) is revisited. The periodicity is based on the two fundamental drivers of criticality, frequency and severity. However, exceptional events may trigger an exceptional review if the changes in the environment are significant.

Monitoring and reviewing risks impacting strategy is a complex process to the extent that trigger events can have very diverse origins from a letter from a professional union to the merger of two competitors, new regulations, consumers' surveys, economic partners' failure, etc. The major issue concerns risk with potentially catastrophic consequences with a level of likelihood that makes leadership and/or stakeholders, 'uncomfortable'. One solution to ensure close monitoring is to establish in the organisation a network of 'sentinels' positioned at key points where they could perceive early signs of the 'dreaded events' and thus trigger early response plans or even abort the event (see Table 5.2).

This activity of data collection and setting up of an information network is part of a wider function known as economic intelligence.

Table 5.2. Examples of Risk Treatment Strategies for 'Critical' Risk Consumers' Market.

What Would Be The Risk If ...?	Frequency/ Likelihood	Treatment
We were confronted with an emerging new competitor who initiated a price war.	High	**Avoidance/suppression** Start a *lobbying* effort to prevent the changes in regulations that would facilitate the competitor's entering the market. **Reduction** Start a Public Relations (PR) campaign stressing our product's superior attributes if a competitor enters the market.
Complying with a new regulation would add twelve or eighteen months to our new products' development time.	Low	**Acceptance** Review the development process to try and cut time in other areas when a new regulation is enacted.
A technology breakthrough that renders our N° 1 product obsolete overnight (the question of substitute rather than competitor)?	Medium	**Reduction** Initiate as early as possible a programme to diversify our offer and include new technologies.
Consumers request 'greener' products than our current line?	Low	**Reduction** Review the processes to develop alternatives to current lines and processes to be ready to launch 'green products' should that become necessary (or even anticipate the move).
Our limited resources (competencies and production capacities, etc) are mobilised for the launch of a new product?	High	**Optimisation/exploitation** Enter into negotiations with developers and producers of the new product to assist in the new line; conversely, find outsourcing for the existing line.

(*Continued*)

Table 5.2. (*Continued*)

What Would Be The Risk If …?	Frequency/ Likelihood	Treatment
Current exchange rates (especially for major currencies like US Dollars, Euros, Sterling, Yuan, Yen, etc.) that provide us a competitive advantage were to be substantially modified.	Medium (with periodic fluctuations)	**Optimisation/exploitation** Increase *marketing efforts* to swamp the European market and gain market shares while the favourable situation lasts.
Frost in Florida would destroy our Floridian competitors' crops?	High	**Optimisation/exploitation** Select control mechanisms in addition to higher prices allowed by the shortage and negotiate with supermarket chains to obtain more shelf space for our products.

5.7. Emerging Legal and Regulatory Issues Concerning ERM

There are many initiatives worldwide to establish standards and frameworks to develop and implement ERM within the strategy process. For example, rating agencies, including Standard & Poors (S&P), are now expecting companies rated to have integrated RM into their strategy process; if they have not always come up with metrics to measure the RM performance, at least in their rating process, they should include a qualitative assessment of the RM performance. The ISO 31000:2018[1] standard proposes guidelines for the organisational framework of RM programmes.

Standards are based on 'good practices', acceptable methods and processes, and result from an international consensus. They are not legal or regulatory documents but have become compulsory if local legislation makes it so and then they are part of compliance.

Compliance with all laws and regulations, and even industry standards, is an integral objective of ERM; this means that compliance issues although separate must be considered within the ERM framework which implies setting up a legal watch for ERM-related issues like:

- Exposures that directors and executives consider as the « most » critical, severity is the key driver, and likelihood is considered in conjunction with severity:

[1]First published in December 2009, the ISO 31000 standard was revised; the present version published in February 2018 should be open for revision in 2024.

'too big to accept such a probability', but again, volatility and velocity have to be considered;
- Frequency of critical risk reviews and the processes that are in place to identify and update them;
- Risk sensitivity influence on managing liabilities/financial decisions;
- Position and mission of the management of risk (and of the risk-manager) within the strategic decision process;
- Organisation's RM culture is identified through the framework, the communication systems, policies, and metrics deployed to manage risks.

Directors and executives should keep in mind that compliance, even when integrating RM into the strategy development process, is not a substitute for a proactive risk policy which is the mission of a matured ERM. Non-compliance may be a killer risk but compliance does not replace RM.

Chapter 6

Contrasting Traditional Risk Management (TRM) and Enterprise-wide Risk Management (ERM)

Traditional risk management (TRM, also called simply RM) is still often limited to managing operational and accidental risks. On the other hand, the *enterprise-wide risk management* (ERM) approach is extended to the whole risk landscape, including financial risks and those impacting strategy. When mature, ERM rests on a global and integrated management of risks that participates in the definition of sustainable objectives in the strategy development phase and ensures that the objectives are met or even exceeded when navigating through the uncertainties, positive (opportunities), or negative (threats).

The four main differences between ERM and TRM are the following (for more details, see Table 6.1):

- Risk categories in the risk-management scope (risk taxonomy);
- Integration in the strategy development process;
- Metrics used to measure performance; and
- Organisational framework.

6.1. Considering Risk Taxonomy

In the traditional approach to risk TRM as well as in an ERM effort, all professionals recognise that risk must be quantified, even if the quantification has its limitations and may result from an expert's evaluation rather than models. This need to quantify to the extent possible is a strong common issue for any type of risk management as it aims at lifting the fog that clouds the future and limiting the range of possible outcomes to define a zone of probable and a tail to be addressed if likelihood remains 'too high to be comfortable with'.

Beyond this shared effort, TRM and ERM differ widely on the risk landscape they consider. Since the beginning of risk management, there has been a strong distinction between **pure risks and speculative risks**; only the first category is managed within a TRM programme. The four quadrants' taxonomy is the most

Enterprise Risk Management in Today's World, Part A:
Enterprise-Wide Risk Management and Strategy, 77–100
Copyright © 2024 by Jean-Paul Louisot and Simon Grima
Published under exclusive licence by Emerald Publishing Limited
doi:10.1108/978-1-83797-406-120241007

Table 6.1. Going Beyond the Traditional Approach to Risk Management.

TRM		ERM	
Risk definition	Operational risk Pure risk only Only perils Only downside risk (threats) Contain the cost of risk	Operational risk Pure, mixed, and speculative risks Strategic risk Risk may result in gain or loss	Events, perils, and change of circumstances Threats and opportunities Creating value while complying with ethics (values)
Link with strategy	Performance indicators include result standards and activity standard	Performance indicators are linked with objectives, at the strategic, tactical, and operational levels RM objectives are aligned with the organisation's objectives	Optimising risk-taking Preserve value and create value
Global and integrated	Does not apply to departments of the organisation not concerned with operational risks	Global approach to all risk/ exposures including: – procurement (and main partners); – GRC (governance and compliance) – Crisis and continuity management	Reputation Disturbances Consultation of all stakeholders (*or interested parties*) Rating agencies
Common vocabulary	Most concepts and vocabulary are derived from the insurance industry	Vocabulary derived from major *management standards and industry tradition*	
Components of risk culture	The *risk manager* is part of middle management, often supervised by a treasurer; it is not part of the strategy development team and is informed only when impacts on operational risks	CRO should be supervised by the board's risk committee and part of the executive team The organisation is split into « risk centres » with a specific risk owner for each risk	Communication and consultation Develop a strong case to justify ERM with executives and board Facilitate a positive risk attitude within the organisation

		ERM, as any « change project » to be integrated into the management system of the organisation	Assist, audit, and promote self-evaluation Risk portfolio approach Involve stakeholders in the process
Exposure space	Exposures linked to operational risk may result only in loss (or no loss) – pure risk	All the risk universe downside and upside risk that may result in loss or gain	
Information system	Traditional risk management information system (RMIS) based on insurance losses and physical assets and liabilities	*Business intelligence systems* (BIS) or *business analytics* that integrate internal data banks, which must be consistent throughout the organisation and the external sources (big data) provided they are assessed for relevance (avoiding the fake news) to develop algorithms that provide insights into the future to assist decision-makers Internal control and financing needs for the short, medium, and long terms can be assessed and aggregated	

commonly used, and it distinguishes hazard, strategic, financial, and operational risks. Hazard and operational **risks** are classified as pure **risks**, while financial and strategic **risks** are classified as speculative **risks**. Whereas other taxonomies of **risk** focus on some aspect of the **risk** itself, the **four quadrants of risk** traditionally focus on the main source of the **risk** and who the risk owner is.

Pure risk

May result in a loss or no loss but not in a gain.

Speculative risk

May result in a gain, a loss, or no loss/no gain.

TRM is limited to pure risk, meaning that the optimal outcome is no-loss; all the other outcomes are losses of varying importance. The four-quadrant approach can create a problem within TRM in that traditional lines of insurance cross the quadrants; an event like a fire may have consequences in all types of losses: direct damages, loss of revenue, staff injuries, liabilities, whatever the original cause of the loss.

When it comes to risk treatment, TRM focuses on risk reduction (prevention and protection) and risk financing (exceptional cash needed to compensate for losses). In reality, reduction measures can be implemented in an array of different practical tools that depend on the cause of risk to be treated, and they can go from simple warning stickers (in lavatories asking staff to wash their hands in food preparation and health facilities especially) to complex engineering project (like sprinklers systems to extinguish fires), and the associated continuity planning to reduce net revenues losses. Other tools include training for first aid, product recall plans, etc. However, the overall approach to risk treatment is to reduce risk to the optimally efficient level (cost/benefit analysis) and finance the residual risk (retention or transfer mostly based on the consequences on cash flow and the cost of transfer).

In contrast, ERM is all-encompassing; it considers the whole risk landscape, whatever the sources of consequences, based on the 'loss of resources' that might impair the capacity to reach specified objectives or the exceptional 'surplus of resources' that should be put to the best possible use. Of course, both pure and speculative risks are considered, and the four quadrants are to be approached in a portfolio fashion. Within the framework of this taxonomy,

- **Strategic risks** include all top management decisions concerning strategic orientations like choice of investments, new product development, mergers and acquisitions, etc.
- **Financial risks** include interest rates, exchange rates, market fluctuations, cash shortfalls, etc.
- **Operational risks** include bid processes, information transfer, construction/project management, accounting processes, ruptures in the procurement chain, electricity shutdown, staff errors and omissions, and all other processes in place to produce goods and services.
- **Hazard risk**s include incidents such as fire, machinery breakdown, natural events, etc.

However, **risks to reputation**, which are at the core of the 'new' ERM and were not on the TRM risk radar, do not find a place in this taxonomy. Reputation has become recognised as an essential asset of many organisations, especially in the age of social media when a reputation can be built or destroyed in minutes. The four quadrants' taxonomy would probably enter them in the 'strategy quadrant' as well as 'cyber-security', which cannot be left to 'operational managers' given the potential consequences.

With its scope limited to pure risk, treating one exposure at a time, TRM was not able to integrate even interactions between pure risks and of course no interaction between pure and speculative risks. This is one of the many benefits of ERM: stressing the interaction between all types of risk and even their combination in one single event of opportunity and threats, for example:

- When maintaining continuity even when a threat materialises, an organisation may gain a competitive advantage; a threat is then transformed into an opportunity, and conversely;
- When accepting a sizable profitable deal that would stretch its resources and threaten its overall reliability, an organisation turns an opportunity into a threat!

ERM focuses on the core mission of risk management in a complex and volatile world, i.e. achieving optimal objectives, whereas TRM's core mission was only to contain the cost of risks, i.e. restore the organisation's financial position and reduce pure risk levels.

The ERM's key to success, and maturity, is to help the organisation seize opportunities, not only during the strategy development process but also during the implementation process as the future unfolds and new opportunities, and threats, appear on the risk radar; such a situation could be a sudden opening to gain market shares, to enter new markets, etc. ERM will offer the directors and the executive team a vision of the threats and opportunities looming and project their consequences, with the help of business analytics and proper modelling. This constant strategic adjustment will keep at all times the organisation as close as possible to its 'efficient frontiers'.

To illustrate the trade-offs involved, social security could benefit from the development of a new vaccine by an independent laboratory as the medical expenses linked with the pathology would be saved in the long run. However, in the rush to bring the vaccine to market, no shortcuts should be taken during the experimentation phase. The public must be informed of the risks associated with the vaccine, as any negative side effects reported on social media could lead to its rejection, similar to what occurred during the COVID-19 pandemic.

6.2. Integration in the Strategy Development Process

In TRM, risk managers were not involved with strategy unless a hazard risk could trigger consequences that could derail the strategy or put into question the Directors and Officers (D&O) liabilities. Within the ERM framework, risk managers should belong to the strategy team. The global and integrated approach of all uncertainties confronting the organisation, which tears down the silos that had been set up to manage risks thus far (*see the four quadrants and other insurance-based taxonomies*), opens up the possibility of optimising risk-taking in a portfolio of projects representing the organisation's strategy. Therefore, there are lessons to be learned from portfolio management models developed in the financial world.

- **Theoretical illustration: strategic integration of ERM**

Low-cost is a regional airline that has three main objectives:

- Keep ticket prices low;
- Continually improve flight punctuality;
- Uphold reputation as a sustainable airline.

In a TRM structure, the chief financial officer (CFO) would be in charge of the hedging policy (purchase of futures or derivatives) to stabilise kerosene costs, while the risk manager would have managed the issue of potential accidental damages to the company's fuel reserves.

Within the ERM framework, the executive at 'Low-cost' must meet the challenge to define an integrated solution where all risks linked with kerosene supplies as pertain to its global strategy and objectives. The following elements have to be considered in the process at 'Low-cost':

- Costs of carrying the kerosene inventory, including the insurance costs, the management of several fuel storage facilities, and the purchase of considerable quantities of kerosene.
- A leakage or fire at a storage facility in a metropolitan area could have several negative impacts, including environmental pollution (affecting air, water, and land) and damage to the company's reputation. Additionally, the incident could lead to increased costs due to the urgent need to purchase kerosene at higher prices. These factors could adversely affect all three strategic objectives of the company.
- Strategic implications for punctuality and low prices, should a hedging policy or schedule risk prove more expensive than anticipated.

After an in-depth study of the pros and cons of a hedging policy on their strategic objectives, Low-cost leadership chose to implement a hedging programme, managing large kerosene storage facilities and buying kerosene in bulk, to optimise its chances to achieve all three strategic objectives. Combining the new policy along with the previous choices under a silo approach, Low-cost was able to project the gain the new policy will bring. In the silo approach, the CFO had underestimated the impacts on two of the strategic objectives, low prices and punctuality.

The portfolio of risk can be represented in a three-dimensional space corresponding to the three attributes that define a risk. This is known as the space of exposures. The three axes are (i) resources, (ii) event categories that form the horizontal plan of 'identification', and (iii) quantification or impact on reaching the objectives, i.e. the consequences on the resource level. This model within an ERM framework provides a visualisation that will help decision-makers at all levels, the risk owners, to identify the critical risks and the level of resources that are 'vital' for the continuity of operations; thus, they can prioritise the actions that will contain resource volatility within 'acceptable' limits to protect the strategic objectives, all the while allowing early recognition of any situation that will bring discontinuity, no matter what.

- **Illustration: TRM and *ERM***

The companies XYZ and ABC are confronted with similar issues. The leaders of XYZ who favour a traditional approach to risk management have assigned their risk manager the task of 'containing the cost of risk', in the pure risk domain.

The **XYZ risk manager** has identified fire as a main accidental exposure. Therefore, he has assessed the return on investing in a new building to be built with fire-resistant materials and equipped with a sprinkler system, while changing the industrial process to use less flammable chemical products, and to project the impact of these measures on insurance premiums and the level of retention. At the same time, the risk manager has considered implementing a strategy of separating risks through the use of several production sites; while increasing the likelihood of a fire in one of the sites, it would decrease substantially the impact and maybe even avoid any discontinuity that a one-site solution would generate if a major fire closed it down, which would provide a competitor an opportunity to enter XYZ's markets and/or attract market shares at the expense of XYZ.

When it comes to ABC company, currently implementing an ERM programme, it is not only concerned with the efficient management of pure risks but also takes into account operational effectiveness and their interactions with controls, staff readiness, and operational manager competencies, and ABC is eager to develop a continuous improvement process. As far as a multi-site strategy is concerned, the main issue for ABC is to assess the effect of the entry into the market of a competitor, or a substitute, when compared to the cost reduction due to economies of scale in the one-site strategy.

Based on a pure-risk approach, XYZ has chosen to split its production among five sites of equal capacity to limit its probable capacity loss to 20% should one be destroyed by a fire. However, this approach did not include in the decision process the effect on the 'cost of operations' and whether the increase might jeopardise XYZ's competitive advantage, as this is a speculative risk. Whereas XYZ's plan aims to limit the chance of entry of a competitor in case of fire, it leaves aside the current risk of opening a wide door to competition by being outpriced and that would not require a fire to be an immediate threat.

With their ERM model, ABC decided on a two-site solution that could operate on a three-shift mode, rather than two should one of the two be damaged by a fire or stopped by any other event for that matter; this means that, should one of the plants be stopped, the other one could, *temporarily*, be operated at up to 75% of ABC's capacity. Productivity gains linked to the management of only two sites of larger capacity in normal times maintain the capability to stay on the market at near capacity in case of a fire, while still avoiding the one-site potential catastrophic consequences.

The illustration demonstrates that even if the two firms are led to choose a risk separation strategy, the conditions of its implementation are substantially different. When integrating speculative risks according to the global and integrated *risk management approach* at ABC (holistic ERM), the optimal solution is a balance between speculative and pure risks, not only containing the cost of risk on the line but also reaching the company's strategic goals. This leads to the 'optimisation of risk-taking', not merely reducing the cost of (accidental) risks at the expense of the overreaching company goals to maintain market share and service to customers.

6.3. Metrics to Measure Performances

In a TRM programme, performance was usually based on two batteries of standards:

- **Result standard** – i.e. the objectives to be met (number of accidents, annual aggregate losses, number of days lost for workers' injuries, cost of insurance premiums, total annual retained losses, etc.);
- **Activity standard** – i.e. the efforts developed to reach the goals, especially those that do not lend themselves to be measured annually but on a much longer period (number of evacuation drills, Business Continuity Plan (BCP) exercises, maintenance budget for risk reduction tools (like sprinklers, etc.).

The distinction between the two can be illustrated in the case of a firm labour intensive with a large workforce, one of the objectives could be to reduce the likelihood and the severity of work-related accidents and organise several days of training on health and safety for workers every year. Training is a way to reduce accidents over the long term. The reduction of the number and cost of accidents improves directly the organisation's performance (*result standard*), whereas the number of days of training is an effort maintained to reduce them in the long run (*activity standard*).

However, not all risks that confront an organisation can be eliminated: there are risks inherent to the activities in which an organisation is involved (like explosion or market risk for a refinery, diagnostic error, and hygiene issues – nosocomial – in a hospital, etc.): suppressing or avoiding could be achieved only by closing down the organisation and ceasing operations altogether. Therefore, ERM will never try to eliminate all risks but rather aim for the optimisation of risk-taking to reach the strategic objectives or meet the missions of the organisation.

Optimisation is both an objective and a process through which the organisation tries to reach the best balance possible between reducing risk and reaching objectives. This means that non-core risks, sometimes called ancillary risks, must be reduced as much as economically feasible, while the core risks are accepted even if contained. The organisation's leadership must define the right balance (risk appetite/tolerance) and then navigate as close to the Efficient Frontier as possible. ERM performance is measured by the adequacy between risk management and strategy, i.e. when key performance indicator (KPI) and Principles for Responsible Investment (PRI) are linked and aligned.

Efficient Frontier:

An efficient frontier is a set of investment portfolios that are expected to provide the highest returns at a given level of risk. A portfolio is said to be efficient if there is no other portfolio that offers higher returns for a lower or equal amount of risk. Where portfolios are located on the efficient frontier depends on the investor's degree of risk tolerance.

6.4. Organisational Framework

Chief Risk Officer (CRO)

The position was established originally in the financial industry to stress the executive status of the risk manager in charge of developing the ERM programme. It has spread to other industries, and it is the acronym 'Chief Risk Officer' as most members of the executive team are 'chief officers' in the discipline identified by the middle initial.

In a TRM approach, the *risk manager* is usually reporting to one of the main functions: finance, legal, and occasionally production. The incumbent has a mission limited to pure risk, i.e. hazard risks, and the management of risk for the organisation is essentially done at the RM office with little need for interaction with the field, except for ensuring that the RM guidelines are followed within the centralised RM programme. Even if there are delegations within the group's entities, the delegation is also limited to pure risks. Thus, a plant manager will typically:

- Supervise health and safety efforts;
- Facilitate training sessions for staff;
- Monitor accidental risk reduction in his/her department; and
- Ensure that sprinklers and extinguishers are properly maintained.

On the other hand, in the case of an ERM approach, efficiency requires that the management of risks be delegated to all levels of decisions in the organisation. Within such a framework, the risk manager, often called a *CRO*, reports directly to the chief executive officer (CEO) or a member of the executive team and should have direct access to the board's risk committee. The mission is very different from a technical manager within a department, he/she is mainly a **facilitator** and a **coach** to make sure the ERM process is understood and implemented by all. The CRO also acts as an internal consultant to coach all risk owners, the operational managers to whom the responsibility and the authority to manage risk are delegated within their sphere of management.

As a facilitator, the director of risk management must ensure that there is a constant dialogue among executives and directors to define strategic objectives in risk management that contribute to optimising strategic goals while due consideration is given to the strengths and weaknesses of the organisation (internal context) and the opportunities it is confronted with (external context). This approach must be regularly revised, to reflect the current rhythm of change in the environment, to monitor and update the understanding of the four elements behind the acronym SWOT.[1]

Contrary to TRM, largely confined to headquarters, ERM rests on the commitment to the risk management efforts of all the organisation's stakeholders. In the acronym, the word 'enterprise' represents the extended organisation including all its stakeholders; this is why developing the acronym ERM as 'enterprise-wide risk management' *stresses* that it is not the management of 'enterprise or speculative risks' but that it is risk management extended to all actors in the organisational system: workers, managers, executives, including directors, and also its main economic partners, suppliers and sub-contractors, customers, and distribution channel; however, consideration must be given also to RM regulatory agencies, local authorities, and populations clearly involved in designing corporate social responsibility (CSR) management.

The responsibility of the director of risk in the strategic process is to assist in the development of:

- Tools to identify, analyse, and evaluate all risks and events that would generate volatility in the resources available that could derail the organisation's path to objectives and missions' fulfilment; and
- Methods to limit and control the volatility within acceptable limits as defined in the risk appetite statement.

As a coach, the director of risk management assists in the development of risk culture within the organisation, which means that he helps the risk owners, operational or project managers, to acquire risk-management competencies needed to fulfil their risk management missions as delegated within the ERM programme. They must assess and manage the volatility their entity or project is confronted with as they attempt to reach the tactical and operational objectives needed for the organisation to reach its strategic objectives. When ERM is fully integrated into the organisation's management system, risk management becomes an important mission of each manager, including project managers, and is part of their job description. Then, the risk-management objectives are truly aligned with the global strategic objectives and the metrics for measuring success; KPIs and KRIs are closely related.

One of the attributes of mature ERM is the development of a communication matrix that ensures information flows freely throughout the organisation

---

[1]The four letters of the acronym SWOT are the initials related to the internal context (*Strengths and Weaknesses*) and the external context (*Opportunities and Threats*).

without constraints and/or distortions, offering all concerned easy and ergonomic access to the information they need to perform efficiently. This means a two-way information flow, top-down and bottom-up, and transversally between departments, breaking silos, including external stakeholders on a need-to-know basis. A common language is required with the director of risk to make sure it is discussed and accepted at all levels; one of his/her responsibilities is to collect the essential vocabulary in a common organisational risk glossary. Whereas transparency is a keyword in risk communication, nevertheless one must exercise judgement in making information public, and it must be vetted with economic intelligence (see Section 8.9.4). Communication efficiency requires that dialogues and discussions be organised at all levels, providing supervisors, managers, and executives with the appropriate training to conduct experience sharing and consultation on risk to enhance the organisation's efforts.

Developing metrics and continuous flows of cognitive data are as important as the communication structure; it means relying on the acute and penetrating look of an experienced professional when identifying risks, and their potential impact. Metrics must be designed to reflect the quality of the organisation's long-term risk management efforts. Matrices and metrics must be integrated with care into the *reporting* structure, which encompasses the entire organisation staff, from individual risk owners to directors, including the economic partners linked to the organisation through contractual agreements, sometimes referred to as the 'extended company'. The resilience of the organisation does not rest on its agility alone. The exercise includes setting up early warning circuits that will facilitate response to emerging risks triggered by changes in the internal and external context and that could impact operational, tactical, and strategic objectives. The metrics and matrices will also help evaluate performances when it comes to treatment for already identified exposures.

The ERM process is both iterative and recursive – iterative as the RM process must be applied to all risks as they change through time and recursive as it must be reviewed regularly to ensure that it remains relevant to the situation. ERM optimise risk-taking through contextual evolutions and the accumulation of new information/experiences. Even if the existing risks are efficiently managed, the conditions giving rise to them change over time, and new risks appear that must be treated in an updated portfolio where risk priorities may prove different: efforts may have to be diverted from one risk to treat another. This means that existing treatments may become sub-optimal in a new risk landscape or even be made ineffective – think of a vaccine with mutating viruses as the experience has shown during the recent pandemic and regularly for annual influenza shots (see Table 6.1 – complete comparison of ERM and TRM).

Of course, when the strategy is substantially modified by important decisions (mergers and acquisitions, change of major stakeholders, regulatory changes, market transformation, etc.), the objectives can be modified in such a way that risk analysis must be revised, including BIA and, as a result, risk-management objectives. Even critical objective priorities can be modified; new critical risks may appear, while others become less significant, and new killer risks may take the front seat both in treatment and monitoring.

6.5. Risk Management and the Management of Change

Change is a good thing in itself, but too much change too fast can become dangerous. Organisations, like living beings, must change continually for different reasons. An organisation may be forced after five years to invest in research and development and develop new products due to changes in consumers' tastes. Another might have to review all its processes and procedures to comply with new regulations.

As already stressed earlier, change is a constant challenge to be met by any actor in the economic and social world. Due to the evolution and increasing complexity of the network in which any organisation must evolve, the face increased uncertainty that weighs its decisions and their execution. In other words, when facing thicker and thicker 'uncertainty fog', selecting an acceptable level of risk requires decision-makers an ever more discerning mind to sort out true opportunities and real threats. It is important to avoid chimeras and mirages. Organisations must constantly adapt to change and even cope with ruptures; it is not a choice but a vital necessity. Every leader, like a captain at sea, spends time making choices, to find the best route to avoid heavy weather and pitfalls. This is precisely how ISO 31000 defines risk as 'the effect of uncertainties on objectives'.

The path to maturity of an ERM project is about assigning the management of risk to risk owners, i.e. operational managers; executives should get directly involved only when the risk impact reaches strategic levels or threatens the outcome of a major investment project. Other risks would be better handled at the supervisors' level like workers' safety on the plant floor even if it may have dire consequences on the organisation's reputation.

Grafting risk management skills onto the existing organisation's culture will require a change project to be continuously modified to cope with evolution in the risk landscape and to bring up to speed newly hired employees. Whereas for the first iteration of the *coaching* by the facilitator it is essential to seed the need for change in the mind of all involved, it will be useless if they do not learn to adapt to circumstances to monitor temporary disturbances and prevent them from turning into a serious situation (discontinuity, crisis). It is like a continuous innovation process that will require each staff member to step out of their comfort zone (work as usual) to test a different future: change is always perceived at first as a threat unless it is adequately prepared and explained.

When it comes to the risk-management project, the CRO is the main actor in change and must understand that these evolutions have to be adhered to by all the actors, even external partners; procurement network resilience is essential for the overall organisation's resilience. Some still use the expression 'logistic/supply chain', but the idea of an open system preferred here gives a better picture of the reality of the inter-connexions in a global and open economy.

Many books offer a vade-mecum for change management, and this proliferation of books does not seem to improve the success rate of change projects. The key advice to the CROs or any other leader in charge of a change project at a time when all organisations have to reinvent themselves constantly is summarised in the following list of common-sense tips on change management:

- **Rules rather than objectives**: Like when dieting, it is better to improve eating and exercising habits daily, which set long-term important objectives;
- **Favour change in daily work, rather than a series of initiatives**: Change does not consist in doing some things differently on the side but tackling daily tasks differently;
- **Specific metrics:** If performance measures are not modified to reflect the change, it will be difficult to get all on board with the efforts needed;
- **Specific motivations**: The imitation effect is important as there is a strong incentive to comply with social expectations and to belong fully to the group, and it is stronger than an individual sense of guilt;
- **Actions are more important than words**: Walk the walk rather than talk the talk, the key to proving leadership involvement is in their acts rather than in their words;
- **Involvement rather than obligation**: Staff, especially associates, is often comfortable with things as they are; therefore, they typically do not like changes that could be imposed on them. They will be more inclined to accept the changes if they are not passive but become actors in the change that directly concerns them;
- **A vital challenge for leadership**: To gain the trust and adhesion of staff, the leadership and management must put in line their position, and at least their bonuses, for the success of the change. They would give up their bonuses in case of failure, that way there is really 'something in it' for them;
- **Principles rather than tactics**: Staff must be convinced that change is morally based and justified so that staff can back it up wholeheartedly;
- **Team loyalty**: More than the overall financial global result, which is not enough to motivate the team, team loyalty and working as a team member is a much stronger incentive;
- **Volunteers, no conscription**: Each staff member needs to engage voluntarily; they must not enter the process through fear or threat. Their voluntary involvement is the pledge of success;
- **Choice of consequences**: Each staff member needs to have a free choice to join or leave the project; however, he/she should also be aware of the consequences on his/her career. There is a fine line between voluntary involvement and the risk of being evicted from the team in case of refusal and retirement;
- **Small steps approach**: Whereas any change is a long-term project, even a continuous one, it is important to design a series of short-term milestones to validate what has been achieved and to reward each individual's efforts.

This list was established by McKinsey,[2] and the last advice is particularly relevant when change is applied to risk management, a long-term change project: decades, centuries, and, in some cases, millennia. Furthermore, from experiments

---

[2]Adapted from Jules, G., & Tony, E. (2012). *Uncommon sense, common nonsense: Why some organisations consistently outperform others* (pp. 161–162). Profile Books Ltd.

conducted, and articles on the subject, so far, an ERM project takes between five and seven years to reach full maturity. Therefore, the project must be split in annual instalments to maintain the interest and attention of all, starting with directors and executives who need yearly results to finance an ongoing project.

Translating all nine ISO 31000 principles in practical terms in developing and implementing an ERM project remains a challenge. However, they can be summarised in a frequent recommendation: keep it simple (KISS). The process must be a natural extension of daily operations for anyone involved, use vocabulary meaningful to all, and start with the identification of employees eager for change and ready to take a leading role in the process. In summary, ERM is an essential performance tool for all involved not only at headquarters but all along the chain of command. ERM enhances the performance of each staff member; the appropriation process will be greatly facilitated if everyone can see improvement coming into their daily life, including work conditions, salary, etc.

Finally, whatever the efforts put into the project, all change actors should keep in mind Machiavelli's warning to his 16th-century readers:

> Nothing is more difficult to organise, less assured of success than the creation of a new system. The initiator will have as enemies all those that benefited from the old system and only as tepid allies those that might benefit from the new.

6.6. Managing Risk to Reputation and the Case of the Insurance Sector

Reputation is a measure of the trust and confidence that all stakeholders have in an organisation. For insurers, who offer a service in the future in return for current payment, it is crucial to uphold a strong level of trust. It is possible that this company is unique in that the sector may face a systemic risk if one insurer fails, which might undermine public faith in the whole industry. For instance, although AIG's recent difficulties were not directly connected to its insurance operations, the sheer number of firms it covered had a significant impact on the business insurance industry, perhaps leading to a rise in the allocation of commercial funds towards insurance alternatives.

6.6.1. Is There a Consensus on What Constitutes Reputation?

Attendees at an International Insurance Society (IIS) meeting in London in 2014 agreed that a strong reputation, based on a single brand or a portfolio of brands, helps improve margins, supports business growth objectives, is a driver of resilience, and serves as a shield against the increasingly competitive environment in which insurers and reinsurers operate. However, attendees mentioned that their clients in various sectors are confronted with similar challenges. Risks to reputation can be approached like other types of risks as threats and opportunities.

In the case of the insurance industry, not only is it an opportunity for increasing market share but also for growth in generating new lines of business for those who dare to innovate. In times of disaster, the impact of the insurers' community on societal resilience is most revealed. Hence, the insurance mechanism creates an opportunity for an insurer to enhance his reputation at the time of disaster while preserving the reputation of the insured by providing the means of continuity of service to the public.

In fact, the importance of reputation is the foundation of the insurance industry and was already in the mind of the founders of Lloyds over three centuries ago since the good reputation of a name was perceived as an essential driver of success. Indeed, two centuries later, Lloyds' reputation had become established in the United States when their representative, Cuthbert Heath, made certain that all victims of the 1906 San Francisco earthquake were compensated, even when the claims could have been challenged. Furthermore, it should be remembered that the Rough Notes Company assisted in the same effort by providing free of charge thousands of claim forms to the agents of insurers who had coverage in the fires that swept through the city.

Conversely, in the course of the discussion in London, participants stressed that the apparent lack of trust within populations, especially in Africa, seems the main hindrance to the development of micro-insurance.

However, the growing awareness that reputation is an asset that must be managed in its right is still relatively recent and has most likely been prompted by the impact of social media and big data. Big data create the source for complex modelling and a better understanding of the roots of trust and mistrust in the public, whereas social media have made swift and devastating campaigns possible and so efficient that 'e-reputation' has become a buzzword in the consultancy world. Financial institutions have been pushed into recognising reputation as an asset by regulators, particularly through Solvency 2 for insurers in Europe and Basel 3 for banks worldwide.

While there is no universal definition of reputation, the trust of many stakeholders is a major component. However, it may prove hard to measure and monitor 'trust' without translating it into an operational model. Academics and consultants have been working since the beginning of the century on developing models, but there is also a need to develop objective measures of a potential loss of reputation that might be covered by an insurance contract. Most proposed contracts include some pre-loss assistance that both reduces the likelihood and the impact of a potential reputation downfall, and the presence of a strong insurer behind a partner would be likely to reassure both its customers and suppliers as a resilience reinforcement.

After conducting a thorough analysis of the existing literature on reputation, scholars at Arizona State University have identified three primary conceptualisations. These include familiarity with the organisation, beliefs regarding future expectations from the organisation, and impressions of the organisation's favourability.[3] The majority of papers and scholarly studies about reputation risk contend that risk is determined by external impressions. Reputation is formed by the collective opinions of external stakeholders, such as the general public,

---

[3]Lange, D., Lee, P. M., & Dai, Y. (2011). Organisational reputation: A review. *Journal of Management, 37*(1), 153–184.

communities, consumers, suppliers, politicians, and policymakers. Therefore, it is crucial to comprehend how these external stakeholders see the company.

In order to mitigate any damage to their reputation, companies must consistently monitor and assess their reputation across all channels and marketplaces.[4]

Precisely because reputation depends mainly on perception, it would not be effective to manage reputation purely based on historical data as these would not usually include a monitoring of public opinion to capture the cause and timing of public mistrust (*the situations provided below for Perrier, Toyota, BP, and Malaysian airlines illustrate how each reputation crisis is specific and without real precedent as the learning curve should prevent a repetition of a previous crisis*). If we define reputation as the set of expectations that stakeholders hold regarding an organisation's influence on them or their interests, then the following equation/principle is logical:

Reputation = Perceptions – Expectations[5]

A strong reputation not only strengthens the organisation's social licence to operate but offers it a 'social licence to develop' as it becomes a more desirable partner, service provider or supplier, and prospective employer. Therefore, the value of reputation as an asset should not only consider current revenues but also the potential for growth as it represents a competitive advantage and a key driver of future business performance.

In a study conducted by the Economist in 2005, 84% of the executives surveyed said their company's risks to reputation had increased significantly over the past five years.[6] And the risk to reputation should not just be assessed on catastrophic development, i.e. whether or not it would make the headlines. A risk can still exist and bad publicity can hinder the reputation of a company when a few angry customers air their dissatisfaction on social media. Although it might never make a headline, if a company does not identify and resolve problems arising from their actions that may have caused a client great disappointment; significant business losses may still follow if this client decides to express his discontent to other clients resulting in a tainted reputation. Risk management alone may not be enough as John Drzik, CEO of Oliver Wyman, pointed out in 2009: 'The Financial Crisis has demonstrated that risk management is not enough; it is imperative now to develop risk governance. For Risk Management to be efficient it must be approached from a strategic perspective, not a mere compliance exercise'.[7]

To avoid the pitfall of a mere compliance exercise, based on Sarbanes Oxley or COSO 2 or any other standard, the delegates of the World Economic Forum

---

[4]Lange, D., Lee, P. M., & Dai, Y. (2011). Organisational reputation: A review. *Journal of Management, 37*(1), 153–184; and see ACE report on 'reputation at risk' – A survey conducted across 15 countries within its EMEA (Europe, Middle East, and Africa) region between April and June 2013.

[5]Oonagh Mary Harpur.

[6]Economist Intelligence Unit 2005.

[7]John Drzik, CEO of Oliver Wyman at the 2009 Davos World Economic Forum.

(WEF)[8] suggested a solution: 'Risk governance is about asking the right questions to the right persons so that it can be assured that the risks taken are within the boundaries of the organisation's risk appetite'. Since the beginning of the century, experts have been developing a global and integrated management of risks that is known as ERM. Full consideration of the economic turmoil of the world was needed for the delegates to adopt it as a reference at the WEFs in Davos.

Many more years may be needed to fully adopt business analytics and big data to provide the 'reasonable assurance' that information received, transformed, and released to all parties is of the highest quality (reliable, relevant, and truthful). However, they might react swiftly because, after a two-year eclipse in the WEF annual survey, risks to reputation were again at the top of boards of directors' agendas worldwide in 2013 and 2014 and remain high after the shock of the pandemic and the war in Ukraine.

When assessing one's reputation, leaders should keep in mind stakeholders are particularly sensitive if behaviours are not consistent with their expectations or when the organisation's promises are not kept. There are many illustrations of this evolution from the famous Perrier's recall in the United States (January 1990) – according to their publicity, Perrier's promised to be perfect, and it was clearly not perfect – to Toyota's massive recalls (2010, 2011, etc.), whereas they pride themselves on the utmost quality and failed to control some sub-contractors in their haste to become World Number 1 automobile manufacturer, not to mention BP surviving the Alaska pipeline debacle, and the explosions of refineries in Texas, only to come close to collapse with the Deep Horizon Oil Platform. And what to think about Malaysia Airlines when a flight vanished in 2014 (Fig. 6.1)?

6.6.2. Is Reputation Essential in the Financial Sector?

As far as the financial sector is concerned, the most salient issues are the problems of audit and rating agencies linked with the subprime mortgage crisis in 2008 and the ensuing financial crisis not to mention a chain of smaller incidents since then and the demise of a California bank in 2023. The limited impact on most (re)insurers went largely unnoticed by the insured public as claims continued to be paid; in Europe, the organisation of 'market solidarity' would have solved any problem. However, directors and top management in the insurance industry are keen on finding ways not only to protect but even to boost their reputation. This was one of the topics in the minds of all the insurance and reinsurance executives gathered in London for the 50th IIS seminar and many conferences worldwide since then. For the last two decades, regulators have developed an interest in ways to quantify reputation to include it in the solvency models as evidenced by their presence and comments at several workshops as well as the International Association of Insurance Supervisors (IAIS) recommendations.

---

[8]The World Economic Forum is an international institution committed to improving the state of the world through public/private cooperation. The World Economic Forum Davos is held in Switzerland for four days (the next session will take place 21/24 January 2015).

> Even before the recent disasters suffered by two flights of the company, the national airline had experienced the worst financial performance ever in the industry. Now; it is time to question the future of the Malaysian brand linked with these horrible tragedies. Some analysts believe that the company cannot survive without a massive injection of capital by the Malaysian government. There is no precedent for the situation since the company has not committed any fault of its own (even if one may question the wisdom of flying over a war zone) yet a survey of potential passengers would probably reveal that they would rather fly any other carrier. However, the company is on a learning curve in matters of crisis communication and seems to have learned its lesson the hard way after the fiasco at the time of the disappearance of flight MH 370. Four months later, when flight MH 17 crashed over Ukraine, communication was swift, compassionate, and as transparent as was allowed by the circumstances. Nevertheless, the situation is such that it will prove necessary to sacrifice both the CEO and the flight director to restore the trust and confidence of both passengers and crews through a strong commitment to safety. Even then, the question of rebranding to save the company has been addressed … Malaysian Airlines still exists but has not regained its previous standing!

Fig. 6.1. Malaysia Airlines. *Source*: From the *Huffington Post*, 29 July 2014.

While stakeholders' trust has significance across all businesses, it is particularly crucial for sectors that directly serve the public, such as the food industry, water supply, medicines, hospitals, and financial institutions. When taking into account the external setting, the reputation equation must consider the following consequences:

- The populace's fury, accumulation of government expenditures, increasing joblessness, impaired food safety, and other related issues.
- Government policy critique and voting for sanctions in many wealthy nations.
- Heightened examination of government entities and regulatory bodies.
- Establishment of autonomous regulatory bodies to oversee businesses under public scrutiny.
- The looming risk of heightened regulation or structural reform in several sectors such as finance, food, and drugs.
- The rapidly expanding impact of social media.
- Increasing investor and rating agency attention on effective risk management practices (ERM).
- Listed firm annual reports must include mandatory disclosure of 'principal risks and uncertainties'. The regulator has the authority to impose a reputational penalty.

Insurers expect an immediate payment in exchange for a promise of future compensations should a loss occur; the public trust is key to continued flows of premiums and long-term solvency. And from the point of view of the insured, especially when holding long tail cover, the best financial protection is the continued flow of premiums of the insurer, rather than the asset side of the balance sheet at the time of the event (claims provision).

Few solutions appear in research papers, and if consultants and/or insurers have underlying models, they are proprietary and in the public domain. However, a model based on seven drivers published by the Reputation Institute in New York mirrors the model published by Jenny Rayner[9] in 2003 and further developed to include nine drivers split into three poles.[10] Risks to reputation, negative, i.e. threats, and positive, i.e. opportunities, are fundamentally linked to the overall organisational risk management policy. All risks have a potential impact on reputation that should be assessed specifically; hence, risk to reputation is a meta-risk, the risk of all risks. The ultimate asset of an organisation is reputation, and it needs to be risk managed. An organisation future hangs on this reputation. While all other assets of the business are important, the tip of the iceberg under which these all fall is reputation. The strategic, tactical, and operational decision-making process and the involvement of stakeholders in a 'communication-consultation' process are essential to enhance a reputation. As stakeholders' trust and confidence is the building material of reputation, decision-making processes at all levels should aim at developing their trust in the future of the organisation and their understanding of its contribution to the sustainable development of society. This is the pillar for establishing and reinforcing 'social licence to operate'.

In such a context, non-executive board members are not likely to feel the need to acquire the skills necessary for monitoring risk management activities in their organisations; in the European Union (EU), this will be reinforced by specific directives putting clearly on the board and the executives a mandate to manage risks. At their level, the issue is long-term sustainable growth, and the key asset is reputation. The implementation guide for Solvency 2 very specifically states managing risk to reputation rests with the board.

Further to the 2007/2008 crisis, the financial industry has experienced individual lapses rather than a systemic crisis; more recently, food and pharmaceutical industries seem to have also suffered the same issues, but they might be signs of systematic risks. Therefore, organisations in all industries need to prepare for a disaster, as the question is more when than if it will occur. In a book on corporate integrity published after Hurricane Katrina in the south-eastern United States, the authors stress that:

> As we found with Hurricane Katrina, being unprepared can cause a disaster that is far greater than the damage caused by the underlying event. The ethical disaster risks facing organisations today are significant and the damage to reputation caused can be far

[9]Louisot, J.-P., & Girardet, C. (2012). Managing risk to reputation – A model to monitor the key drivers. A key to long-term solvency for insurance and reinsurance companies. *International Journal of Banking, Accounting and Finance, 4*(1).

[10]The traditional seven drivers for the Reputation Institute are visions/promises to others, CSR profile, human capital, leadership/governance, outreach, regulatory profile, finance & value, to which are added sector profile and operations.

> greater for those companies that find themselves unprepared for an Ethical Misconduct Disaster. Although we can't predict an ethical disaster, we can and must prepare for one.[11]

However, even if ethics are important, there are several drivers to reputation and many stakeholders whose confidence has to be nurtured. Common sense would not be enough for robust decisions in such a complex network of intertwined relationships. This is the reason why a model to pilot reputation efficiently is needed. Left to their devices, decision-makers would typically: 'tend to avoid the problem [of interacting criteria] by constructing independent (or supposed to be so) criteria'. The same expert points out that: 'the distinguishing feature of the fuzzy integral is that it can represent a certain kind of interactions between criteria, ranging from redundancy (negative interaction) to synergy (positive interaction)'.[12]

6.6.3. The Findings of a Survey on Reputation and ERM

Whereas insurers must embark on the ERM journey with a special interest in the meta-risk, the risk to reputation, what about the other side of the coin: the potential new market for innovative insurers?

In a report published in July 2013, the ACE Group,[13] it is observed that 81% of the surveyed organisations consider their company reputation to be their most valuable asset. Nevertheless, a staggering 77% of organisations had challenges in assessing the monetary consequences of reputational risks on their business, rendering it more arduous to gauge compared to conventional vulnerabilities. Moreover, a significant 68% of firms express the belief that locating knowledge and guidance on effectively handling reputation risks is challenging. Captive Alternatives incorporates these significant assets, which are generally excluded from the business' balance sheets and cannot be covered by the conventional commercial insurance market, into its strategic business strategy.

A further 66% of surveyed organisations express a sense of being insufficiently equipped to address these particular risks in terms of insurance coverage, while 56% of enterprises acknowledge that social media has significantly intensified the likelihood of reputation-related risks impacting their business. Captive Insurance Company can provide insurance coverage for damages to the intangible assets of reputation or business goodwill. In the case of global players, especially, where the amount of coverage needed may exceed market capacity, the use of Captive Alternatives could help in creating a working layer for their reputation losses,

---

[11]Brown, M. T. (2005). *Corporate integrity: Rethinking organisational ethics and leadership.* Cambridge University Press.

[12]Louisot, J.-P., & Girardet, C. (2012). Managing risk to reputation – A model to monitor the key drivers. A key to long-term solvency for insurance and reinsurance companies. *International Journal of Banking, Accounting and Finance, 4*(1).

[13]ACE report on 'reputation at risk' – a survey conducted across 15 countries within its EMEA (Europe, Middle East and Africa) region between April and June 2013.

maybe through a finite insurance program, thus opening new venues for covering higher trenches of potential losses through the reinsurance market and even the financial markets.

6.6.4. Reputation Essential to Sustainable Development

In order to achieve long-term success and stability, a firm must establish a strong degree of resilience. This can only be accomplished by gaining the trust and confidence of all stakeholders, which requires aligning deeds with words. Practically, this entails incorporating into the overarching plan the essential components of fostering trust: corporate governance, risk mitigation, CSR, and reputation management.

Through their analysis of the context in which an organisation operates or in response to new legislation, such as the directives on governance in the EU,[14] practitioners, directors, and officers have recognised the necessity of implementing a comprehensive worldwide business risk management plan.

Nevertheless, there appears to be a significant increase in the number of new specialised areas within risk management, like sustainable development risk management, procurement risk management, marketing risk management, and so on. Due to the societal need and the advancement of CSR, adopting an integrated approach to risk management is not only a choice but an essential requirement. Trust can only be acquired, maintained, and improved via the practice of openness and ethical conduct. Therefore, in any company, particularly for publicly listed firms, the management of reputation risk has become crucial for achieving the desired integration. This requires executives and board members to recognise that a reputation must be developed from both internal and external perspectives.

Moreover, a business reputation functions as a store of positive sentiment that may be utilised in times of adversity and obstacles. In the current crisis, which has been caused by a reasonable decrease in trust in the financial industry, it is crucial for leaders to make a concerted effort to establish a genuine business. Niels Croft wrote in 2005: 'A defining feature of an authentic business is that its profound and positive purpose shines through every aspect of what it does, whether paying invoices (claims), parting with a member of staff, or presenting at a conference'.[15]

6.6.5. Insured Search for Reputation Loss Coverage Presents Innovative Insurers With an Opportunity

Captives should be available to fund the smaller, more easily containable losses, again, because risk transfer can be limited and expensive. Having emergency funds available to immediately address loss issues can help contain a situation and prevent

[14]The 8th European Company Law Directive Article 41 states, 'the audit committee will, inter alia, monitor the effectiveness of internal controls, internal audit, and, where applicable, risk management systems'.

[15]Crofts, N. (2005). *Authentic business – How to create and run your perfect business.* Häftad.

it from getting out of control, creating situations where limited abilities to pay or fund claims can adversely affect reputation. More interesting is the idea of having the captive fund for acceptable layers of risk (based on the balance sheets of the captive and the parent/associated entities) and then to participate in a side-car vehicle that would access catastrophe bond cover for the truly catastrophic exposures.

As companies continue to expand into global markets, this could prove to be a major area of expanded use for captives. It is yet another example of captives being used to address complex exposures far beyond the traditional predictable risks of the past.

General insurance policies do not cover the risk of reputation losses; although more specialised policies protecting a company against reputational harm are available and can be attached to an umbrella policy by way of endorsement (see below). Traditional business interruption or product liability recall policies do not provide first-party revenue protection following a loss. In light of this gap, a more responsive risk to reputation insurance policy is needed to provide coverage in the event of an adverse media blitz that could damage the policyholder's ability to exploit their products and brands.

What is the state of the market for coverage of risk to reputation for organisations? Here are some of the products on the market followed by a table extended to an additional insurer:

- **AIG ReputationGuard**[16] – ReputationGuard offers an insurance policy that provides cover to help policyholders cope with reputational threats. It delivers the benefit of both access to world-class reputation and crisis communications professionals and coverage for costs associated with avoiding or minimising the potential impact of negative publicity. The result is cutting-edge coverage against publicity that puts reputation and brand image at stake.

  ReputationGuard gives policyholders access to a select panel of the internationally recognised and award-winning communications firms of Burson-Marsteller[17] and Porter Novelli.[18] These firms are committed to providing strategic guidance and implementation support on critical communications issues on global, national, and local scales.
- **Allianz Reputation Protect in practice**[19] – Allianz Reputation Protect covers a wide range of scenarios and provides funding for crisis management for their

[16]www.aig.com/reputationguard_295_393319.html

[17]Burson-Marsteller is a leading global public relations and communications firm operating across 96 countries. It provides companies in crisis with strategic counsel and programme development across the spectrum of public relations, public affairs, digital media, advertising, and other communications services. For more than half a century Porter Novelli, a global leader in public relations, has been providing counsel in crisis management to clients in 90 locations around the world.

[18]Porter Novelli is a global public relations leader, has been providing issues and crisis counsel for nearly 40 years, and serving clients from 90 locations around the world. Last year, the agency introduced its real-time reputation specialty, which recognised that a world in which social media can damage hard-won reputations in just minutes.

[19]http://www.agcs.allianz.com/services/financial-lines/reputational-risk-management/

clients in the event of a crisis. Through the services provided by their expert partners, their clients receive the analysis and professional consultation necessary to deal with a potential public relations (PR) situation. A first risk to reputation assessment is conducted by Media Tenor International, a leading media analysis consultancy, to gauge current perception by the media and public. During the crisis period, Media Tenor will continue to monitor media perception and work hand in hand with the client and a selected expert consultancy, which will support a tailored response to the crisis.
- **Aon Corp. and Zurich Financial Services Ltd.**[20] – Aon has launched a product to help companies affected by an event that could negatively affect their reputation. The product, underwritten by Zurich Financial Services Ltd., provides up to $100 million in limits of coverage. The policy would be triggered should one of 19 named insured perils occur and should a company suffer financial loss and adverse publicity after an event. An important element of the policy is that as soon as it is purchased, the insured company receives PR advice from London-based marketing communications company WPP P.L.C. The policy provides for pre-loss consulting from WPP every quarter whether or not an event has occurred and crisis consultancy when an event occurs for up to a year after that event.
- **Finch Insurance Services**[21] – The insurer works with their clients to protect against the claim and ultimately their reputation. The questions that are asked, the processes that are followed, and the team selected to 'fight' the claim could really make an important difference to the business in the long run when it comes to their brand. If a business's reputation matters, Finch's advice is not to gamble on a policy in the first place – it's all about managing risk practically and, secondly, to have business advice from professionals when facing a claim.

Other insurers have joined the rank, but the shortcomings in the products mentioned in the list above remain at the heart of covers: they finance remediation tools but not really the long-term cost of damages to reputation.

6.6.6. Innovation Needed to Boost Insurers' Profits

The role of insurance is changing rapidly. Although many technology and privacy (cyber) policies in the industry do not currently address a company's financial loss due to a security breach or privacy loss, a select few are introducing important data and network security policies and privacy policies designed to fill this void. Equally important is the advent of risk to reputation insurance designed to protect the very valuable, but somewhat intangible, corporate reputation. Most contracts offered today are insufficient to meet these needs as they tend to be limited to assisting in public recall and advertising/communication expenses.

[20] www.businessinsurance.com/article/20111004/NEWS06/111009972
[21] www.finchgroup.net/2013/11/insuring-your-reputation

With improved coverage, corporations can react faster to adverse issues, be more effective in protecting the organisation and secure the trust and confidence of clients while at the same time securing the bottom line. In this way, the practices of insurers both in contract generation and claims payment and other activities can enhance not only the insurers but the insured's reputation and hence contribute to societal resilience.

The strategic question that all insurance and reinsurance CEOs should address with their boards is the following:

> Do we believe the risk to reputation is the next big development in insurance coverage? Can/will the coverage be profitable? How could we determine whether the initial rates are adequate? What pitfalls could we foresee in offering this coverage and how susceptible is it to fraudulent claims?

Other gaps in cover have been unearthed during the pandemic with a chain of litigations on the issue of business interruption linked to confinement, and the lack of cover for consequences of the war in Ukraine and resulting geopolitical unrest.

Chapter 7

The Management of Risk and the Management of Change

Risk management (RM)'s mission is to consider all the uncertainties that could interfere with the organisation fulfilling its missions and reaching its objectives, be they accelerators (opportunities) or retarders (threats). Resilience engineering is the construction of the organisation's capacity to respond to disturbances or stress and maintain its major functionalities under all circumstances.

There is a continuing debate on the Internet centred on the idea of a new activity called « resilience management ». In such a context, the issue for RM is how to integrate this « new » function into RM. The original discussion was launched by the Scottish Widows Bank, already involved in solvency issues a few years ago, who asked the question of whether RM (or resiliency management) has real content beyond the name.

7.1. Contrasting RM Objectives and Change Management Objectives

The minimum RM objective in any organisation is to ensure survival and so long as it has enough cash to avoid bankruptcy, this minimal goal is achieved. But that would be the typical task of the treasurer assisted by RM for troubled times. For RM, the task would be to ensure that when suffering a loss, the organisation has enough cash to live through the following period when its cash is depleted. However, this is enough only if it is further assumed that it can maintain its stakeholders' trust and confidence until it is again up and running and can thus preserve its 'social licence to operate'.

However, there are exceptional circumstances in which even this « minimal » objective may prove elusive, especially when liability losses and damages to the environment are concerned. The Exxon Valdez comes to mind, as well as BP's Deepwater Platform explosion[1] in the Gulf of Mexico, which caused millions of dollars in damage and fines to their companies. The real question was whether the

[1]For further information, go to https://echogeo.revues.org/12099

Enterprise Risk Management in Today's World, Part A: Enterprise-Wide Risk Management and Strategy, 101–108
Copyright © 2024 by Jean-Paul Louisot and Simon Grima
Published under exclusive licence by Emerald Publishing Limited
doi:10.1108/978-1-83797-406-120241008

deep emotion in the media and the avalanche of social media interaction would be stopped by the punctual safety measures taken in the wake of the explosion and would allow the oil companies to continue *business as usual*. Or, whether the economic and political cost would create enough of a shock to bring a systemic change, boost renewable energies, and put climate change back on governments' agenda? The answer over a decade later is at best mixed. How hard it is to learn from mistakes and draw conclusions as soon as the citizens' attention turns to other issues! The same could be said about the 2008/2009 financial crisis that triggered an economic upheaval from which the world had not entirely recovered when it was hit with the pandemic.[2]

When it comes to managing a potential 'black Swan' or extreme catastrophic scenario developed during the risk-assessment step, it may be that RM will have to content themselves with limiting the likelihood of their occurrence below a magic number (one in a million chances, one in a billion chances? or the centennial or millennial event?) that will allow stakeholders to 'live with it', i.e. have a perception of the risk that makes it acceptable in exchange for the societal or financial benefits that the risky activity brings in (see Deepwater). This is what the 'social licence to operate' already mentioned is about.

But, in most situations, an objective limited to « survival » cannot prove enough to answer stakeholders' expectations. This is particularly true in the case of 'medium exposures' which, although uncertain every year, become probable for a 5 to 10-year horizon. 'Survival' would take care of the cash issue but not of the impact on the financial markets as the organisation's return on assets would be on a roller coaster that would not only displease the first circle of stakeholders (stakeholders, directors, staff, and financial institutions) but would also raise concerns with suppliers, sub-contractors, as well as customers; major stakeholders would legitimately question the organisation's long-term sustainability.

State authorities, local communities, and 'citizen-consumers' or simple spectators could be alarmed by what they could perceive as short-view chaotic management. This is precisely why leaders have to assign more binding objectives to RM, especially when compared with corporate social responsibility (CSR) discussions. Such objectives can include maximum acceptable downtime or downgraded operation, stability of financial results, and watching for societal interests, in line with the values and ethical choices of the organisation. This is a question linked to disturbance and continuity management to prepare for optimal bouncing back following a serious event, even catastrophic, and to prepare the elements of a post-event strategy to further 'the mission'.

When escalating the scale of objectives assigned to RM for a post-event situation, there is an increasing need to allocate resources, including finances that are diverted from normal operations. This means that the decision to open a better future in the case that an undesirable event occurs will lead to a suboptimal

---

[2]Wemer, D. (2020, October 2). *Can we compare the COVID-19 and 2008 crises?* Atlantic Council. https://www.atlanticcouncil.org/blogs/new-atlanticist/can-we-compare-the-covid-19-and-2008-crises/

economic performance on an ongoing basis if the event does not occur. Protecting the future reduces ambitions for the present.

All this means that on a short-term horizon, an organisation that would not devote any resources to RM would seem more efficient, at least when it comes to medium and critical risks, as the financial results would be better. In the short term, the return on assets would be higher but vulnerable.

This is why the resources devoted to RM might seem superfluous, and they can be justified only with the introduction of a concept that is more and more discussed in the RM and strategy literature so that the long-term horizon can be assessed in a time of short-term stock purchases. How to measure the impact of decisions on sustainable development, even in a financial framework? The much-debated concept is resilience.

RM practitioners and academics are regularly using the word resilience, without necessarily offering a practical definition or content. The first attempt to develop a definition for resilience emanated from the Canadian auditors, and their association published a guide for its members during the last decade of the 20th century.[3]

The concept was first used in metallurgy to measure the capacity of a metal to regain its qualities, especially elasticity after a stress, thermal or mechanical. In sociology and psychology, it is the capacity of an individual or a society to adapt to change.

Resilience is defined in the Glossary of the IIA[4] as 'the adaptive capacity of an organisation in a complex and changing environment', credited to ASIS International, a global community of security practitioners. The main definition is embodied by:

1. The organisation's ability 'to resist being affected by an event or the ability to regain an acceptable level of performance within a limited period after being affected by an event'; and
2. The 'capability' of a system to maintain its functions and structure in the face of internal and external change and to degrade gracefully when it must.

When applied to RM, resilience is an assessment of the organisation's capability to rebound after a major disturbance and to survive a crisis. Thus, this means that the organisation is in a position to do the following:

- For society, to comply with all its obligations;
- For staff, to maintain employment;
- For economic partners, to ensure continuity of exchanges; and
- For stockholders, to provide dividends.

---

[3]The role of the Internal Auditor in business resilience 1303A-16, business resiliency article. https://chapters.theiia.org/IIA%20Canada/Thought%20Leadership%20Documents/The-Role-of-the-Internal-Auditor-in-Business-Resilience.pdf

[4]Institute of Internal Auditors.

7.2. RM Evolution and Explosion and Change Management

In order to comprehend the significance of the notion of resilience in the present RM environment, it is imperative to examine the progression that RM has seen over the past 25 years. RM has been more prevalent in many businesses, to the extent that several professional degrees in universities now incorporate RM as a key component of the management sciences. Only a small number of scholars and professionals foresaw this transformation, but they saw that maintaining continuity and effectively managing crises would become crucial procedures in every business. And is it not the essence of resilience?

Resilience is the primary goal of RM in this particular setting. This concept is applicable to many sectors of business and services, although financial institutions appear to be leading the way in its implementation. According to one participant in the recent blog debate, resilience refers to the extra financial resources that an organisation has to deal with a significant disruption, in comparison to the potential losses it may suffer. The participant argues that the level of resilience is directly proportional to the difference, or margin, between these two factors. Nevertheless, the scope of this vision is constrained by its limited financial resources, so neglecting the consideration of human, technological, and information resources, as well as the evaluation of the organization's reputation in light of changes in social media.

An organization's ability to produce an appropriate response depends on its agility and flexibility. Management style and structure directly influence the resilience of the company. In a highly hierarchical and bureaucratic company, employees are required to adhere to rigid procedures without any flexibility to adapt to specific conditions. Even during a crisis, any modifications, such as the implementation of a continuity plan, necessitate obtaining prior authorisation from the organisational hierarchy. Only organisations that possess the ability to adapt can endure, much like structures constructed to withstand an earthquake. This matter exemplifies a continuing dispute that remains unresolved by the ISO 31000:2018 standard. It asserts that 'risk-owners', who are the operational managers responsible for managing risks at their level, must possess both the accountability and the power to effectively execute enterprise-wide risk management (ERM).

In a novel approach to resilience, the notion encompasses a wider scope than just RM, including even its cognitive processes. Resilience refers to the ability of an organisation and its employees to effectively adjust and respond to many situations, including changes, difficulties, failures, and even severe disruptions or crises. Therefore, resilience is the paramount goal for any effective approach in an exceedingly unpredictable future. Resilience appears inherent in the cultures of companies that promote individual efforts. For instance, in the event of tripping and falling, it would be advantageous to get the Euro currency discovered on the floor before standing up! Bertrand Robert has proposed the concept of 'creative rupture' as a means for organisations to adapt to changing circumstances. This involves conducting a new SWOT analysis to redefine the organization's strategy, taking into account both internal factors (strengths and weaknesses) and external factors (threats and opportunities).

For instance, in terms of good or bad connotations, the corporations who provided services to the notorious FEMA[5] trailers had to modify their distribution strategies from targeting summer fun seekers to catering to those affected by the tragedy, providing them with temporary housing. The challenge at hand revolves around the ability of an organisation to exploit disruptions by devising innovative applications for their existing products or developing novel products that align with the economic and societal context following a catastrophe. In the event of a fire in the printing shop of a daily regional paper in France, which would result in its complete destruction, the available resources could be utilised to establish an online newspaper and repurpose the land for the construction of apartments. This particular location holds significant value in a medium-sized city situated in the central region of France. In change management, communication systems play an important role, all the more critical in times of stress, communication must be the subject of a continuous process linking the organisation with its stakeholders and building or comforting their trust, communication about risk is only a part of the bigger picture. Communication at a time of crisis is efficient only in so far as it rests on institutional communication. Resilience also requires the development of a consistent and robust communication process with all stakeholders at all times.

7.3. Differing Visions of Resilience: The Substance of the Debate

Failure is strictly unacceptable in certain sectors, such as aeronautics and space. Resilience is a fundamental aspect of every project, and it is imperative to establish a structure that guarantees achievement. Given such circumstances, it is imperative that the entire organisation is effectively managed, equipped, and educated to guarantee the durability of all its activities. What is the correlation between resilience and RM? The system undergoes a system safety analysis as part of the RM framework.

RM is an integral component of the system's mission, initiated during the conceptual phase and implemented prior to system operation. It involves identifying all potential risks and providing relevant information to the team responsible for system development. This approach is highly effective in minimising the likelihood of adverse events and improving the ability to handle unforeseen circumstances. Conversely, if RM concerns are postponed until operations commence, there may be deficiencies in the process. RM has the capability to detect and assess developing risks, novel threats, vulnerabilities, and exposures in order to prioritise them and suggest an enhancement procedure. However, it is now considered an additional component rather than an integral part of the whole process, resembling an afterthought.

Some experts and scholars recommend adding RM into project engineering as a component of comprehensive project management. This should include the

[5]Reports of health issues relating to Katrina-issue FEMA trailers began to appear in July 2006. A federal report in July 2006 identified toxic levels of formaldehyde in 42% of the trailers examined, attributing problems to poor construction and substandard building materials. https://en.wikipedia.org/wiki/FEMA_trailer

integration of 'lean management' and 'compliance' principles. Opting for holistic and integrated RM, such as ERM, appears to be a more efficient approach. A comprehensive system safety strategy involves the early assessment and mitigation of hazards throughout the design process, with the ultimate goal of ensuring the system's resilience. This concept may be succinctly expressed by a proverb: 'Prevention is preferable to cure'.

7.3.1. Resilience and Standards

In the United Kingdom, the organisation in charge of standardisation, the BSI published in 2022 a revised version of BS 65000[6] centred on resilience but from a public perspective. It should be noted that several other standards address the subject.[7] Risk and resilience are interconnected ideas. However, resilience is not only a mere function but a crucial goal for all organisations. They strive to effectively manage their resources in order to successfully adapt to various changes, even drastic ones and disruptions.

However, within this expanded context, the goal of resilience applies to all the protective duties, encompassing information technology (IT) security, physical security, health and safety, environmental management, and more. Hence, it is imperative to conceive it through a comprehensive 360° methodology that integrates culture, strategy, and transformation. Mature ERM incorporates continuity management as a strategic approach to mitigate the consequences of future disruptions. ERM must build robust learning mechanisms that enable prompt decision-making under high-pressure situations, especially when faced with little information during a crisis.

7.3.2. Engineering Versus Ecological Resilience

The concept of resilience is so widely used that it covers different realities including the following:

- *Engineering or reactive resilience*: Engineering resilience aims at the speed of return to a new stable state following a disturbance which implies that the emphasis is on the rapidity of the effect. At stake is the organization's reactivity, including the acceptable time for degraded functioning and/or downtime a key parameter of any continuity management effort.
- *Ecological or proactive resilience:* Ecological resilience considers the unavoidable change within and outside of a system, like entropy, and aims at finding a new equilibrium within the altered contextual framework, thus reflecting the capacity of the organisation to adapt and thrive. This proactive resilience rests

[6]First version published in 2014, second in 2022 – *Organisational resilience, guide on practice*. BSI.

[7]*Among others*: ISO 22301:2019 – *Business continuity management*, ISO 31000:2018 – *Risk management*, BS 11200:2014 – *Crisis management*, and BS 11000:2010 – *Collaborative business relationships.*

on the agility of the organisation that allows it to find efficient answers to disturbances and could be also defined as a 'pre-event resilience' built on environmental sciences, thus a key to sustainable development.

7.3.3. Risks and Resilience

Under this emerging framework of resilience, several experts perceive RM as an integral component of resilience management. Nevertheless, this approach suggests that RM is confined to the management of threats that are already identified and understood. To clarify Donald Rumsfeld's statement, RM is responsible for addressing neither the 'known-unknown' (rising hazards) nor the 'unknown-unknown' (Black Swans). Woods and Wreathall[8] create a resilience model that is analogous to the stress-tension technique. The initial response to an occurrence is identified as the collective and consistent reaction of the entire organisation when it is capable of effectively addressing the problem. Is the concept of RM being considered when referring to the initial stage of reactive capacity? The second level of reaction refers to the ability to adapt to a new circumstance. This level of resilience goes beyond relying on pre-planned responses, procedures, and resources. Instead, it involves finding solutions that beyond the limitations of first adaptations.[9] In their framework, RM would only allow for anticipation of the probable and the possible, and true resilience would come only with an appropriate response to the second order of change.

7.4. The Appropriate Response to Disturbance Levels

Within a comprehensive and interconnected framework, RM must extend beyond familiar dangers or scenarios where pre-existing contingency plans may be effortlessly executed to overcome unforeseen challenges. In reality, RM must tackle both reactive and proactive resilience. Efficient RM is employed in intricate systems, which interact within a constantly expanding network of interdependencies, ultimately existing in an unstable equilibrium. When the system deviates from its inherent equilibrium, remedial actions must be taken to reinstate equilibrium. Nevertheless, these deviations from the norm are frequently referred to as 'crises', even though not all emergencies lead to a crisis. Labelling any unforeseen or unlikely situation as a crisis can have adverse consequences, including:

- An exaggerated response that may escalate the situation into a crisis; and
- A weary and apathetic attitude among staff, resulting in delayed and inadequate response when a genuine crisis is imminent.

[8]See bibliography.

[9]Woods and Wreathall. *The stress–strain model of resilience operationalizes the four cornerstones of resilience engineering – Article 2008.* www.resilience-engineering-association.org

This situation of 'unenlightened catastrophism' is identified in a recent book by Dylan Evans,[10] in which he suggests that 'transforming low probability events into quasi-certainties when these events are perceived as particularly formidable by stakeholders is an approach of worst case scenario that can induce dreadful decisions'. It is imperative for the organization's existence and resilience that leadership and the chain of command respond progressively to the nature and potential seriousness of specific events.

The amount of disturbance in a complex system exists on a continuous spectrum. This concept may be shown by the description of four states mentioned in the November 2007 edition of the *Harvard Business Review*, as well as in other sources.

- **Simple state:** This refers to the initial state of the system that is established based on best practices. It is an unstable equilibrium that is rarely maintained, but it possesses the following characteristics: stability, with clear cause/effect relationships; slow evolution, with emphasis on order and accomplishment; avoidance of complacency.
- **Complicated state**: This state requires specialised knowledge and falls under the realm of 'best practices'. Operational managers, who are responsible for managing risks, are able to effectively manage daily fluctuations within the realm of what is feasible. This state is characterised by the following: multiple potential responses and the ability to analyse various solutions; willingness to consider unconventional ideas; it is important to note that making timely decisions is more crucial than waiting for the optimal solution.
- **Complex state**: This refers to a circumstance where operational managers need to explore new alternatives before taking action. However, it necessitates a structured planning approach. Business continuity plans are most effective when the following conditions are met: a thorough understanding of the sequence of events is achieved through feedback based on experience; embracing innovation, creativity, and new management models is crucial; caution must be exercised to avoid reverting to the pre-event situation without considering the new context.
- **State of chaos or rupture:** This refers to a situation where quick action is crucial, but it requires a strategic vision that goes beyond the capabilities of operational managers. It may even necessitate involvement from top management and the board of directors. This level of disruption calls for a strategic redeployment planning (SDP). The state is characterised by the following: inability to identify stable cause/effect patterns or manageable schemes; the need to restore a reasonable degree of order, which may differ from the previous equilibrium; clear and specific communication from top management, providing instructions for implementing swift strategic changes if necessary (there is no time for dialogue).

Caution: This is an opportune scenario to adopt novel ideas and strategic pivots (alterations in management).

[10]Dylan, E. (2012). *Risk intelligence*. Simon & Schuster, Inc.

Chapter 8

Emerging Risk Management Issues

In the complex and volatile world, organisations have to cope with several emerging issues that create challenges for risk-management (RM) professionals.

8.1. Economic Crisis and RM[1]

Many observers blamed the financial crisis on the failure of RM, and many officers and directors complain that making strategic decisions has become a nightmare in the current context, more complex and more volatile than during the last years of the 20th century.

However, in those days, forecasting tools were not as robust as today, whatever the limits of today's toolbox despite the cloud and 'big data'. Nevertheless, solutions must be found to improve the comfort level of decision-makers; the first step is to analyse the underlying causes of the current situation, be it reality or perception.

It is not so much that leaders are not equipped to make decisions in an uncertain future (see developments above). The US defence has developed war games since the cold war, and the schools of management have trained their students in quantitative methods based on decision trees and time value of money (NPV – net present value) combining return on investment and probabilities where risk is measured by volatility (standard deviation).

These were tools that considered an uncertain future that could be framed within set boundaries and to the extent that the future could be inferred from the past. They prove not so reliable in a time of ambiguity and chaos when integrating uncertainty must transcend mathematical models.

When the 'fog of uncertainty' is thick as in the foreseeable future, it is essential to be able to react rapidly as soon as some 'low-level signals' point to a somewhat clearer future; thus, allowing anticipation of where the volatility leads. Being the first to seize the opportunities that suddenly start shaping, including mitigating threats, offering a competitive edge, a way to fend off substitutes, and remaining relevant to stakeholders. This requires being on the alert and ready at all times

[1]McKinsey. *Economic crisis and risk management.*

Enterprise Risk Management in Today's World, Part A: Enterprise-Wide Risk Management and Strategy, 109–126
Copyright © 2024 by Jean-Paul Louisot and Simon Grima
Published under exclusive licence by Emerald Publishing Limited
doi:10.1108/978-1-83797-406-120241009

to process new information with an open mind, transcending purely quantitative information to forge the future, even more than anticipating it!

8.2. Structural Issue for RM?[2]

The financial crisis shed light on RM shortcomings, especially in large banks and financial institutions. Rather than a failure of RM, it seems more reasonable to conclude that these organisations did not have a robust RM system in place.

It is in this context that the *Economist Intelligence Unit* surveyed 364 RM professionals in May 2009. Despite the overall thought process the practitioners have undertaken, it appears that many organisations are reluctant or incapable of a complete overhaul of their RM system.

Inflation in cash positions, staff attrition, and lean management together with a lack of resources are still obstacles to RM short-term redeployment efforts.

In a summary of a report on governance, Rob Mitchell, editor of the *Economist Intelligence Unit*, stated: 'Risk-management is undergoing a transition. It is currently under scrutiny by top management and is in for renewed interest and an important revision'.

The report shows that important improvements direly needed are not undertaken. However, professionals hoped then that process improvement and training investments were likely to be made. Whereas RM is slowly rising on the organisation's chart, the report has highlighted some anomalies not really addressed so far.

First of all, too many doubts remain regarding the skills in RM at all levels in organisations. Only 50% of the professionals interviewed believe the non-exec directors have enough expertise in RM. Furthermore, they recognise that the time and attention that the board allocates to RM is still insufficient.

However, the survey was conducted before the publication of the current UK code of governance,[3] which may well prove a game-changer as the obligation to prepare an annual report on long-term value preservation imposes to think beyond the next four quarters, and beyond the end of their term in office as the code, stipulates that: 'Each company must be headed by an efficient board of directors collectively responsible for the long-term success of the company'.

The survey findings raise serious doubt as to the involvement and the competencies of non-exec directors. These are questions that the Walker[4] report tried to address. The report highlights that *risk managers* remain focused on threats and are still often not expected to bring a framework and directions for the conduct of RM operations in the units.

---

[2]This paragraph is inspired by the article 'Has risk management a structural problem?' John Liver, *Compliance and risk management*, partner with Ernst and Young.

[3]*The UK corporate code of governance 2018* (current edition) by the Financial Report Council (FRC). www.frc.org.uk

[4]Sir David Walker wrote a report for the British government in 2012 to evaluate and recommend improvements to corporate governance in the United Kingdom, addressing flaws in bank management and contributing to the drafting of a new governance code.

The report finds that *risk managers* do not spend enough time and effort on identifying new risks. Control, monitoring, and compliance issues consume most of the RM department resources: three out of four professionals confirm that they spend most of their time on these files. They also stress that they rely on mediocre data and insufficient technology to tackle the assessment step efficiently.

While recognising the reality of these challenges, organisations' leaders seem reluctant to hire the talent they need to find solutions. It is difficult to find out if this is due to the lack of competent RM professionals on the market, the lack of real interest in the recruitment process, or the insufficient incentive to attract the right candidates. Whatever the reason, RM issues need to be taken seriously if they are to be met with solutions.

One of the ways to further the evolution is to set up an independent risk committee. Their mission would be centred on the analysis of risk information but should also be involved in executives' compensation plans so that they would include risk/return assessments and their decisions and performance alignment on the board strategic objectives and risk appetite statements. Thus, the boards would deliver their obligation to the shareholders. These provisions will put heavier responsibilities on non-exec directors and not only to members of the risk committee.

However, this is feasible only if additional resources are put at their disposal, to ensure their information and training so that they gain a deeper understanding of the organisation and its risk landscape, as well as the system put in place to manage them. The Walker report stresses the need to put this knowledge in perspective of the external context.

Whereas the Walker report was mainly concerned with the financial sector, the target assigned to Sir Walker by the prime minister, it must be noted that the financial crisis impacted many sectors of the economy by contagion. Therefore, it would be pointless to seek solutions limited to the confines of finance. However, when extending the conclusion of the report to the whole economy, as in the UK code of governance, the potential consequences must be considered seriously.

One area of particular concern is the governance rules that the banks and financial institutions have to comply with given their impact on the life of the city; they may not be suited for all economic actors when they could unduly increase their operating costs. Other industries may not have to manage so serious a systemic risk. The high stakes of systemic risk in the finance sector alone justify that the sector be submitted to a high level of strict RM regulations.

It would be ironic that a hasty extension to all economic activities have a counter effect and not reach the objectives the government had targeted; could it not challenge the governance principles of the new combined code of governance[5] that contributed to the act on companies of 2006,[6] to the setting up of 'good governance rules' in most UK firms.

The British government has accepted most of the Walker report recommendations, and they are included in the current governance regulation. It specifically kept the intentions of the report not to impose new rules unless they are targeted, relevant,

---

[5]United Kingdom's combined code, revised in 2018 (see Notes 10 and 53).

[6]Companies Act 2006.

and economically justified. The government probably kept in mind the cost of implementing the Sarbanes-Oxley Act, and all governments should avoid this pitfall.

8.3. From Three Lines of Defence to Five Lines of Assurance

The 'three-line of defence approach' is supported by auditors worldwide and is part of the response of the profession to the Enron debacle and ensuing Sarbanes-Oxley regulation in the United States. It remains a reference and is presented by many consultants to their clients as 'the' answer when setting up efficient governance in an organisation. However, it has two major flaws; it seems to exonerate the directors and officers of their responsibilities and introduces RM as a defence when it should be part of an offensive strategy.

The approach[7] introduced here is not widely used, but it offers an expanded vision of 'defense' with five lines instead of three, explicitly including directors and officers. By seeking 'assurance,' it aims to verify that the risk strategy and risk appetite defined for the organization are appropriate and implemented with integrity.

This approach in the hands of the organisation's leaders is focused on the following seven elements:

1. Objectives register

When visiting the issues of exposure through the lenses of their impact on strategic objectives, i.e. what might happen to prevent the organisation from reaching its strategic objectives, the approach of the management of risks is elevated to the strategic level, which is one of the foundations of enterprise risk management (ERM). Thus, the chances of reaching the objectives are enhanced, and the relevant risk information is brought to the attention of the directors to help them find the optimal allocation of resources while assessing the levels of uncertainty.

2. Leadership involvement and cost/benefits analysis

The objective register must reflect the elements that are susceptible to generating value (opportunities) and those that could destroy it (threats), with the proviso mentioned earlier that this is not a fixed dichotomy when uncertainties can be transformed into value creation whenever it is managed in the interest of the organisation. Thus, ERM is 'naturally' integrated in the strategic process and also into the performance assessment in executives' compensation. But it is even more when cyber-security and compliance issues are included in the picture. It leads to the integration of a global vision of all silos control and brings transparency to the board of directors.

---

[7]'Board and C-suite driven/objective centric and internal audit approach to fives lines of assurance'. Conference Board Director Notes, June 2015, from an article by Parveen Gupta and Tim Leech, *The next frontier for boards: oversight of risk culture.*

3. Clearly defined responsibilities

Whereas earlier ERM approaches mainly aimed at identifying risk owners, the present approach rests on 'objective owners' who are responsible for managing the risks that may impact the capacity to reach the objectives assigned to them, enhancing opportunities and curbing threats. This is why they are to report to their boss not so much on losses but on the status of their objectives, thus indicating the residual uncertainties, both positive and negative, bearing on them.

However, the distinction may not be as drastic as it may seem at first sight: why would an operational manager be designated a risk owner if he/she does not have objectives to reach? This is a lingering question that consultants and professionals have to address when working on a project operational managers tend to reject the concept of 'risk ownership', except for risk impacting directly their performance, their objective, and their bonus plan.

4. Definition of a rigorous risk diagnostic process and specific « assurance »

The risk committee must come up with a clear definition of the effort levels they expect in the development and updating of diagnostics concerning the strategic objectives and the level of 'assurance' by an objective eye (internal or external audit) that they require to enlighten the monitoring and review of strategy and orientation changes that might prove necessary.

5. Establishing the range of risk treatment options

Optimisation requires that all risk treatment options be considered, and this is not limited to financing. In other words, all previously mentioned options – including sharing, contractual transfer, avoidance/suppression, segregation (with or without redundancy), prevention, protection, and even exploitation to potentially create a competitive advantage – should be considered. At this stage, the operational risk committee convenes specialists from various fields and experiences to engage in discussions with auditors and insurance buyers. Focusing on the overall objective, rather than individual exposures, is essential to finding the optimal solution.

6. Focusing on residual composite risk acceptability (portfolio approach)

Focusing on key objectives allows for identifying a global residual risk on the 'risk portfolio' that weighs on a given objective. In addition, the analysis extends to the consequences on the entire organisation of a deficit in reaching a given objective. Equipped with this information, the staff involved, the 'objective-owners' and the line he/she reports to can find improved solutions. These may include reviewing an objective that would appear overambitious and/or with little impact on the overall strategy. This is also a good time to review risk criteria and risk appetite in light of the new information, including the internal and external context evolution.

7. Risk treatment optimisation

Once a consensus is reached on the composite residual risk acceptable for a given objective, the treatment plan is to be reviewed to optimise the cost/benefit ratio for all the risks impacting the objective.

Whereas the major benefits of the five lines of defence approach to major objectives, rather than on each exposure, are already listed above, the following clarifications are important:

- Directors and executives are not mere spectators of the RM process but key actors, especially when it comes to risk-impacting strategic objectives, which some risk taxonomies label « strategic risk » – see four quadrants – when it is probably more judicious to call them strategy-impact risk;
- Leaders (chief executive officer [CEO], mayor, or managing partners) answer directly to the board of directors for strategic objective risks;
- RM mission is 'risk-taking optimisation' with a balance between offence and defence, enhancing opportunities and controlling threats;
- An approach is aligned with supervisors' expectation that a framework must be defined for risk appetite (in the case of financial institutions);
- Internal audit role and mission are confirmed and aligned with the organisation's strategic objectives, which reconcile the consultant and controller roles;
- Other specialities such as prevention, dependability, economic intelligence, insurance covers, legal, and continuity are companions of the ERM exercise and serve the same objectives;
- Risk treatment optimisation is at the heart of the system to cap the cost of risk in a dynamic and proactive vision, rather than a defensive and reactive one;
- The choice of words is important; replacing the word 'control' with the word 'treatment' makes a clear difference between the measures that aim to limit the level of risk (threats) or take advantage of the risk (opportunities) and those that aim to verify the efforts of all. Note that in the United States, the ambiguity of the word 'control' has blurred directors' understanding of RM for a long time and has reinforced their vision of RM as a costly compliance exercise, rather than offering them a value-creation tool;
- A clear answer to the request by supervisory authorities who stress the total responsibility in RM for RM policy, development, and implementation (see the eighth EU Directive, Basel 3, Solvency 2, etc.);
- Resource allocation optimisation is a strategic goal, not only at the initial stage of a strategy but also throughout implementation as ERM facilitates adjustments to the constant evolutions of the external and internal context. In other terms, it is an essential component of the steering mechanism that assists the organisation in optimising its real-time performance.

All the preceding elements call for serious consideration to be given by directors and officers of any organisation, to the proposed approach as it efficiently combines strategy, RM, and change steering.

8.4. Integrating Quantitative Risk Analysis (QRA) in All the Organisation's Processes

One major issue when an ERM programme is on the path to maturity concerns risk quantification. As for existing standards, they all recommend using Monte Carlo simulations, though there are obvious limitations in the method when the context is fast evolving.

On the other hand, even if there are differences in vocabulary, which creates a problem for the development of RM as an academic science and as a transposable practice, the method to incorporate uncertainties, the 'Risk-Management process' that they suggest is always a version of the one already mentioned and repeated below (see Fig. 8.1 – a repeat of Fig. 3.1).

In all cases, the weak stage is always risk assessment, for which standards provide objectives but no real practical implementation tools, even considering ISO-IEC 31010:2019.[8] Risk identification is essential, and as far as analysis and evaluation of identified risks is concerned, i.e. a quantitative or qualitative measure of risk, it remains precarious so long as the data concerning risk and the impact of the treatment are not sufficiently robust to be reliable. Of course, there is also the issue of context setting as it is the point of immersion in the strategic

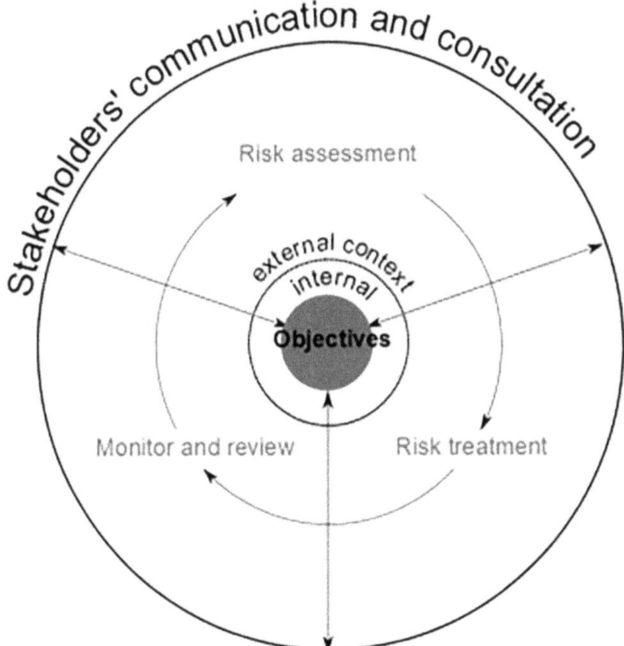

Fig. 8.1. The Circular Process of RM.

[8]Risk management – Risk assessment techniques.

effort and supposes that economic intelligence is up and running, that the risk treatment plan selected is properly implemented, and that controls to measure their efficiency are in place.

QRA is the cornerstone of the process that facilitates the passage from qualitative to quantitative, but it is important to remain cautious about the precise details that might not be reliable in the world of uncertainty. Surveys have shown that only one out of four organisations use simulation in their strategic planning process and the reasons invoked are diverse: models are too complex; they are like black boxes; the leadership does not trust that the analyses are reliable; they do not bring robust information and are not really useful for decision-making. In many organisations, scepticism is fed by the idea that approximate data are transformed into numbers so volatile that they are hardly usable, if not completely false.

Probabilistic risk analysis provides decision-makers with realistic confidence intervals but not precise figures and also a better understanding of uncertainty drivers; thus, they can pilot the organisation efficiently through contextual hazards to enhance opportunities and curb threats. In truth, a robust quantitative analysis offers the organisation a competitive advantage in the selection of its activity portfolio to optimise risk-taking within the boundaries of their risk appetite and, thus, select the risk they are ready to accept, core trade risks or strategically induced risk, and those they have to suffer, ancillary risks.

The following method offers a way to introduce quantitative analysis in an organisation to strengthen its RM process and develop competencies in all staff through a continuous learning process so that the quantitative approach becomes embedded in all departments, projects, and processes; it must become business as usual maintained by repetitive analysis. The method in 10 steps will incorporate the main elements of strategy–risk–change (SRC) described further (see Section 8.9.7) so that the continuous strategic process rests on RM and change management.

Step 1. Top management engagement

To the extent that a course on RM is a relatively new addition to MBA curricula, outside of the insurance track, the current leadership generation, often still « insurance oriented », and the next generation, until the Millennial generation takes over, are not familiar with the concepts and methods of RM and try hard to get involved in business analytics. However, QRA requires efforts and resources that the directors and officers will not easily allocate unless they are more familiar with these concepts and show publicly their interest in engaging all staff. To get directors' and executives' interest, here are some relevant questions:

- What are the major (killer, critical) risks of the organisation? How are the decisions concerning risk made in the organisation? How is their analysis conducted today? Often, the analysis appears fragmented and conducted within functional silos, resulting in reports that cannot be consolidated due to the use of different concepts. Consequently, leadership cannot obtain a comprehensive overview or rely on the assurance that risks are being managed efficiently within the organization.

- Would it make sense to bring in an external consultant with broad experience and relevant education and training? The appropriate curriculum should include modelling and provide information on the results obtained in other organisations to make sure that it is capable of producing histograms and maps of critical risks (*heat-map*). However, the leaders should question the approach and be reasonably convinced about the deliverables they need and the level of trust they can put in the models. This means also that they must define the in-house competencies and resources that will be needed for the consultant mission to be a success.
- Have you already considered the progressive development of a risk analysis programme in the organisation? The unfolding of the programme must consider the organisation's culture, specifically the level of maturity in risk awareness. If the concept of uncertainty is new for the organisation, then resistance to the programme will be stronger, and the department will have to be trained to understand how uncertainty and risk apply to their activities, processes, and performance. As the timeline of the project will encompass several years until it becomes automatic, it will be important to share the progress of the new risk analysis plan as new departments are involved in the process. Communication is essential, and peer comments will do more to generate enthusiasm than hierarchical pressure. Experience shows that, as in any change project, failures are mostly due to a lack of involvement of middle management. The project is lost in the sands of middle management!
- Middle management[9] has a vital role within organisations but often feels undervalued. Local managers and supervisors face pressures from above and below, they tend to be both underdeveloped and powerless, and they face increasing pressure to offer flatter, faster, and leaner organisational structures; thus, they are underutilised and not appreciated, whereas they are the key to success in change management.

Step 2. Quick pre-study

Before formally launching the analysis programme, it is essential to take a look at the current situation: were there any risk analysis methods used in the past, and/or still currently implemented? Does the organisation currently develop risk reports and risk registers to build on? For example, in France, all organisations must update yearly a 'document unique', a legal document referencing professional risks and the efforts to improve them. It should never be assumed without checking that risk identification is complete. A survey conducted should allow spotting unrealistic evaluations, and departments that do not take seriously risk issues or see RM as superfluous. But it is essential to stay tuned to the information needs of the organisation's chain of command.

---

[9] *Stop wasting your most precious resource: Middle management*. Mc Kinsey & Company. https://www.mckinsey.com/capabilities/people-and-organizational-performance/our-insights/stop-wasting-your-most-precious-resource-middle-managers

Step 3. Training the analysis facilitator

For executives and managers with a solid education and relevant experience, a week's training on modelling techniques should prove enough. However, the seminar will have to be split into three or four sessions so as not to distract them from their job or disrupt normal operations. In-house, hands-on training sessions where the participants will be coached into developing apps relevant to the specific needs of the organisation should be considered. Basic techniques are the same but the attendees' attention will be awakened only if they find their daily life and concerns illustrated in the examples used in the training.

Training content must include, but cannot be limited to, fundamentals in statistics, trend analysis, and the use of risk analysis apps. The attendees from upper and middle management, but no part of the executive team, must develop a strategic vision so that they see the organisation and the context through the directors' lenses. Thus, they will understand what issues are essential to them, and what their information expectations are. The attendees must also learn how to conduct expert interviews so that they can quickly throw out fake data or data misrepresented in the recordings. Models must be as clear as possible to lend themselves to auditing; the underlying assumptions must be spelled out and justified; the results must be displayed in a readable fashion so that their realism can be assessed easily and so that tweaking the drivers provides a clear vision of the impact on the 'expected outcome'.

Step 4. First risk diagnostic – simplified

The goal of this step is to put into practice the skills and knowledge learned during the training so that staff acquires experience of the process and further the adjustment of the risk analysis process to the specifics of the organisation and the leaders' expectations. Typically, the methodology will be implemented for an investment project, and for the assessment of cash flows, it would perform well, when the impact of risk is brought into the picture. The following steps will be required:

- Work on risk issues with the leadership;
- List all relevant data available;
- Suggest and get approval for a plan to find, and solutions for, the issues deemed essential;
- Build a quantitative analysis model with the appropriate algorithm and introduce evaluations;
- Run the model, preferably with different sets of assumptions and formulate the resulting risk analysis;
- Present the analysis to leadership for an open discussion and gather their reactions and proposals; and
- Summarise the comments, develop a recommendation as well, and experience feedback.

Step 5. Developing a risk register focused on objectives

The risk register is an interactive database where all risks are consolidated at the headquarters level. Each risk must be documented with the necessary qualitative and quantitative information, gross exposure, and residual risk when the impact of risk reduction measures in place is considered. Depending on the risk taxonomy, the link with strategic objectives should be easily traced.

What will be presented to the board and executives is an edited version of the risk register limited to those that have a potentially strategic impact on the organisation, with a specific reference to the objective involved in the consequences. In all circumstances, it is important to keep in mind that all risk consequences are not quantifiable in financial terms: the impact of a strategic product recall, or an accident causing environmental impairment, cannot be precisely assessed but only estimated; on the other hand, the impact on reputation can be revealed only over the long run.

A word of caution when entering the residual risk in the risk register: If the valuation of residual risk is to be realistic, it is essential to validate the reduction measures: they have been put in place and are still running. Therefore, if there is a plan to develop new measures, the register must provide a brief description, the 'measure-owner' and the target date for completion, so that the internal auditor can verify easily in due course.

Step 6. Identify and develop forecasts for the organisation

In case the quality of some of the imported data is not assured, they could be quarantined in a separate database (imported data for simulation, DIS – distributed interactive simulation). This database contains the elements needed for Monte Carlo simulations for the organisation. It combines data from the internal and external context of the organisation. The DIS allows reliance on common assumptions, which avoids disparity and inconsistency in forecast during the consolidation phase.

Step 7. Implement the analysis in all departments in the organisation

Once the methodology is selected, the executives must inform the management team to ensure that they will support the programme and to make sure that their teams will get on board. This is an essential element of the *top-down* phase so that the analysis can spread through the organisation and the construction of the risk register the *bottom-up* process bringing the proof that all the risks are taken care of.

Step 8. Create dashboards to facilitate top management monitoring

Dashboards allow executives to focus on key risk issues. This means undertaking the following actions:

- List main events, with a description and an analysis for each of them;
- List main projects underway and assess the probability that they will be completed on time and budget;
- Estimate the volatility of cash flows, for each project, and their aggregate at the level of the organisation;
- Analyse the sensitivity to measure the project risk drivers' impact on the outcome and the effectiveness of existing risk reduction measures;
- Gather all other information that leadership deems necessary.

Dashboards must offer directors and executives an up-to-date risk overview of the risk universe with which the organisation is confronted and the quantified impact of uncertainties on its various activities. This aggregated presentation is based on the DIS and models selected that provide a realistic consolidated image of individual risk analysis.

Dashboards are useful if they provide the information in as visual a format as possible. Risk analysis does not provide certainties about the future; it aims only to provide enough information to provide decision-makers with the confidence to make decisions and that is why they need to visualise the impacts of alternative decisions.

Although it is used mostly as an investigative tool, the presentation as a bowtie of causes and consequences may prove useful for decision-makers especially in the form below (see Fig. 8.2) where decision-makers can have a grip on their potential level of control on the various causes and consequences.

The bowtie in itself does not provide quantitative information but helps visualise the different strategies and the uncertainties that may influence its execution.

Step 9. Implementing monitoring and review processes

Evaluations developed in organisations regarding their drivers' confidence intervals are influenced by several prejudices, known as cognitive biases such as representativeness, adequacy, fixed value, optimism/pessimism, etc. An experienced analyst can work on these prejudices and limit their impact on the output during the evaluation process. Some will remain nevertheless but the feedback loop should assist progressively, especially through the assessment workshops suggested in the method.

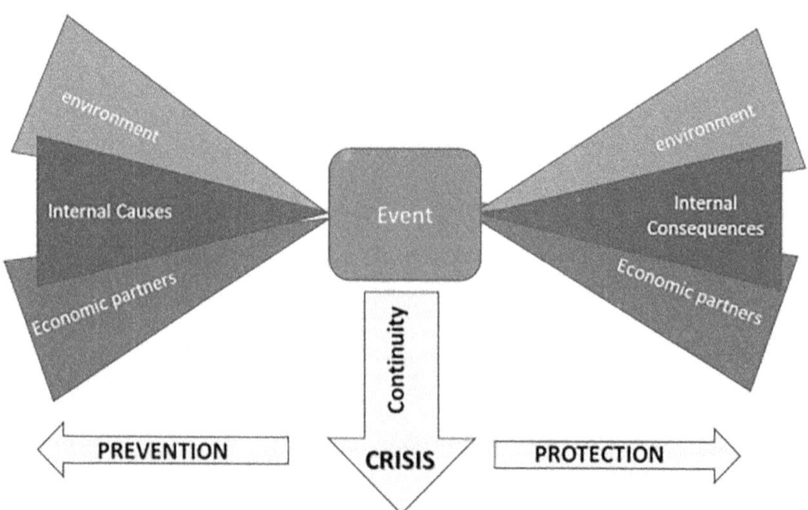

Fig. 8.2. Bowtie Revisited. *Source*: J.P. Louisot.

Step 10. Iterative process

Of course, risk analysis is not a one-time process, and to make valid decisions, it needs to be updated regularly. An organisation's risk universe is in constant evolution, and the risk analysis must be revised regularly and prompted after a new risk is identified or a new event takes place bringing in new experiences and lessons. This is why computer systems that collect data, generate and run models, provide reports and dashboards, must allow reprogramming to take into account evolutions in the internal and external content.

In summary, QRA is not an option but a must, as the information provided to the leadership would be of little value for decision-making if it was not quantified. When many directors and executives still have reservations as to the importance of RM, beyond compliance, it would be easy to convince them if they are provided with relevant information to make decisions and transform hazardous wagers into rational decisions that are expected of them in the governance regulations in many countries.

The training may have to start at the board level where expectations should be summarised to develop the training/coaching needed by all the management staff. Grafting the right RM competencies will require setting up coaching sessions with a competent external consultant, who will bring in a broader experience than the in-house team. Then, the directors and executives will consult the dashboards that will provide the information needed to take the organisation to a safe harbour despite the high seas, with the help of a watchtower to scout the horizon for weak signals announcing tempests.

8.5. Optimising the Organisation's Performance in an Uncertain Future

The ultimate objective of RM is the level of uncertainty that all decision-makers face when making decisions. This is why the key question is to optimise the performance using uncertainty in a proactive mode to leverage results rather than retreating from uncertainties and remaining in a reactive mode.

8.5.1. How to Capitalise on Synergies Between RM, Security, and Economic Intelligence?

At a time when private security services are evolving and going through regulation changes in many countries,[10] it may seem strange that economic intelligence is often not included in the picture. There is an obvious synergy between all actors involved in uncertainty as already mentioned. Will the road ahead require professionals and academics to open a new front where economic intelligence, RM, security, health and safety, and continuity will merge in a new all-encompassing function?

---

[10]France, for example, has gone through a series of legislations after 30 years of stability: Law No. 2015-912 of 24 July 2015 for intelligence, Law No. 2017-258 of February 2017 concerning public security, Law No. 2017-1510 of 30 October 2017 to reinforce internal security and fight terrorism.

8.5.2. Uncertainty and Risk Revisited

Uncertainty is at the core of all thinking in the micro and macro economy as in essence every future is uncertain. However, economic theories tend to consider uncertainty as being contained within limits, confidence intervals and even in a probabilistic future. Such is the case of the financial model developed by Harry Markowitz[11] when he used the standard deviation as a measure of the risk to include a risk premium in his theory of return on capital, with the underlying assumption of a normal distribution.

The mission of RM is precisely to take the issue one step further and allow the organisations' top management to prepare for the improbable and modify the model to consider a limited time horizon. This is why continuity and crisis management have become so important in RM efforts, and Bertrand Robert[12] goes further to suggest exploiting ruptures that result from the 'rise of the absurd'. This is why it is so important for RM to be involved in testing the sustainability of strategic objectives even before they are published and then in making sure they are reached or corrected as events dictate throughout the strategy implementation.

The French philosopher Alain[13] stated that 'all humans retain in the depth of their unconscious a Savannah hunter wired to see risk', and the risk manager's enemy is the posture 'we have always done it like this' when confronted with any suggestion of change. However, attempting always to draw the future from the past is not good enough. Who has ever tried to drive using only rear-view mirrors rather than looking through a clean windscreen? In a few words, drawing from past experience should never absolve one from the need to screen the future.

As a matter of fact, in the labyrinth of life, humankind is guided by the future, and if the present is the accumulation of the past, one should never forget that the future also contributes to shaping the present. The game is to see opportunities even if the cloud ceiling is low and may obscure the light. Alain Panisse[14] sees the opportunities the world offers *risk managers* in the current difficulties the world is going through, provided they learn to:

- Be noble, in the sense of noblesse oblige, i.e. put their talents and competence to the service of all, including their leadership, provided they pursue the social good;

---

[11]Harry Markowitz – 1952. Portfolio selection. *Journal of Finance,* 7(1), 77–91; 1959. *Portfolio selection: Efficient diversification of investments.* Reprint. Wiley, 1970; and http://www.businessinsider.com/harry-markowitz-best-thing-beginning-investors-can-do-2016-2

[12]Notes 6 and 65.

[13]Alain, pseudonym of Émile-Auguste Chartier (born 3 March 1868, Mortagne – died 2 June 1951, Le Vésinet), a French philosopher whose work profoundly influenced several generations of readers.

[14]Alain Panisse rose in the rank of Marseille (France) staff from labourer to work supervisor in cultural affairs. https://fr.linkedin.com/in/alain-panisse-5bb61648

- Cultivate doubt, as the French philosopher René Descartes[15] suggests in his writings in the Socratic tradition, i.e. to learn to always question the certainties that prevail in an organisation's culture while maintaining a secure path so that the mission remains clear for all;
- Refocus the leadership to help them contrast their self-centred vision with stakeholders' visions so that they can make enlightened decisions by the information received and the future prospects.

8.6. Risk Universe and the Regulatory Turmoil

The wind of regulatory changes that has been blowing since the beginning of the century, triggered by the Enron debacle and further fed by the financial crisis, does not seem to be abating as it is fuelled by climate change. It has a considerable impact on the governance of organisations and adds to the costs of management, especially the management of risks, in private and public organisations due to duplications, even contradictions, when new regulations are piled on existing ones, as is the case in France.

This continuous flow of reforms has forced organisations to re-engineer their RM system, framework, and processes to comply with the new « risk governance » provisions, the industry codes of conduct, prudential rules, and diverse legislation.

If RM has risen in the organisational hierarchy, it is most of the time thanks to ambiguity as the directors saw mostly the issues of governance and compliance. The contraction of the legal and regulatory net has made corporate officers interested in, even worried about, the consequences for their responsibilities and accountability to different stakeholders, no longer only to shareholders. If directors are more involved in risk issues, it is not always for the right reasons. Most directors are mostly interested in compliance and legal risks that might put them in a hot spot, and that means they tend to be risk averse.

The major consequence is that many organisations are buried under expensive and time-consuming compliance programmes, based on list-checking exercises that lose sight of the main mission of developing and implementing a 'winning strategy' through risk-taking optimisation … But that presupposes some risk appetite!

For[16] high-performing organisations, the rise in rules worldwide is not an obstacle but rather a significant catalyst for success. Regulations facilitate the worldwide expansion of enterprises, safeguard their interests, and promote steady growth. Furthermore, effective adherence to regulations may serve as a powerful competitive edge, earning companies the confidence of customers, investors, and other stakeholders.

---

[15]René Descartes (31 March 1596–11 February 1650) was a French philosopher, mathematician, and scientist. Dubbed the father of modern Western philosophy, much of subsequent Western philosophy is a response to his writings, which are studied closely to this day.

[16]These five paragraphs are derived from '5 Best practices to future-proof compliance'. Metric Stream.

Nevertheless, achieving compliance is becoming increasingly challenging. Regulators are implementing more rigorous inspections, despite the rapid evolution and expansion of compliance requirements in tandem with fast-paced markets and technological improvements. However, the growing frequency of non-compliant and fraudulent situations, such as the manipulation of income, indicates that the mere implementation of controls may not be adequate. Compliance functions are always facing new demands and expectations, which need them to adapt their working practices and utilise technology.

Amid this situation, what distinguishes great achievers is the efficacy of their compliance programmes, allowing them to utilise compliance as a chance rather than a hindrance. These programmes are crucial in shaping an organisation's culture by translating intricate legislative requirements into clear commercial terms, fulfilling the needs of top-level management, and enabling stakeholders to assess whether the intended cultural framework has been successfully implemented throughout the company.

8.7. Constantly Evolving Risk Universe and the Need to Anticipate

Several determining factors influence the risk universe in this third decade of the 21st century[17]:

- Organisations recognise that their existence and profitability rest on their capacity to accept socially useful risks;
- The notion of risk, as a rational and objective analysis of a random variable, is questioned by the rise of the absurd[18];
- A purely financial approach to risk as volatility of outcomes leaves out the human and social dimensions of risk;
- A silo approach to risk is not acceptable anymore, especially when limited to hazard risks, all risks must be integrated into one global system;
- The integrated approach to managing risk presupposes the consideration of RM as an integral component of the organisation's strategic process;
- The RM executive function is still in the making as its working frontiers are not set;
- At the core of the current evolution is the risk ownership at the operational level, where both responsibility and authority must be delegated.

The key to managing anything is knowledge and understanding. Therefore, the initial step in managing risks is to learn to know them: to identify, analyse,

[17]Louisot, J.-P. (2023). *Comprendre et mettre en œuvre le diagnostic des risques.* AFNOR Éditions.

[18]Bertrand, R. (2002). Nouvelles pratiques en management des crises. Dix ruptures pour passer d'une logique de procédures à l'apprentissage de la surprise, Argillos. *Environnement, Risques & Santé, 1*(1); and (2002). *La gestion de crises en agroalimentaire: Anticipation et pilotage.* AFNOR Éditions.

and evaluate risk. Collecting data becomes the cornerstone of RM and is the risk analysis cornerstone as mentioned above (see Section 8.6). Without reliable data, there is no improved risk information for decision-makers at any level: strategic, tactical, or operational. However, data are the 'raw material', and they are transformed into information only if all decision-makers, engineers, managers, or elected officials are trained in using risk analysis tools. Perhaps, this should become part of civic education for all citizens.

In a continually changing legal environment (see Section 8.6), managing legal risk has become a real challenge for organisations. Compliance and governance are not optional; however, the framework must be such that it does not kill all initiatives and create an environment of aversion to risk such that the organisation ends up totally paralysed. It is even so complex sometimes that total compliance cannot be achieved, especially where regulations contradict one another.

Thus, the legal wake-up call should include prioritisation of rules and regulations, and the directors must set risk tolerance limits for 'minor non-compliances' keeping in mind that stakeholders' concerns and expectations change over time and that regulations may lag behind their shifting interests. In this post 'subprime' era, let all leaders keep in mind that practices tolerated before 2008 would not be acceptable today, be they legal or not![19]

8.8. Change Fatigue – A Risk to Be Managed

The need for continuous change is increasing to remain relevant in a constantly evolving context; change fatigue has become a top developing concern among risk managers according to surveys.

Conducted among 138 global risk professionals, Gartner's quarterly emerging risks report for the second quarter of 2017[20] found that change fatigue remains the top concern for the second consecutive quarter, and the following editions did not overturn the situation.

According to the research and consultancy organisation, the most successful companies navigate change by implementing gradual changes and prioritising incremental enhancements. In addition, executives in ERM may assist in evaluating the possible risks associated with change efforts by leading talks and conducting scenario exercises to identify potential areas of failure.

The poll encompasses feedback from risk, audit, and compliance executives located across North America, Europe, and Asia Pacific. An emerging risk, as described in the study, refers to a systemic issue or business practice that has either not been recognised before, has been recognised but inactive for a long time, or has not yet become a matter of substantial concern.

---

[19]See ISO 31022:2020. *Risk management – Guidelines for the management of legal risk.*
[20]Change Fatigue Top Concern Among Risk Leaders. (n.d.). *Strategic risk global.* https://www.strategic-risk-global.com/change-fatigue-top-concern-among-risk-leaders-/1422289.article

The research and advisory company said that the best companies advance through change by taking small steps and focusing on incremental improvements. Furthermore, ERM leaders can help assess the potential risks of change initiatives by facilitating discussions and scenario exercises to uncover where they could go off the rails.

The survey consists of responses from risk, audit, and compliance executives in North America, Europe, and Asia Pacific. An emerging risk, as defined in the survey, is a systemic issue or business practice that has not previously been identified, has been identified but dormant for an extended period, or has yet to rise to an area of significant concern.

'Business leaders are relying on change initiatives to help drive innovation and stay competitive, but they risk overwhelming and alienating their employees in the process', said Matthew Shinkman, risk practice leader at Gartner, who supervised the initial study. 'The end result of too many poorly communicated change initiatives is, ironically, that organisations are more vulnerable to productivity losses & errors that in the end slow things down'.[21]

This conclusion verifies the tenets of change management: all involved in a change must be 'partners' in the change project and embrace it. This is why communication and consultation with all internal stakeholders are essential; they must see 'what there is in it for them'. But there need to be 'quiet times' scheduled to help staff recover from a sequence of changes.

[21]Change Fatigue Top Concern Among Risk Leaders. (n.d.). *Strategic risk global.* https://www.strategic-risk-global.com/change-fatigue-top-concern-among-risk-leaders-/1422289.article

Chapter 9

Risk Management Projects and Change

As a science and profession in the making, risk management is a construction endeavour with continuing projects to improve methods and deliverables. Current projects include issues of governance, big data, analytics, cyber-security, and coping with climate change (conversion risk). These risks are compounded due to a complex web of interactions between actors in society in a rapidly changing environment.

9.1. The GRC Triangle (Governance/Risk Management/Compliance)

This context led academics and practitioners to conclude that governance and compliance issues had to be managed rigorously provided the future is better grasped through risk management, i.e. the information it provides improves understanding of the future. This is how the acronym GRC was forged and a triangle was drawn to provide a visual aid (see Fig. 9.1). It is a way to stress that the three poles are intertwined and that only integrated solutions can knit together the requirements of these three poles, distinct, and yet intrinsically mingled.

As mentioned in the previous chapter (see Sections 8.6 and 8.7), managing legal risks requires directors and officers to be presented with legal dashboards allowing them to make sure that the 'Risk management' and 'Compliance' teams work together although they come from different if complementary perspectives. There is probably a need for a hybrid professional able to manage the three components of the GRC triangle consistently while integrating sustainability to enhance 'social licence to operate'.

As[1] regulations become more intricate, organisations must develop a strong vision and strategy for compliance to prioritise what is truly essential. This includes identifying and addressing areas with the highest compliance risk and

[1]These four paragraphs are derived from '5 Best practices to future-proof compliance'. Metric Stream.

Enterprise Risk Management in Today's World, Part A:
Enterprise-Wide Risk Management and Strategy, 127–137
Copyright © 2024 by Jean-Paul Louisot and Simon Grima
Published under exclusive licence by Emerald Publishing Limited
doi:10.1108/978-1-83797-406-120241010

Fig. 9.1. GRC Triangle.

promoting a culture of consistent compliance. Simultaneously, efforts should be made to streamline compliance processes, reduce costs, simplify procedures, and ensure reliability.

Compliance management initiatives in high-performing businesses are tightly integrated with the business's strategic vision and goals. The primary objective is to optimise the efficiency of compliance management workflows by integrating individuals, procedures, and technology and establishing distinct points of integration among them.

In essence, this technique enables businesses to establish a compliance culture that is both enduring and adaptable, capable of accommodating future regulatory and operational shifts.

It represents a novel approach to understanding and implementing compliance initiatives in businesses. These programmes are not only a routine task but rather a crucial instrument for safeguarding the organisation's brand and reputation, as well as strengthening its resilience.

9.2. The Contribution of the ISO 31000:2018 Standard and Its Implications for ERM

Within the context of the ISO 31000 standard, *risk management guidelines* is becoming an international reference for risk management. When it was first published in 2009, the definition of risk was a breakthrough as it went beyond the engineers' vision (a combination of the probability of an event and its consequences); the international standard ties the definition of risk to uncertainty and the organisation's objectives. ISO 31000 includes the following risk management process[2] proposed here in a circular image (see Fig. 9.2 – repeated from Fig. 3.1):

---

[2]Louisot, J.-P. (2022). *Gestion des risques*, collection « 100 questions pour comprendre et agir » (3rd ed.). AFNOR Éditions.

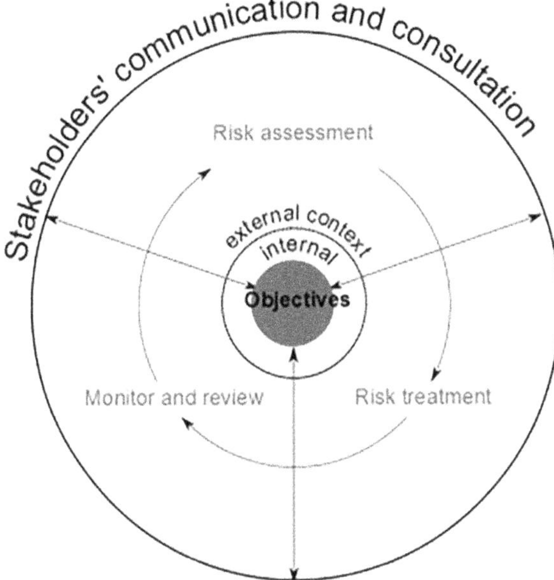

Fig. 9.2. Circle of Risk Management. *Source*: J.-P. Louisot.

The increasing complexity of organisations and the web in which they operate has made obsolete the silo-based approach to managing risk and has led to the development of a new global and integrated approach to risk. The actual management of risk is delegated to operational managers, the risk owners, who need to be empowered so to do. They must have the responsibility and the authority to manage the risks arising from the activities they supervise. This is known as *enterprise-wide risk management* (*ERM*) which assumes that decision-making includes risk considerations at all levels, strategic, tactical, and operational.

To help decision-makers venture into uncertainty with more confidence to tame uncertainty, Jim DeLoach,[3] a partner in the consulting group Protiviti, suggests a six-step process:

- Draw profit from pioneers' well-timed value creation: this means size an opportunity and get out before threats materialise;
- Be aware of the limited value of historical data, anecdotes, surveys, and specialised articles: facts must be validated by questioning methodologies and underlying assumptions;
- Accept that change must be embraced, as it is unavoidable: change must be anticipated through sentinel signals that allow for preparation and even building of a desirable change;

[3]Jim, D. (2013, November 27). *Knowing, what you don't know – Six steps organisations can take to manage uncertainty*. NACD Directorship.

- Avoid 'blind spots' in the organisation: they are resource destroyers, and all models are built on underlying assumptions that may prove dead ends, as the future will not be a carbon copy of the past;
- Make sure that strategic assumptions are aligned with realities: it is important to stay in touch with the external environment at all times so that relevant data are uploaded into the system to verify assumptions and change them as necessary;
- Verify that all the directors' and officers' fears and concerns are on the table: if needs be, workshops should be organised based on creative thinking to discuss not only the 'improbable' but also the 'impossible' to imagine the type of response that would be needed should it happen.

9.3. Strategy and Risk Management in a Complex and Fast-Evolving World

Performance optimisation in a highly volatile world can be reached only if uncertainties are managed to benefit the organisation. The strategy must be built on realistic assumptions and with due consideration to constraints, current and future; time and resources must be allocated to provide for uncertainties and imagine the range of potential scenarios that could derail the strategy; this is part of preparing efficient responses for situations of rupture.

The concept of strategic risk is not new as it appears in the 'four quadrants' representation, but it should be called a strategic impact risk. The list and ranking of such risks are constantly evolving as the context and the risk universe are both complex and constantly changing. However, the management of risks that impact strategy has gained more top management's attention, as evidenced by the latest Forbes[4] survey as the list of 10 risks and threats that can be forerunners to crises for companies and organisations including supply network, damages to reputation, succession planning, etc.

However, implementing the strategic component of risk management requires including the risk-management effort all the functions to ensure sustainable development for the organisation despite, or even maybe thanks to, a volatile environment. When the revolution of 'big data' and 'cloud computing' are taken into account, all functions' ultimate mission is to strengthen the organisations' and society's resilience. However, this requires that all functions cooperate more closely to implement the strategy defined by the board, including risk management. It is the only way to ensure that management will extend to exposures that Donald Rumsfeld used to call the 'unknown-unknown' and Patrick Lagadec[5] the 'unknown', i.e. uncertainties not even yet on the emerging risks radar.

---

[4]Segal, E. *The 10 biggest risks and threats for businesses in 2023.* https://www.forbes.com/sites/edwardsegal/2023/01/01/the-10-biggest-risks-and-threats-for-businesses-in-2023/

[5]Patrick Lagadec, former senior research scientist at the Ecole Polytechnique, Paris, France, and consultant in global crisis. https://www.crisis-response.com/about/editor.php?num=24

But compliance remains an essential piece of the puzzle. One[6] major benefit of implementing a highly effective compliance management system is that it enables businesses to effectively pursue and achieve successful strategic initiatives. It allows stakeholders to comprehend the compliance risks associated with significant strategic choices, like mergers and acquisitions, which are often significant due to their substantial financial implications. By providing stakeholders with immediate compliance and risk insights, they may more effectively detect the risks connected with such initiatives. This allows the company to take proactive measures to prevent any potential reputational or regulatory harm. An effective compliance management programme aids businesses in evaluating behavioural risks, overseeing the control culture, and incorporating security and ethics into the fundamental structure of the firm. Given its numerous capabilities, the compliance function serves as a crucial strategic ally inside the firm.

This is why the cooperation, already mentioned, of risk management, security, compliance, and economic intelligence (EI) is an absolute necessity to enlighten decision-making and provide warning to consider the 'unknown' as soon as it appears on the radar, even if only through weak signals. A route to reunification could be found in Henri Fayol's[7] fifth executive function, security, and Hubert Seillan[8] by global management in his proposal to create value and optimise performance.

9.4. EI as an Engine to Bridge Security and Risk Management

In 2007, Serenus Conseil, one of the *leaders* of EI in France, decided to partner in the creation of a security service company called Amarante.[9] In those days, the *leitmotiv* was: 'provide private firms the same level of service as the state by its best specialists'. Amarante aims at a high-end market, protecting firms' assets in sensitive areas, offering advice, audit, and training, and do not limit its involvement to physical security. At the time, professionals in this activity thought that this type of joint services made sense and that the branch maturity would bring about a multiplication of such initiatives.

It seems that merging these activities and possibly including broader risk management services makes a lot of sense especially when it comes to small- and

[6]This paragraph is extracted from '5 Best practices to future-proof compliance'. Metric Stream.

[7]Henri Fayol (1841–1925) was a French mining engineer, mining executive, author, and director of mines who developed the general theory of business administration that is often called Fayolism.

[8]Hubert Seillan, lawyer and former lecturer in risk analysis at Bordeaux University.

[9]Ruello, A. (2007, October 2). *Serenus Conseil se lance dans le domaine de la sécurité*. Les Echos. https://www-lesechos-fr.translate.goog/2007/10/serenus-conseil-se-lance-dans-le-domaine-de-la-securite-541507?_x_tr_sl=fr&_x_tr_tl=en&_x_tr_hl=en&_x_tr_pto=sc

medium-sized enterprises (SMEs) and medium-sized companies. However, in recent years, the movement has not gained momentum as it still seems difficult to bring together specialists who until recently ignored each other: on the one hand, EI participates in the strategic process, whereas security is seen as a 'physical guard', all muscle and little brain. On the other hand, a security specialist viewed EI at best as fuzzy and of little interest. However, the landscape is slowly changing for two main reasons.

As far as private organisations are concerned, the current business environment, in many countries, is such that they cannot think strategy without making sure that security issues are considered. When it comes to international development or outsourcing, the organisation's survival cannot be assured unless it gives due consideration to the protection of persons (expatriate and their families, but also national staff), assets, and even more information with the rising issue of cyber-security. When it comes to international business, safety, and security policies are not only a competitive advantage, but also a significant cost.

International support has for a long time been within the realm of EI, but it is progressively shared with security, especially when there are terrorist threats. This has a corollary: the new security department tends to manage some aspects of EI, especially when it comes to security in foreign countries. This means that the 'security landscape' is changing and if EI consultants want to remain relevant, they have to broaden their range of services and bring in security competencies. It is therefore no surprise if ADIT, a *leader* of EI in France, chose Jean-Pierre Vuillermé, one of the most renowned French security directors and former security director for the very secretive Michelin group, as the leader for their 'risk management' pole![10]

On the other hand, the association of French Security and EI directors (Cercle des DIrecteurs de Sécurité (CDSE)) and security supports the establishment of service providers that become credible or trustworthy partners for large multinational groups and thus create an alternative to Anglo-Saxon service providers, global security services that may even include due diligence as well as VIP close protection. In most countries, security services and EI consultants are too small to offer serious alternatives to trans-frontier providers, whereas in some industries, it might prove important to contract with national firms to preserve national interests. Some companies are integrated into large groups.

9.5. A Market to Meet Actors' Expectations

Finally, an interesting perspective was developed by Mark Casson in his book *The Entrepreneur: An Economic Theory*, in 1983[11]: what interests enterprises is not the market as it exists, but as they create it. In other words, the only market that interests a company is the market of its 'potential customers'. This is even truer today with

[10] Adit. (n.d.). Team. https://www.adit.fr/team/

[11] Loasby, B. J., & Casson, M. (1983). The entrepreneur: An economic theory. *The Economic Journal, 93*(372), 931. https://doi.org/10.2307/2232766

the constant technological revolution that offers opportunities to develop new products, new services, and new apps that Millennials seem prompt to seize and the number of successful start-ups is an indication of where the economy is going.

When it comes to the development of security services, a large conglomerate that tends to outsource security should seek service providers that can answer their diverse needs as they want to open 'their secret coffers' to a limited number of highly reliable partners.

Each country should be interested in promoting national actors as they are part of societal resilience. It will be possible only if private and public actors work hand in hand but that may require some legal and regulatory adjustments and maybe the creation of a 'national watchdog' to maintain the separation of powers at the national level, which private companies usually do not do. But, after all, private companies are not democracies, or are they?

9.6. Security Management, Risk Management, Compliance, and Value Creation

A main part of value creation by risk management comes from information brought to decision-makers of all levels; they have a better outline of the future as the fog of uncertainty is partly lifted; thus, they can navigate closer to the reef, with more assurance and surf on uncertainty creatively and proactively rather than stay on a defensive attitude in dread. Business analytics fed by internal and external data develop models based on algorithms that narrow down the range of impact based on several assumptions and provide scenarios involving risk interactions that the human mind alone could not decipher, i.e. human intelligence is enhanced by artificial intelligence. Continually adjusting strategy to adjust to contexts' evolution will allow for optimising strategic objectives under any circumstances. However, this can be achieved only through constant cooperation between all the functions involved in managing the many facets of uncertainties with a common goal of ensuring resilience; they include risk management, compliance, EI, security, quality – Total Quality Management (TQM) –, health and safety, continuity, and crisis management. Ultimately, all these contribute to reputation management, and the CRO might also be seen as the Chief Reputation Officer; some would develop the acronym as Chief Resilience Officer (see Section 7.3.3).

To truly add value,[12] a cutting-edge compliance management system should embrace a proactive strategy, placing less emphasis on past occurrences and instead directing attention towards predicting potential dangers and identifying early warning signs. Data frequently hold the key to predicting the unknown. Many businesses possess substantial amounts of data that may be employed to forecast compliance issues through the use of predictive data analytics and sophisticated statistical techniques. These systems efficiently analyse data in almost real time, providing essential insights about both existing and emerging dangers.

---

[12]These four paragraphs are derived from '5 Best practices to future-proof compliance'. Metric Stream.

A company may significantly mitigate risks by continuously monitoring and analysing both structured and unstructured data. Additionally, there exist collaborative compliance technologies that aid in the correlation of various risk categories and facilitate the timely identification of compliance concerns. This, in turn, grants businesses the opportunity and assurance to successfully address these issues.

Data analytics play a crucial role in compliance initiatives by providing important and timely insight to the company.

9.7. From GRC to SRC: Strategy, Risk Management, and Change

Some academics and professionals question the validity of the GRC triangle (see Section 8.9.1). Due to the rapid changes and the increasing complexity of the internal and external context in which organisations must find a successful path, directors and officers have no other choice than to clear their path through uncertainties. This means they have to take measured risks thanks to a constant adjustment of strategies to perceived realities and emerging developments. The price to pay to preserve, and reinforce, the organisation's relevancy to remain a key node in its web of partners, and a reference for stakeholders, is evolution and anticipation at all times; continuous innovation is the name of the game, taking chances is not a choice but a vital necessity! (see Fig. 9.3).

Under such circumstances, forward-thinking leaders who shape the future are instrumental in building the resilience of their organisations and even society as a whole. However, as there is only a fuzzy vision of the future, they need a systematic process to bring to their attention emerging evolutions thanks to collective wisdom. The solution is to implement a new triangle where a continuous strategic thinking process is fed through a holistic, integrated, and systematic management of risk. This can be achieved by developing and implementing ERM programmes providing information gathered by all operational staff in their daily interactions with stakeholders and instilling a culture of change for survival.

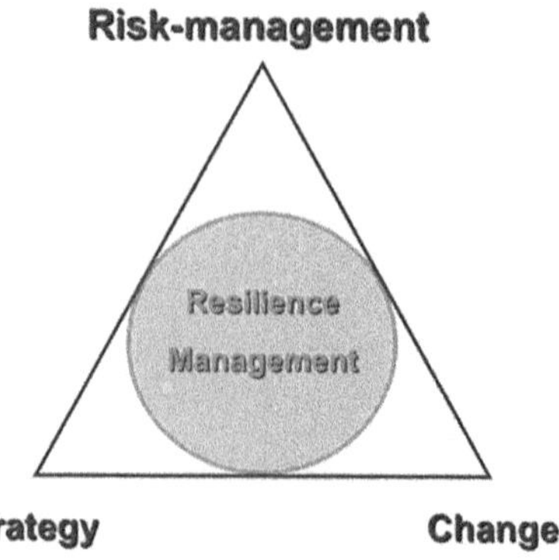

Fig. 9.3. SRC Triangle: Continuous Strategic Process.

This is why compliance must be revised to integrate risks. A[13] risk-based approach to compliance involves identifying and focusing on the most critical areas of compliance risk inside the business while conducting compliance assessments. The primary objective should be to allocate compliance resources towards the areas that provide the highest level of concern. This methodology results in improved allocation of resources and enhanced operational efficiency.

Ensuring that the organisation's internal policies are in line with all regulatory standards is a crucial aspect of implementing a risk-based approach to compliance. This type of mapping or alignment assists stakeholders in identifying the business processes and places that are affected by a certain rule. Additionally, it aids in formulating a strategic course of action to minimise the related regulatory compliance hazards. Furthermore, it enhances comprehension of issue tracking, facilitates the identification of the reasons behind these difficulties, detects ineffective controls, and expedites the resolution of the issue by implementing suitable action plans.

However, to cross-reference information channelled through the bottom-up process, EI is necessary for enhancing top management's capacity to take ownership of the future; the tool for this is called business analytics which can integrate the latest advances in modelling including learning capacity built into the system (Fig. 9.3).

However, at the end of the day, until such times that artificial intelligence will assist them, leaders must develop capabilities to discern the major trends for the future amid an overflow of information, even if their risk manager and intelligence specialists select only the 'essential'. But if their vision is to materialise, leaders must generate a culture of change and bring the tools of change management to give staff the means for a successful change to transform their vision into an economic and social success.

There is an ongoing debate among risk and security professionals and academics on a common definition of resilience, especially when applied to society; however, for a private or public organisation, the key to resilience is to retain stakeholders' trust and confidence. Hence, resilience rests on the capacity to remain relevant through evolutions in the internal and external context, even when evolutions are rife with ambiguity, or bring chaos. An efficient reaction to change, expected or unexpected, must be 'on time' and 'to the point', i.e. resulting from staying continuously alert.

9.8. Putting the Fun Back into Risk[14]

Half a century ago, the focus of management was mostly on the concept of 'dominate or perish'. Only the most resilient individuals in an industry were able to prosper, while others were forced to withdraw because they recognised

---

[13]These two paragraphs are extracted from '5 Best practices to future-proof compliance'. Metric Stream.

[14]From the article by Hans Læssøe, former senior director of strategic risk management at the LEGO Group and founder of AKTUS, published in *Strategic Risk*, 28 August 2017. http://www.strategic-risk-global.com/putting-the-fun-back-into-risk/1422288.article

the necessity of adhering to the regulations established by the dominant figure. Subsequently, the game underwent a transformation and shifted its focus towards managing expenses and delegating tasks to external entities. Given the present circumstances, it is no longer feasible to get a significant competitive edge just through the practice of outsourcing.

Strategic risk management has evolved into a crucial factor for determining whether entities are able to survive and thrive. Risk managers must collaborate with company executives whom they perceive as advocates. Subsequently, they provide assistance to such leaders in order to enhance their achievement beyond that of their counterparts. The firms who are most adaptable will experience survival and prosperity, since success leads to further success, similar to the concept of Darwinism. The upcoming decade will focus on agility as a key aspect of strategic advantage. The utilisation of risk management tools and information will help businesses in attaining this objective.

In order for risk management professionals to have a significant influence on the strategy, they must engage in conversations with decision-makers to capture their attention, comprehend their thought processes, and discuss risks with them during the decision-making process. This necessitates acquiring a comprehensive understanding of the strategic challenges confronting the organisation.

9.8.1. A Rapidly Changing World

The upcoming generation of risk managers, consisting of millennials and post-millennials, will bring a greater sense of enjoyment to the job, which is indicative of a shifting work environment. Adolescents are creating applications in their private rooms and conceptualising the world in a fundamentally distinct manner from previous generations, with the inclusion of risk potentially contributing to the enjoyment of life.

The millennial generation is likely to find the process of auditing a firm enjoyable due to the implementation of a software game. Many jobs are likely to transition in that direction. The rate of change in the world has always been relative, but the overall speed of change has grown and will continue to do so.

In the future, the Fourth Industrial Revolution will involve the automation of anything that can be standardised. Artificial intelligence will possess the capacity to comprehend a multitude of intricate information and data, allowing it to make highly accurate judgements through a series of 4,000 quick steps, surpassing the limitations of human humans.

According to Jack Ma, the CEO of Alibaba, he believes that robots will be the most competent CEOs in the next 30 years.[15] The process of looking for data that used to take four months in 1981 may today likely be accomplished within a few hours using a mobile application. To progress, it is crucial to acquire and integrate

[15]Low, A. (2017, April 25). Alibaba's founder Jack Ma says AI will likely replace CEOs. CNET. https://www.cnet.com/science/alibabas-founder-jack-ma-says-ai-will-likely-replace-ceos/

both agility and inventiveness, as both qualities are now beyond the capabilities of computers.

9.8.2. Beyond a Tick-Box Exercise

As professionals, risk managers must acknowledge that seeing risk just as a simple compliance task does not ensure future success.

With the evolving global landscape and increasing disruptions, it is imperative for individual organisations to comprehend this reality. Strategic risk cannot be easily quantified using a quantitative equation. Success requires a strong sense of business acumen.

Instead of only reporting to compliance boards, risk professionals should aim to have greater influence at a high level within businesses. In the United States, the accounting scandals that occurred in the 1990s and the subsequent legislation, including the Sarbanes-Oxley Act,[16] resulted in risk management becoming too focused on completing routine tasks without considering the actual risks involved.

Companies have developed the belief that being compliant with the Sarbanes-Oxley Act (SOX) ensures effective risk management; however, this is not the case. Indeed, it is comprehensible that risk management services must provide documentation to demonstrate their efforts in mitigating the company's risks. However, this matter is not currently being discussed on the board's agenda.

The board is employing strategic thinking and deliberating on whether to expand into a certain region or sector. Should we design a novel product category or consolidate with this company? The inclusion of risk is crucial in that debate.

Any competent company manager would never make choices without taking into account the costs and advantages involved. In a for-profit firm, the financial outcomes hold utmost importance. The board should engage in discussions on the company's strategic pursuits, risk exposure, and corresponding mitigation strategies.

The issue arises when risk management is excessively linked to compliance, which perpetuates the mistaken belief that risk solely pertains to avoidance and expenses, rather than embracing proactive measures to enhance performance. Embracing calculated risks is crucial for ensuring survival in a world characterised by upheaval. Inaction is not a viable choice.

Every leader must always undertake strategic risks, while it is not morally wrong to make an unintelligent choice. If a leader takes decisions without being aware of the dangers, it is not only foolish but also demonstrates a lack of responsibility. A leader has the capacity to make suboptimal judgements, yet it is worth questioning the reasons behind such choices.

---

[16]https://sarbanes-oxley-act.com/

Chapter 10

Conclusion and Perspectives

Managing resilience, complexity, and change coherently and aligned is a significant challenge for boards, executives, and management professionals throughout the organisation. The challenge of resilience cannot be overcome when resilience is left to department heads that approach it from a compliance or continuity angle, and not as an integrated discipline of decision-making at the strategic level with performance in focus. This becomes even more complex when business continuity is disconnected and not integrated into the enterprise risk management (ERM) programme.

Organisations need strategic tools to manage risk, i.e. enhance business opportunities, and curb threats both internal and external to strengthen their resilience, ensure future development, and proactively manage risk to reputation. The proposed methodology complies with the governance requirements for integrated organisational risk management, also called corporate governance, and aims to effectively implement recognised management standards. The proposed methodology is based on the application of risk management.

The coordination and potential integration of business risk management systems is now potentially easier with the increasing convergence of standards. In the community's increasingly influential concern with corporate social responsibility (CSR), CSR indexes serve as indicators of probity in safety, environment, and other areas. Therefore, companies must demonstrate their CSR[1] level through the use of recognised management standards.

In any organisation, the chief executive officer (CEO) and the governing body need to evaluate and differentiate the decision-making process affecting their risk management activities and how accreditation to management standards that are integrated within CSR-focused activities will impact their business performance.

So long as it is truly integrated into the existing strategic management processes of the organisation and grafted on the existing management system of

[1]Among others, the Dow Jones Sustainability™ World Index comprises global sustainability leaders as identified by S&P Global through the corporate sustainability assessment (CSA) and check consensus ESG ratings. https://www.csrhub.com/csrhub/

Enterprise Risk Management in Today's World, Part A:
Enterprise-Wide Risk Management and Strategy, 139–143
Copyright © 2024 by Jean-Paul Louisot and Simon Grima
Published under exclusive licence by Emerald Publishing Limited
doi:10.1108/978-1-83797-406-120241011

the organisation, ERM constitutes a booster for the overall performance while focusing on the essential (vital/killer?) risks that can mean success or failure for the organisation. Both threats and opportunities are jointly considered for the directors and officers to dare to take risks within their defined risk appetite.

However, the expected benefits can be reaped only if the organisation's leadership accomplishes the following tasks:

1. Develop ERM objectives *(after establishing the internal and external context of the organisation)*;
2. Identify exposures *(the first step in risk assessment);*
3. Analyse, evaluate, and prioritise critical risks *(the second and third steps in risk assessment);*
4. Treat critical risks, based on residual risks prioritisation *(risk treatment)*;
5. Monitor and review critical risks *(monitor and review).*

The legal and regulatory environment of risk management is in constant evolution, reflecting increasing governance expectations; therefore, an ERM programme must be initiated and monitored at the organisation's highest level of decision, but leaders must maintain a constant dialogue with all transversal functions that contribute to the organisational and societal resilience. This requires a risk-management professional to be in charge of the ERM project and report directly to the risk committee of the board and the CEO.

All national and international standards stress the need for a two-way dialogue with all stakeholders but insist also on the leaders' direct involvement in the development of the ERM programme and the effective implementation of a robust risk management policy; this programme must be consistent through space and time, relevant and tailored for the organisation's specific needs.

For several decades, traditional risk management (TRM) was essentially limited to managing hazards or accidental risks that an organisation is faced with; the limits of this traditional approach were brought to light during the last decade of the 20th century prompting academics and professionals to embark on a re-engineering process for risk management. Already initiated by the Australian Standard in its first version in 1994, ERM encompasses all risk categories of the traditional quadrant taxonomy, hazard, financial, strategic, and operational, thus both pure and speculative risks. However, ERM provides the assurance that all risks are managed, while drawing directors' and executives' attention to risks with potential strategic consequences, especially 'critical' or 'killer' risks that would damage the organisation's reputation.

Beyond the explosion of its domain and presence throughout the organisation, ERM helps to understand interactions between the different exposures and evaluate their combined impact on the organisation strategic path, trajectory as well as volatility. ERM is not only integrated into the strategic development process but also at all levels of its implementation and must become integrated into the organisation's culture so that all staff are aware of any unusual signs and can report them even before any change takes place. ERM's objective is to assist in optimising risk-taking by working on uncertainties to one's advantage.

Of course, risk management's core objective must be aligned with the organisation's core mission. For example, in the case of a for-profit listed company, it will integrate threats and opportunities to optimise value creation for the stockholders or owners. For public entities or not-for-profit, ERM will aim to create social value for its interested parties (citizens, beneficiaries, etc.). But in all situations, through the involvement of all stakeholders, internal and external, and due consideration given to their concerns and expectations, ERM will contribute to the organisation's CSR programme and ultimately to societal resilience.

In all instances, it is a decision support tool that reduces the field of future uncertainties and makes sense of absurd situations, thus offering better information to make objective decisions that can lend themselves to rational explanations when communication and consultation with all stakeholders is undertaken: it is a key performance tool for all to shape a better future.

Many standards deal with uncertainty and risk and offer frameworks, processes, solutions, and points for consideration when implementing ERM in an organisation. Some even use the expression 'management system' (see ISO 22301), but most experts prefer to envision risk management as inserted in existing management systems. Referring to such standards is most often voluntary, and the choice is quite open. However, some organisations must comply with industry and national standards based on their activity (highly polluting industries, medical devices, pharmacy, food, etc.) and others on their financial structure or profession (Sarbanes-Oxley, Basel 3, Solvency 2, etc.). The obligation may result from a clause in a contract with a principal if a sub-contractor accepts a clause that provides specific rules for his risk management efforts.

The globalisation of the economy and the increasing complexity of dependency networks that clamp each economic actor in a procurement web combine to the necessity of an internationally recognised reference for risk management. Given definite inroads worldwide, it is clearer and clearer that ISO 31000 is becoming such a reference, with support from leading risk-management associations like RIMS, FERMA, etc. The publication of the current version in 2018 was advertised widely which gave a boost to the 'guidelines', now COSO-ERM 2017 compatible. It is adopted by many global players, both public and private, and several countries have introduced implementation guides to help small- and medium-sized enterprises (SMEs) and middle-sized organisations implement the guidelines.

To summarise, risk-taking is at the core of any strategy, and it would be unreasonable to leave the management of risk in a silo managed from headquarters by a risk-management specialist with a mission limited to hazard risk and insurance buying. Only an all-encompassing approach, embedded throughout the organisation will provide a 'reasonable assurance' to all stakeholders that risks are managed efficiently. This is why, in line with most governance initiatives by regulatory authorities worldwide, the ultimate duty to define and oversee the management of risks rests with directors and executives, who delegate to the operational managers, the risk owners, the responsibility and authority of managing risk daily with the assistance of risk management professionals.

Therefore, the risk-management professional, whatever the title, must be in a position to play fully his role as facilitator and coach to all, starting from the directors and executives, all the way to associates on the plant or shop floor. It is through a continuous process of change that risk management remains relevant as a performance enhancer for all stakeholders, internal and external, and preserves the organisation's 'social licence to operate'.

The road ahead is still quite open and will have to incorporate millennial and post-millennial-specific concerns. When addressing a meeting of researchers during a study conducted by a specialised[2] media, John Ludlow, Senior Vice President of Global Risk Management at InterContinental Hotels Group (IHG), stressed the intimate link between risks and strategy while addressing the issue of the relationship between the risk manager and the board members:

> Directors are serious about risk-management. But the risk-manager must understand the Board's mission to increase the organisation's value. Yet, this value is now more and more nested in the reputation. Whereas directors can be convinced easily to get involved in the management of risks that impact strategy and change programmes, they have more difficulties in getting excited about operational risks. However, they can get into it if they are shown their impact on reputation. It is a matter of making the case for the intrinsic link between the concepts to get their attention.

As a temporary conclusion, due to the constant evolution of science and profession, I would like to share the optimism of the authors[3]:

> Our deep feeling is that the potent cocktail of scientific thinking, and market intuition that characterise our open society is the dynamic that will propel world economy to new heights for individual success, prosperity, and personal development accessible to all.

Organisations need a 360° risk periscope to gain awareness of their context and visibility into their processes, operations, and objectives. The exponential effect of risk on the organisation makes this complicated and requires constant vigilance. Organisations operate in a chaotic world where even a small event can cascade, influence, and develop into what ends up being an important issue. Dissociated siloed approaches to risk management that do not encompass all processes and systems can leave leaders with a fragmented truth, and they fail to see the big picture for the extended enterprise, as how it impacts strategy and objectives. Boards and executives need visibility into objective and risk relationships across processes and activities.

---

[2]*Global risk survey 2014 – Commercial risk Europe*. www.commercialriskeurope.com. Rubicon Media Ltd. © 2013.

[3]Adapted from Jules, G., & Tony, E. (2012). *Uncommon sense, common nonsense: Why some organisations consistently outperform others* (p. 229). Profile Books Ltd.

Complex and intricate business, as well as the interconnections between risk data, requires the organisation to implement an ERM programme with resilience as the ultimate objective with robust monitoring of risk enforced with automated processes.

To be successful in resilience, the organisation needs to develop an integrated strategy, process, information, and technology architecture. Thus, leaders can gain a comprehensive, straightforward insight into resilience to assess, manage, and monitor risk in all the organisation's operations, processes, and services. The organisation must develop the capacity to continuously monitor the external and internal context and capture evolutions in the organisation's risk profile from internal and external events that can impact objectives as their occurrence is increasingly probable. This allows organisations to monitor their current state and plan for an expected future state of increased resilience maturity.

The growing importance of climate change risk has prompted ISO to issue a guide[4] to ensure that developers of ISO standards and other deliverables make sure to include provisions in standards to address climate change impacts, risks, i.e. threats and opportunities.

Long before our time, aware of the need to change, Confucius reminded his fellow men that they 'must reinvent themselves at all times, but who could be constant in wisdom and happiness?'

[4]ISO Guide 84:2020.

Appendix 1: Exposure Identification and Risk Assessment

Introduction

This appendix serves the purpose of focusing on a specific topic that is not covered in the globally published RM standards, including both versions of ISO 31000 and even ISO 31010. As a result, we provide a practical tool for identifying, analysing, and categorising the range of risks, opportunities, and threats that an organisation faces when planning for its future.

The concepts of 'space of exposure' and 'risk centres approach' can be valuable tools for readers who are undertaking the enterprise-wide risk management (ERM) journey. These concepts aim to clarify uncertainties in decision-making and implementation, as expressed by Felix Kloman.

How Can One Effectively Navigate and Address Uncertainties in Order to Effectively Manage in a Dynamic and Evolving World, Considering Both Potential Risks and Potential Advantages?[1]

The future is inherently uncertain and unpredictable. 'What tomorrow holds remains unknown'. However, effectively overseeing companies is the process of making informed judgements based on information obtained from many sources that provide insights into the future.

Throughout history, humanity has endeavoured to enhance its destiny by exerting influence over the forces that shape the future. The initial method employed was making sacrificial offerings to the deities. Pascal, Fermat, and their successors began devising methods to access future possibilities based on past and current experiences, although this progress only occurred towards the end of the 17th century. The initial method to overcome uncertainty was through the utilisation of probability and trend analysis.

[1]Kloman, H. F. (1992). Rethinking risk management. The Geneva papers on risk and insurance. *Issues and Practice, 17*(3), 299–313. https://doi.org/10.1057/gpp.1992.19

Enterprise Risk Management in Today's World, Part A: Enterprise-Wide Risk Management and Strategy, 145–173
Copyright © 2024 by Jean-Paul Louisot and Simon Grima
Published under exclusive licence by Emerald Publishing Limited
doi:10.1108/978-1-83797-406-120241012

In the late 20th century, the advancement of global and integrated risk management (RM), supported by increasingly sophisticated forecasting models, shifted its focus from just considering the negative aspects of risk, such as threats, to also considering the positive aspects, known as 'opportunities'.

The tragic occurrences of 9/11 and the AZF explosion in France, as well as the more recent Tsunamis and tropical storms in the United States, have highlighted the necessity of being prepared for catastrophic events. The pandemic and the war in Ukraine further intensified this urgency, catching many organisations off guard. Being prepared is crucial for survival during a period of emergency. Nevertheless, when faced with the unknowns of the future, businesses are realising that 'threats' and 'opportunities' are inseparable components of risk, representing contrasting aspects of the same situation.

Directors, officials, and investors should promptly revisit the fundamental principles of economic and financial theory. Engaging in a profitable venture inherently involves risk. Undoubtedly, institutional investors anticipate a certain amount of risk in order to achieve the projected return on investment. In finance theory, the anticipated rate of return is defined as the aggregate of two components:

The basic return refers to the risk-free investment, often defined by the yield on US government bonds with a similar maturity.

The risk premium refers to the extra return that an investor should receive for assuming a higher level of profit volatility in order to support a certain social objective, such as advancing technology or developing a new treatment.

Naturally, not all volatilities are equivalent. In scientific literature, there has been a long-standing distinction made between a future that can be predicted with probabilities (referred to as 'risk') and a future that cannot be predicted with probabilities (referred to as 'hazard').

In practical terms, decision-makers find themselves in the first scenario when they possess sufficient dependable data to calculate a probability distribution or plot a trend line for future occurrences. They may then establish confidence intervals, which are the boundaries that separate the probable from the improbable outcomes. For instance, when examining previous economic circumstances, it should be feasible to obtain a realistic estimate of the quantity of automobiles that will be sold in the European Union, the United States, or Australia. The rapidly growing and relatively new Chinese market may not readily conform to this sort of dependable pattern. Consequently, an automobile manufacturer can accurately forecast its future sales in well-established regions globally but has challenges in predicting sales in developing areas.

Conversely, when introducing a new model, particularly if any flaws are discovered during the initial year of sales, it becomes far more challenging to rationalise investments without dependable sales projections. Banks encountered comparable circumstances when they started the handling of operational risks in order to adhere to the Basel 2 and Basel 3 regulations. When a database is unavailable, it becomes necessary to formalise experts' opinions using methods such as the Bayesian network approach and scenario analysis.

By just focusing on the negative aspects of risks, the aforementioned instances may be subject to criticism once more. Operational risks present a notable potential for banks that allocate more resources than their competitors in this pursuit, leading to a competitive advantage. Not only would they likely reduce their internal expenses, but they may also acquire valuable skills that will assist their clients in the long run.

The prevailing approach in RM is to eliminate isolated risk compartments in order to achieve comprehensive optimisation of RM. This involves examining both potential threats and opportunities for each individual unit, process, and project. Therefore, an organisation is examined as a collection of risks, each with its own potential benefits and drawbacks, which should be maximised, similar to how an investor would maximise their investment portfolio.

Practically, the consolidation of all risks is more readily accomplished for the financial repercussions, namely at the level of risk financing. Increasingly, economic entities view their risk financing endeavours as an integral component of their comprehensive, long-term financial strategy. Integrating risk assessment and loss control is feasible by including the chain of command in the RM process, known as ERM, where managers assume the role of 'risk-owners'. The globalisation of RM is achieved by adhering to the principle of subsidiarity, which dictates that directors and officers should focus solely on the exposures that directly affect the strategy. They can have confidence that the RM process implemented across the entire organisation will handle 'minor' threats and seize 'tactical' opportunities.

A Definition of the Term 'Risk'

The term 'risk' is utilised by RM professionals and others in their daily lives, particularly in the context of RM, risk mitigation, and risk finance. However, do we possess a clear understanding of the concept of risk? The Australian RM standard defines 'risk' as the probability of an event occurring that might affect the achievement of objectives. Therefore, has the matter been resolved? However, there are several widely accepted interpretations of the term:

- **Risk (pure, speculative, hybrid)**

Specialists typically utilise these, which are consistent with the Asset Safety (AS) definition, depending on the nature of the relevant repercussions.

- **Distinction between systematic and unsystematic risk**

Systematic risk, also known as non-diversifiable risk, arises from non-hazardous factors that have the potential to occur concurrently. Consequently, it is not suitable for diversification. For instance, any participants in the economy might be impacted by a decline in economic activity or an increase in interest rates.

Unsystematic risk, also known as diversifiable risk, arises from specific sources and may be analysed using probabilistic methods. These portfolios are tailored to individual economic entities and provide the opportunity to create a 'balanced portfolio' for risk distribution. Consequently, insurance coverage may be specifically tailored to protect against these risks.

An insurable risk refers to a situation or event that can be covered by an insurance policy. This definition is more stringent since it specifically pertains to incidents that have an existing insurance market. In addition, insurance professionals frequently utilise the term 'risk' to denote the entity that is exposed to potential harm, the specific danger that is covered, the effectiveness of the entity's RM strategies (degree of risk), and the comprehensive evaluation of a location ('favourable risk for its category').

Excluding the realm of 'psychological wordplay' by French psychoanalyst Lacan, individuals must confront the actual hazards associated with employing the term 'risk' within a social and economic context. It is important to exercise caution since this often used 'four-letter word' might have varying interpretations for various people. It is essential for all participants to recognise and consider the variety present while interacting in a boardroom or with various stakeholders.

It is important to remember this fact while conveying dangers, regardless of the medium used. Every RM professional must be cognizant of a significant difficulty and danger: ensuring that their risk perception is accurately understood by decision-makers and stakeholders, which is more crucial than any scientific evaluation of risk. It is advisable to avoid using a term with several meanings if you can. Instead, go for less popular words like exposure, danger, opportunity, hazard, impact, and others, depending on the specific aspect of 'risk' you are referring to. It is advisable to provide an explanation for a subject that is not widely known, including professional terminology, rather than assuming that the recipient of the message would comprehend it without any assurance of their actual understanding.

An exposure refers to the state of being subjected to or coming into contact with anything, such as a substance, situation, or event, that has the potential to cause harm or have an impact on an individual or a group.

The term 'risk' encompasses several definitions and can be deceptive when employed in a professional setting, particularly when an entity is disseminating information about risks to a wider audience. Consequently, professionals and scholars in the field of RM must establish a more exact and specific notion. Fifty years ago, George HEAD, the inventor of the Associate in RM credential, selected the term 'exposure'. However, at that time, only potential negative outcomes were taken into account. Therefore, a new definition that is more suitable for the current global approach is needed:

An exposure refers to the financial impact caused by an unforeseen incident that alters an organisation's resource levels.

This definition permits the identification of an exposure based on three factors:

The risk object: refers to the resource that is vulnerable and crucial for the company to achieve its objectives and missions.

A random event (PERIL): sometimes known as a peril, refers to an occurrence that might permanently or temporarily change the amount of organisational resources. This change can either create an opportunity by increasing the level or quality of the resource or pose a threat by decreasing the level or quality of the resource. The probability of the event will determine the degree of occurrence.

Potential IMPACT (severity): Organisations often aim to measure the financial consequences of the identified exposure by assessing the resources at risk and random events. Nevertheless, it is important to note that the aims and objectives of an organisation may not always be expressed solely in financial terms. It is imperative to additionally take into account ethical considerations and corporate social responsibility. Nevertheless, it is important to note that the concept of 'severity' is typically quantified in terms of monetary value.

Nevertheless, it is important to acknowledge that the repercussions do not just impact the organisation. Therefore, it is crucial to differentiate, particularly when considering the potential negative outcomes.

Primary and secondary damages refer to the effects on the organisation itself and its resources.

Tertiary damages refer to the consequences that affect third parties and the environment. Particular emphasis should be placed on the effects on the organisation's partners, including both consumers or clients (downstream), suppliers or subcontractors (upstream), and temporary collaborators for specific projects. The study should encompass all ramifications and not be restricted to liabilities, as long-term repercussions without immediate legal ramifications can be expensive, particularly in terms of reputation. Conversely, 'tertiary damages' encompassing contractual, tort, or criminal obligations will have an effect on the organisation's resources through its leaders, workers, finance, and perhaps its 'social licence to operate'.

When carrying out a thorough study, it is important to consider the potential positive outcomes, since the risks faced by one company might potentially present an opportunity for another.

Once a thorough understanding of the concept of 'exposure' is achieved, it offers a framework for developing a systematic approach to RM. This approach views any organisation as a collection of exposures and challenges that need to be addressed in order to implement an optimal strategy. The risk register, as recommended by the Australian standards, serves as a comprehensive list of the different 'risk assets' that need to be managed. Consequently, decision-making tools derived from finance, such as portfolio theory for managing investment portfolios, are applicable in the rational decision-making process of RM, ultimately leading to effective governance.

Exposure is a crucial element in incorporating RM into an organisation's strategy. It helps to capitalise on opportunities and minimise hazards that arise throughout the pursuit of excellence.

Which Resources are Under Jeopardy?

An organisation is a dynamic entity that combines resources to achieve specific goals and objectives. RM is centred around the development and communication of these objectives. Therefore, for RM purposes, an organisation can be seen as a collection of exposures, threats, and opportunities that need to be efficiently managed in order to achieve these goals and objectives, regardless of the circumstances. In a competitive economy, efficiency refers to either achieving the most ambitious objectives using the available resources or accomplishing the assigned goals with minimal resources.

While there is general agreement on this straightforward approach, the question remains as to how many categories of resources should be considered. The proposed model restricts itself to a small number of categories, specifically five. This allows for the inclusion of all resources involved in organisational management, while also facilitating the listing of resources within a specific organisation. This approach enables a systematic and comprehensive identification, as the categories of exposure are directly connected to the categories of resources. Each of these categories necessitates specific measures to control losses. Therefore, the five categories of resources are as follows:

H = Human: In this context, 'H' refers to all individuals associated with the organisation through employment or executive contracts. Their specific experiences and competencies are valuable assets for the organisation, although they are not always evaluated and recognised in financial statements. When considering this resource, factors such as age, gender, and marital status, which may affect actual capabilities, should be carefully monitored. The potential risks associated with human resources should be examined, including both the importance of key individuals and the costs and obligations related to labour and social benefits (such as pensions). Risk managers are particularly interested in what is commonly referred to as 'knowledge management or talent management'.

T = Technical: These encompass the physical assets of the organisation, including buildings, equipment, and tools. The legal ownership of these assets is of lesser significance; the organisation may possess, lease, rent, or hold them on behalf of a third party. The crucial aspect is that the organisation exercises full control over these assets and can directly manage the associated risks.

I = Information: The entirety of data circulates within the organisation, regardless of its format (digital, physical, or stored in human memory). This encompasses information pertaining to the organisation itself, as well as information about external entities (such as medical records of patients in a hospital). It also includes information that others may seek to acquire about the organisation (such as open-source intelligence or industrial espionage), and vice versa. Additionally, the organisation's ability to conduct business relies on the trust it establishes with others. The perception that all stakeholders hold of the organisation is a crucial 'asset', and the risks associated with damaging the organisation's reputation are a growing concern.

P = Partners (upstream and downstream): These are the economic partners with whom the organisation is connected, specifically suppliers, service providers, sub-contractors, customers, and distribution channels. Among them, there are key partners who are crucial for the organisation's operations and efficiency. Identifying these key partners is necessary to address dependencies in the supply chain. This is particularly important in an economy where outsourcing is prevalent and poses significant risks.

F = Financial: It encompasses all the monetary inflows and outflows of the organisation, both in the short term (cash, liquid assets, short-term liabilities) and in the medium- or long term (capital and reserve, long-term debt, project financing, etc.). This encompasses all the risks associated with the financial strategy of the organisation and the trade-off between profitability and financial stability.

However, the analysis would be incomplete if the organisation did not take into account its non-contractual interactions with the environment. These are the resources that the organisation does not directly pay for but are crucial for its smooth operation. These 'free resources' are not recorded in the organisation's accounting books, but they are essential. Economists refer to them as externalities, which include factors such as air quality, access to sites, and social licence to operate.

Ill-considered choice: Furthermore, when a leader takes judgements without being aware of the potential hazards, it is not just foolish but also irresponsible. A leader may occasionally make unwise decisions, but one must question the rationale behind such actions.

The Space of Exposures

The three following figures (Figs. A1–A3) summarise all of the above in a graph to help implement the tool.

When potential damages to the environment and society are perceived as insufficiently managed, stakeholders' trust and confidence may be lost and the

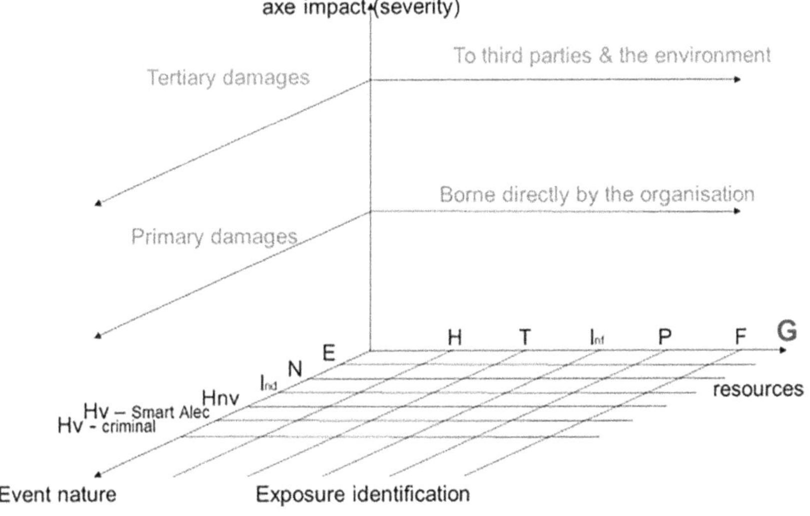

Fig. A1. The Space of Exposure – Threats.

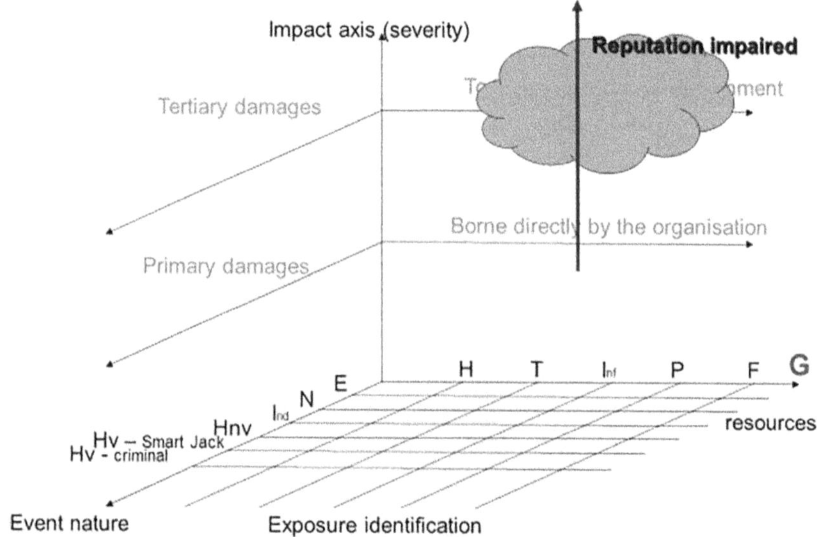

Fig. A2. The Space of Exposure – Including Reputation.

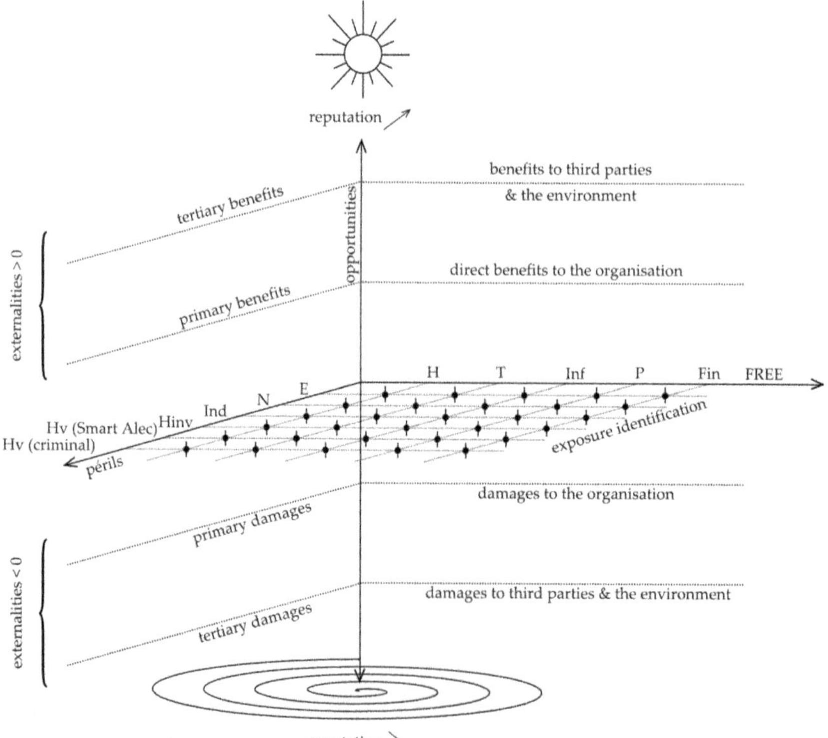

Fig. A3. The Space of Exposures – Threats and Opportunities.

reputation impaired; sometimes, it takes a series of events, as in the case of British Petroleum (BP) in the first 15 years of the 21st century so that a cloud has built on the company's reputation (see Fig. A2).

A mature ERM approach must consider both upside (opportunities) and downside (threats) risks; therefore, the complete space of exposures is the following (see Fig. A3).

How to Manage Risks Caused by Partners' Resources?

The process of market globalisation has created intricate networks that connect several organisations throughout the globe through the externalisation process. In recent times, major conglomerates have increasingly prioritised the processes of ideation, promotion, and production, which are supported by a global network of suppliers. Several small- and medium-sized enterprises (SMEs) function as a single component within an extensive supply chain.

Procurement systems often have a hierarchical structure rather than a linear one in the majority of cases. Procurement and the supply chain have become essential components of organisations that produce products and services, since their production increasingly depends on outsourcing a growing number of functions.

Hence, the term 'partners' resources' encompasses essential elements such as raw materials, components, machinery, and services, as well as distribution networks that companies rely on for their day-to-day operations. The available resources may be classified into three clearly defined categories:

Upstream resources refer to the materials and supplies that are acquired by suppliers, service providers, and sub-contractors and then transported to production locations by transporters.

Lateral resources refer to the goods and services that you supply to your clients, which are then incorporated into complex systems, projects, and products, where your contribution is merely a component. Although you may be unfamiliar with them, there exists an inherent solidarity that connects you. For instance, you can create tyres that are compatible with specific wheel hubs produced by a third-party company. However, if the supplier of the hubs goes bankrupt, your customer will no longer want your tyres.

Downstream resources refer to consumers or intermediaries involved in the distribution process, such as distribution networks, transporters, and financial institutions that ensure the effective completion of transactions.

During the RM assessment, it is crucial to identify all the components belonging to this particular class of resources. The principles governing this process remain consistent across different categories. However, the challenge lies in the fact that the security of the organisation relies on actions and attitudes that cannot be monitored on a daily basis, unlike the resources directly controlled by the organisation. Consequently, whether intentionally or unintentionally, the organisation has delegated a crucial aspect of its RM function to a third party.

Hence, the pivotal inquiry in procurement RM is to discover methods to guarantee the organisation's comprehensive ability to withstand any failure in the delivery of resources by its partners, both in terms of timeliness and required quality.

Essentially, the primary principle is to avoid excessive reliance on a single partner, whether it is a supplier or a client. The principle of diversification is applicable in this situation, as it is unwise to concentrate all of one's resources or investments on a single entity. It is generally advised to always have a minimum of two or three sources. Nevertheless, achieving this may be challenging, particularly in cases where intricate technology or specialised expertise is required. In addition, the selection of various sources must be carefully weighed against the heightened vulnerability to economic espionage when the partnership entails the exchange of any kind of proprietary information.

In addition to this fundamental premise, the same guideline is applicable both before and after, which I refer to as the '3 Cs' rule.

The user's text is empty. Select – It is important to meticulously select **(Choose)** the partners you wish to engage in business with. Prioritise assessing if the items or services provided align with your requirements in terms of quality, quantity, and punctual delivery. It is important to analyse their financial robustness as a partner that would experience swift failure would be futile. Moreover, it is crucial to evaluate their 'ethical compatibility' with your values, particularly the ones you emphasise during interactions with stakeholders. It is worth noting that a prominent sports goods manufacturer faced significant challenges in 1998 during the Football World Cup. The media exposed that a supplier of a supplier was employing underpaid, underage children to manufacture the balls.

Contractual agreements **(Contract)** must ensure that the partner's activities maintain a high standard of RM. It is particularly crucial because there is now no globally recognised standard, unlike quality. I am responsible for granting you access to the site and documents in order to guarantee the effective design and implementation of RM. In addition, it is advisable to incorporate conflict resolution clauses into contracts to address any problems and ensure the partnership maintains harmony, even under challenging circumstances. Lawyers sometimes allocate excessive effort to defining the items or services encompassed in a contract, while neglecting to adequately address conflict resolution before any issues arise.

Control – It is important for your team to consistently visit your partners and stay updated on their progress in order to ensure that they remain the dependable sources you desire to engage with. It is imperative that you be cognizant of significant alterations in their leadership, ownership, atmosphere, and strategy.

Regarding lateral resources, they often refer to partners whom you have not selected and with whom you have no contractual agreement. Hence, the sole means of guaranteeing the quality of RM is by relying on a shared partner, project manager, or reputable corporation. When interacting with him, it is important for you to have access to the comprehensive roster of individuals participating in the project that you both collaborate on.

When risk transfer occurs, the principal remains socially accountable for the welfare of all stakeholders involved in the whole process. In the event that a team member breaches their trust, all other team members will experience negative consequences. Ultimately, reputation risks cannot be transferred.

Are There 'Free' Resources?

Who would have the audacity to assert that there are unpaid resources in the global economy? An organisation requires both internal and external resources, as explained before. By 'external', we refer to resources that are traded with economic partners, both upstream and downstream. These resources need payment. Nevertheless, there are also non-transactional interactions with the environment that are crucial for the growth and even the survival of the organisation. As previously stated, materials obtained from the environment without any kind of monetary payment are referred to as 'free resources' since they are not recorded in the organisation's financial records. Nevertheless, the term 'environment' could be excessively comprehensive; in every circumstance, the subsequent aspects should be examined:

- *Physical environment:* It comprises air, water, and earth.
- *Political, legal, and social environment*: It requires looking at all aspects of the conditions of life and the organisation of society, including cultural differences.
- *Competitive environment*: It entails looking at all aspects of the current competition, technological breakthroughs, and shifts in consumers' tastes, but also substitutes for the organisation's products and services. Furthermore, one should always analyse the reason for the appeal of our offering; the notion of a 'magnet site' allows investigation of the circumstances outside of our management sphere that are keys to our success.

Economists refer to these transactions as 'externalities' since they are not included in a contractual transaction between economic partners. To reiterate, externalities can either be positive (where society gains a benefit from a private transaction) or negative (where society faces an additional cost that is not accounted for in the private transaction). It is important to acknowledge that the scope of these externalities can differ between countries. Regarding pollution, the establishment of regulations to safeguard the environment has compelled private producers to bear the expenses of cleaning up sites or limiting the release of contaminants. This has resulted in the transfer of certain 'social costs' to their operations.

When an organisation is considering diversifying or entering new markets through local manufacturing, it must consider the availability of necessary resources in the potential locations or nations. These resources may not be readily accessible. To be more explicit, a highly successful SME may not be aware of the exact factors that contributed to its success in its original location. These factors may not exist in the potential new locations or may be lost due to mergers or acquisitions.

Several particular scenarios can exemplify the notion. However, it is important to note that they are only typical instances, and every organisation should do a methodical examination of its unique circumstances.

There are industrial operations that require a significant quantity of 'cooling water'. This water is discharged downstream without any chemical or biological contamination, but it is released at a higher temperature than the water taken in upstream. Have we envisioned winters of great severity, characterised by frozen rivers, as well as summers with excessively hot temperatures that hinder proper heat exchange and prevent fish from surviving due to oxygen depletion at the release temperature? Is there a chemical facility located upstream of the suggested site that has the ability to emit pollutants, which might potentially damage our installation or disrupt production? Moreover, what will be the outcome of the phenomenon of global warming?

Throughout the factory, the air must meet the standards necessary for human survival and also comply with local regulations for 'workplace conditions'. Is there a nearby plant that has the potential to emit a hazardous cloud? Conversely, many production processes need the purification of the atmosphere from any particulate matter. Could minute particles potentially bypass our filters, therefore contaminating our products, such as optical lenses or medical devices?

The user's text is empty. There is only one antique bridge that provides direct access to a factory. Following a mild earthquake, there are questions over its long-term durability. The local authorities have implemented restrictions on entrance, allowing only lorries weighing less than 5 metric tonnes. The extended distance of the new route from a crucial supplier to the facility may result in significant delays and cost escalations, rendering the unit economically unviable without any straightforward solution.

Production in a new nation may result in significant savings on salaries and salary costs. However, it is important to consider the political stability of the country. Is there a risk of nationalisation if an opposition party gains control? Will the social and political environment continue to be conducive to foreign investment?

The precautionary concept has been incorporated into the French constitution. The repercussions for the firm based in France, whether in terms of its domicile or activities, are yet uncertain. Is it possible that foreign corporations will sell new items in France?

Local cultures can influence company operations, including factors such as working hours. Upon entering a new nation or province, has the organisation examined its commercial and human resources processes to ensure they are in accordance with local norms, going beyond simply adherence to local laws?

Do people choose our company primarily for the exceptional quality of our products or services, or do they just opt for convenience? A store operating in a commercial centre that attracts clients due to the presence of a well-known national brand hypermarket should consider the following question. Alternatively, this may also apply to a restaurant located near an industrial area, which mostly attracts its customers from there. What would occur if the industrial organisations decided to construct their own restaurant for their employees?

What Are the Perils?

In the context of RM, an organisation may be defined as a collection of risks or exposures, encompassing both potential threats and opportunities. The definition of each exposure is based on three key dimensions: the resource that is at risk, the specific peril or hazard involved, and the resulting impact. Therefore, the danger is the second of these variables.

An event, with uncertain likelihood, that might significantly alter the quantity of a resource inside an organisation, either partially or completely, for a permanent or temporary duration. Typically, in the majority of businesses, the assessment would focus solely on the negative consequences.

The vector resource/peril, which operates in two dimensions, serves to identify the level of exposure. During the analysis phase, the possible effect will be measured, with a focus on quantifying the financial or other repercussions.

Ideally, the danger is assessed by determining the likelihood based on experimental probability derived from historical data and/or mathematical models. Oftentimes, due to insufficient or untrustworthy data, only a qualitative assessment can be made. This assessment may categorise events as exceptional, rare, infrequent, or frequent, provided that the evaluating group has a shared understanding of these terms (such as once a decade, once a year, twice a year, once a month, etc.).

Several phenomena have normal distributions, characterised by bell-shaped curves, which are fully determined by two parameters:

- Mean or 'average', i.e. hurricanes will hit Florida four times a year on average.
- Standard deviation which allows the definition of a confidence interval, i.e. the lower and higher level of a given phenomenon, if the standard deviation is 1, the confidence interval at 68% is that there will be between three and five hurricanes hitting Florida next year, 95% between two and six, and more than 99% between one and seven).

Historical data indicate with a high degree of certainty that Florida will have a minimum of one hurricane annually and a maximum of seven.

When dealing with phenomena that can be controlled more easily than natural events, such as the number of accidents in a large fleet of vehicles or the number of fires in plants belonging to a multinational firm with over 2,000 sites globally, the occurrence of multiple events that fall significantly outside the confidence interval provides valuable information for predicting long-term losses. Based on the indications of divergence, improvement, or worsening, the situation will require an explanation of this assessment and an examination of the underlying reasons.

When the danger can be represented by a numerical probability distribution, it is referred to as 'probabilistic'; in other cases, it is referred to as 'non-probabilistic'. The differentiation between these two concepts is crucial since the effectiveness of decision-making tools for uncertain futures is strongly dependent on the accuracy and reliability of the data. The purpose of the risk diagnostic is to enhance the information available in order to facilitate informed and reliable decision-making.

Regardless, the probability distribution of occurrence combined with the probability distribution of impact or severity is crucial for making reasonable decisions. This enables for the justification of investments or recurrent expenses for suggested loss control measures, as well as the premium offered by insurers.

It is important to emphasise that for events that occur very seldom, the average number of occurrences over a lengthy period of time (according to the Law of Large Numbers) does not have much significance for the decision-maker. During such circumstances, the decision-making process primarily relies on assessing the amount of effect and severity. The objective is to minimise the likelihood of occurrence to a level that is considered acceptable by the key stakeholders. When executives in an organisation responsible for overseeing nuclear power plants evaluate 'nuclear risks', they prioritise assessing the probability of a significant accident happening in the near future, rather than focusing on the average cost over an extended period of time, such as 1 or 10 million years. They must take into account the threshold of probability at which the populace would refuse to reside in proximity to one of their facilities.

The kind of danger will determine the specific loss control methods that can be put into effect. For example, while dealing with a vehicle fleet, if the problem is related to the drivers' driving abilities, the solution would involve providing instruction to the drivers to alter their mindset while driving, specifically by adopting defensive driving techniques.

Defining an Efficient Taxonomy for Perils and Hazards

1. There are several methods to categorise the events that might potentially impact the circumstances in which a company makes its strategic decisions. While some individuals may focus on the causes, others may direct their attention on the results. Our focus will be on examining the knot of the bow tie, rather than the two wings. Therefore, the suggested categorisation does not claim to be scientific but rather aims to offer RM professionals a first framework for identifying suitable loss control measures to reduce the potential risks involved. Perils and dangers are categorised based on two criteria:
2. **Where it originates**
    - *Endogenous:* The genesis of the issue lies inside the organisation itself, namely within the boundaries it oversees, whether they be physical or procedural. For instance, it may be a fire occurring within the premises or an employee using a procedural oversight to transfer funds to an offshore account. The resolution must be sought inside within the business, and frequently, prevention will prove to be the most effective strategy.
    - *Exogenous*: Its genesis lies external to the organisation, namely beyond the boundaries it governs, whether they be physical or procedural. For instance, a strike occurring in a facility nearby, where employees are occupying the premises, so obstructing other employees from entering the building; a strike by long-haul drivers; water contamination caused by a chemical spill, resulting in the cessation of production at a brewery. In order to decrease the likelihood of a rupture or unfavourable occurrence, it is necessary for third parties to commence the solution. Internally, 'Plan B' will play a crucial role in managing and minimising losses. This includes activities such as business continuity planning, disaster recovery, and strategic redeployment planning in the event of a worst-case scenario.

3. **Its nature**

Economical: The event would be a significant alteration in an economic factor in the organisation's surroundings, resulting in an unforeseen opportunity or a significant threat. Possible factors that can impact business opportunities include the bankruptcy of a significant international competitor, fluctuations in currency exchange rates that affect long-term prospects, and shifts in consumer preferences. Additionally, the current oil situation is another example. To respond effectively, it is crucial to rely on accurate forecasts and closely monitor the global economy.

Natural: It would normally refer to events categorised as 'Force Majeure' in insurance plans, such as hurricanes, earthquakes, floods, tsunamis, or global warming. However, this phrase is rather broad and should be further divided into its specific repercussions for proper analysis and handling. Prevention is not feasible as it is impossible to 'preclude' the eruption of a volcano or the formation of a storm. However, the examination of facts and scientific information may still be beneficial in selecting more suitable locations and better planning for any future events. Hence, the strategies to reduce losses before and after the occurrence will serve as the means to mitigate the impact. When it comes to natural catastrophes, a crucial factor in selecting the right investment may be summarised by the acronym TAI, which stands for 'Threat, Alert, Impact'. The greater the duration between the increase in the level of likelihood (Threat) and the occurrence of the event (Impact), the more convenient it will be to make preparations when the event becomes highly probable, allowing for the allocation of previous resources to other risks (such as comparing earthquakes with floods near a river's estuary).

Industrial occurrences encompass all outcomes arising from broad human economic activity, excluding direct involvement of human factors in the specific situation. Possible causes of damage include fire, non-flood water damage, mechanical malfunction, and so on. These risks are usually non-systematic and the insurance market is well prepared to handle them, both in terms of sharing financial risks and controlling losses. The insurance business has extensive expertise in managing such incidents and will benefit from efforts to mitigate risks across its full portfolio of covered buildings. As a result, insurance companies and reinsurers have acquired extensive expertise in this field. They are occasionally known as 'unintentional hazards'.

Human: Therefore individuals of the *Homo sapiens* species: Human involvement is often present in most accidents, with fires occurring in areas where welding activities are taking place being a notable example of this.

Nevertheless, the fact that the phenomena originates from humans is insufficient to comprehend its underlying explanation. It is necessary to make a more distinct distinction:

The involuntary human peril: The unintentional human hazard mostly arises from a mistake, omission, or neglect. The event can be triggered either immediately (such as when a lit cigarette is dropped upon combustible material) or with a delay (such as when the basement of a house in a flood-prone location lacks sufficient insulation). Identifying the individual accountable and attributing blame to a 'wrongdoer' will not be beneficial. If significant damages arise from a 'involuntary human act', it is imperative to examine and evaluate the system and its procedures. Human mistakes are certain to occur, and it is crucial to manage and mitigate their repercussions. Quality and RM share a clear and inherent responsibility.

The voluntary human peril: Human risk arises only from a purposeful and intentional action taken by an individual or a group of individuals. However, it is important to note that not all conscious actions are carried out with the intention of causing damage to others. As a result, we can further differentiate:

Intentional acts of harm committed by individuals with criminal intent, aimed at causing negative consequences for the organisation, its procedures, or its stakeholders, and

Unintentional acts of harm committed by individuals without any intention to cause harm, resulting in risks that affect the organisation, its procedures, or stakeholders without any planned negative impact.

Regardless of their intent, whether intentional or naive, 'voluntary human perils' are consistently the most difficult to combat. It is crucial to acknowledge that we are facing a highly intelligent entity that has the ability and intention to adjust to every novel method of loss prevention that we conceive and will patiently await the opportune moment to exploit our vulnerability. An example of this would be information systems, where new worms and viruses are generated on a daily basis, necessitating constant updates to firewalls and other security measures. In addition, employees may develop a sense of complacency if they are not consistently reminded of the ongoing challenges they face on a daily basis.

Why Must Risk-Management Objectives Be Defined?

According to ISO 31000, under the ERM framework, the RM objectives should be in line with the strategic objectives of the business, with a primary emphasis on navigating challenging circumstances.

The objective is to strategise for the allocation of necessary resources to accomplish the aims of the organisation, particularly in the face of a significant event or crisis. Essential resources for the company include financial flows required to offset losses, regardless of their source. The function of risk financing, which is addressed at headquarters as part of the overall finance strategy, remains consistent regardless of the level of decentralisation in operational RM.

The fundamental principle of RM stays consistent regardless of whether it is considered in terms of potential threats or potential opportunities. This principle involves preparing for circumstances characterised by significant instability.

Failure to do so would directly impede the cost control objectives of any manager. Professionals have identified two sets of objectives in RM, referred known as 'pre-loss' and 'post-loss' objectives, due to the intrinsically unpredictable nature of RM performance. Nevertheless, from a comprehensive perspective, it would be more advantageous to designate them as 'pre' and 'post' occurrences, so refraining from making premature assessments regarding the potential good or bad consequences of the event.

It is essential to establish objectives in advance, taking into account the contrast between the pace and time frame of significant events and the routine activities.

Post-Event Objectives (Continuity of Operations)

In any case, the first objective is the organisation's survival which could be achieved if there is enough cash at hand when the financial demands of the event are due. But there is a continuum of objectives depending on how resilient the organisation should be. If we look at it from the perspective of the resources at risk:

1. **Technical, information, and partners**

Continuity of operation is the key. However, the question is rarely that of absolute continuity but rather how long an interruption the organisation and its partners can get through and continue to survive. The longer the acceptable downtime can be, the lesser the investment necessary in 'continuity measures' to mitigate the threat. However, when public service is at stake, the acceptable interruption may be very limited: birth and death certificates must be issued daily; schools should open every day to educate children, not to mention the utilities of a hospital where surgeries and intensive care units need electricity without any break.

2. **Financial**

Even when there is enough cash to survive, that may not prove enough for the community of the investors, who may require as proof of the executives' foresight that, under any circumstances, they were able to:

- 'Maintain a profitable situation' even in a year when a disaster occurs.
- 'Maintain the expected level of profit' *(the median over the past three years for example)*.
- 'Maintain the growth rate' (of earnings per share).

As a reminder, the financial markets do not take it lightly when publicly traded companies show erratic results. In such situations, the share price may sink, thus providing some sharks with a tempting target, and tremendous risk for the independence of the organisations and the job of the 'executive team!'

3. **Human and social**

In terms of social responsibility, the question is how to limit the impact of an event on the firm's environment for stakeholders: employees, economic partners up and downstream, and the whole society both now and in the future. That is the impact on the « social licence to operate » and its reputation.

Pre-Event Objectives

These are the ongoing objectives; like any other department in any organisation RM is expected to be as economically efficient as feasible, i.e. contain ongoing costs as much as possible. However, the higher the post-event objective, the costlier it will be to reach.

Other Possible Secondary Objectives

- *Contain uncertainty*, i.e. the volatility of the organisation's financial result, to a level acceptable to the executive (risk appetite/tolerance).
- *Compliance with legal and regulatory requirements*. When an organisation operates globally, the issue becomes: what legal framework (?), where (?), should it state its standards beyond local legal requirements (?), etc.
- *Society's expectations,* i.e. alignment of the organisation's goals and objectives with the citizens' expectations should be ensured through the:

  1. *Laws enacted in the land* that the legislative branch should vote following their popular mandate;
  2. *Ethical behaviours* that should guide any executive and they would therefore act for the common good in the interests of all stakeholders.

Managing Risks or Containing the Cost of Risk: Is It the Same Objective?

The stated RM objectives emphasise that the primary goal of RM in any organisation is to ensure the continuation of operations and minimise disruptions during periods of instability, enabling the organisation to achieve its strategic objectives, even in the event of a significant disruption. The primary responsibility of risk managers is to ensure the availability of the resources required to meet the post-event objectives established by the board.

Nevertheless, this goal must be accomplished with little resources. In order to achieve the highest level of economic efficiency, it is necessary to quantify risk-management processes. Illustrating a measure, such as minimising the long-term cost of risk. What is the financial impact of risk inside a certain organisation?

Historically, the cost of risk has been divided into four components in the following manner:

- *Administration costs:* These are the expenses directly linked with the implementation of the RM process throughout the organisation. They include salaries, office expenses, and travel and communication expenses for RM office personnel, and costs for outsourced services, whether for risk assessment or other aspects. These costs are relatively easy to track. However, it is essential also to include the costs of the time and efforts devoted to RM in the operational units and other executive branches; and these are far less easy to evaluate properly and objectively.

- *Loss control costs:* They include not only the annual depreciation of loss control investments but also recurring costs linked to risk mitigation efforts. For instance, when dealing with automatic systems for detecting and extinguishing fires ('sprinklers') the initial investment is substantial, but the system must be maintained regularly and receive major overhauls over the 20 years of their lifetime. For individual protection, there may be the cost of purchasing adequate equipment, and replacing it regularly, but sometimes 'control' is achieved through modifying processes that may increase the production times, hence costs. These are not always easy to identify and measure precisely.
- *Transfer risk financing costs:* For the most part, they represent the insurance premiums paid to insurers or reinsurers (through a captive company). These costs are quite easy to track and consolidate as they should appear as such in the accounting documents. However, with the new Alternative Risk Transfer (ART) instruments, some of which operate through financial markets or banks, one should be careful to include every element, especially in a large global conglomerate. Furthermore, the cost of contractual clauses of sharing risk financing with non-insurance economic partners is extremely difficult to 'price' as they are part of an overall deal.
- *Retention risk financing costs:* These represent all the claims and fractions of losses that remain on the books of the organisations. This includes those that are not insured or not insurable but also the deductible and or the portion above policy limits, especially in the liabilities area. For the losses, outside of the realm of insurance, they will be reported only if the RM accounting practices provide for their tracking.

At any rate, this breakdown of the 'cost of risk' concentrates on the downside, the threats, and does not consider the upside of risk, the opportunities. A 'fifth' component should be added, an opportunity cost:

- *The cost of investments deemed 'too risky' is made possible thanks to a robust RM process*, but it is extremely difficult to assess the potential opportunities that are passed by. However, this impact should always be kept in mind when running any investment analysis.

In all organisations, executives are always tempted to benchmark against competitors and partners. A typical question would be 'Is our cost of risk in line with competition?'

This answer is difficult to come up with as no two organisations have the same risk profile (*each has its specific portfolio of exposures*), and no two executive teams have the same risk appetite.

If the high-frequency losses that should be treated as quality failures are excluded, in the short run, an organisation with no RM in place might seem more efficient as it incurs little 'cost of risk'. This appearance will disappear when a catastrophic event happens and the organisation cannot rebound. In summary, the cost of risk should always be assessed in light of the organisation's resilience.

How to Conduct a Diagnosis of Exposures?

The initial stage of the RM process involves creating an exposure diagnostic for a specific company. This step may be divided into three distinct phases: identification, analysis, and evaluation.

An ongoing challenge in the field of developing RM science is the presence of several vague and undefined ideas, notwithstanding the release of the latest edition of ISO 31073. By 'identification', we refer to the acknowledgement of the possibility of an unfavourable event. 'Analysis' involves measuring the impact of this event on the organisation and its stakeholders, without taking into account any control measures in place. On the other hand, 'assessment' incorporates these control measures in the most effective manner. This can be compared to the insurance concepts of maximum possible loss (MPL) and expected reasonable loss (ERL).

The likelihood of the event happening, its frequency, as well as the significance of the consequences, the severity of possible damages are all measured and expressed in numerical terms. However, comprehending the phenomena necessitates taking into account the level of volatility in the repercussions, namely the extent to which the effects are dispersed. Ultimately, RM experts must prioritise the potential impact on the organisation's capacity to accomplish its objectives and fulfil its missions, regardless of the circumstances, which is sometimes referred to as its level of resilience.

The diagnosis is a crucial element in the RM process. The quality of choices relies heavily on the accuracy of the information they are founded upon. Failure to identify a risk can result in missed opportunities or the inability to mitigate a potential danger. Conversely, if a risk is recognised and accurately measured, RM mitigation tools may serve as proof to the seasoned risk manager. The diagnosis should be included as a continuous procedure inside the organisation's feedback loop.

One occurrence can have a significant effect on several companies. However, the idea may be exemplified by the following: A stockpile of old tyres is currently ablaze near a densely populated town, causing the release of hazardous fumes that are being carried by the wind towards an adjacent industrial and commercial park. The analysis of this event's impact should be conducted from several viewpoints, with primary focus on the corporation responsible for the inventory and site management. The study will encompass the assessment of property and equipment damages, the evaluation of staff losses, and the calculation of net revenue losses. It is essential to evaluate the repercussions for all economic collaborators in order to determine the possible losses in contractual obligation. Nevertheless, it is important for each spouse to independently assess the repercussions as well. If the context has been adequately described, the likelihood of an external incident should be incorporated into their risk register as a 'exogenous' hazard. It is important to consider the potential negative effects on the reputation and image of the owner of the tyre inventory, as this might have a detrimental influence on their business partners. However, the affected businesses may also experience a detrimental effect on their reputation, even if they are not at fault, if they are unable to demonstrate enough readiness for such a predictable occurrence, as it became evident to everyone afterwards.

When addressing semi-open or open systems that may affect external stakeholders without contractual obligations to the organisation, it is necessary to expand the scope of the investigation to include the broader environment. This includes engaging with neighbours, local communities, regional and national authorities, as well as various private entities. Hence, it is imperative to undertake an inquiry into the potential effects on all parties involved in order to further evaluate the civil and criminal responsibilities that may arise from the fire, as well as any further non-legal repercussions. Indeed, this is ultimately an inherent danger that might potentially impact a wide-ranging ecosystem.

Moreover, the risk manager of a healthcare institution situated within a one-mile radius should have recognised the 'tyre treating plant' as a possible danger during the process of developing the context. Failure to do so would suggest that he may have neglected to consider the influence of air quality on the health of his lung patients.

Essentially, the exposure diagnostic is an ongoing process of regularly updating the organisation's risk register to ensure it is comprehensive and up to date.

During the second phase, it is necessary to conduct a comprehensive and quantifiable assessment of the effects on the organisation's resources and objectives. This can be accomplished by utilising probability and trend analysis to assess the 'frequency risks' using existing data, employing other quantification techniques like expert advice and Bayesian networks for the median risk category, and conducting scenario analysis for 'catastrophic' events, particularly when multiple stakeholders could be affected.

As previously said, open systems require a strategy that takes into account the surrounding environment. This is evident in the case of Malls, Healthcare facilities, and even municipal administrations, where many stakeholders are not directly subordinate to or have contractual relations with the organisation. Managing the risks of a manufacturing plant is made simpler when the majority of individuals involved can be taught and educated to identify risks and take responsible actions to minimise their impact. This should be seen as a way to improve the skills and abilities of all employees.

Lastly, there is a unique scenario that arises when working on projects that involve several partners who may not necessarily have completely aligned aims and objectives. To get the most effective solution for RM, it may be necessary to find a compromise between conflicting interests.

How to Analyse and Assess Risks?

The potential outcomes that might occur in a situation of uncertainty for a certain organisation are boundless. While RM often focuses on assessing and mitigating potential negative outcomes, it is crucial to have a comprehensive viewpoint on their potential consequences, if only to prioritise efforts in controlling risks.

Frequently, even in the present day, the assessment of risk effect is typically confined to the two conventional factors employed by the insurance sector. This industry attempts to determine the anticipated value of the claims that may arise from a collection of policies. These variables are:

- The probability, also called frequency, as claims do occur even in a well-balanced portfolio (law of large numbers).
- The severity, or essentially financial impact, is most of the time measured within the scope of the insurance covers granted to the insured by the contract.

In the long term, if the portfolio is sufficiently big and well evaluated, the insurer may anticipate paying the product of the frequency and severity, also known as the anticipated value, in claims on its portfolio.

Nevertheless, when employed within the context of a singular entity, regardless of its size, the formula fails to provide a comprehensive understanding of the unfavourable circumstances it may encounter, with the exception of infrequent and narrow claims such as bodily harm to a group of cars. One crucial factor that is absent is the unpredictability of the yearly losses and the adverse cash flows resulting from the happening of risky incidents. Let us provide a concise illustration using an example derived from the nuclear sector. Assuming a 1 in 10 million chance of a major catastrophe occurring at a nuclear power plant, with a cost of $2 trillion, the long-term annual 'cost of risk' for Électricité de France (EDF), the main electrical utility in France, which operates less than 100 sites (currently 56 nuclear reactors in France), is less than $200,000 per year. EDF bears a rather manageable responsibility in this regard. Nevertheless, it does address the public inquiry over the safety of the nuclear business in France, namely in terms of guaranteeing a consistent energy supply and the well-being of those residing near power plants. Why does it matter if the minimal cost over a 10-million-year period is insignificant in the long run? Ultimately, the matter is connected to sustainable development and Environment, Social and Governance (ESG) concerns, rather than the anticipated cost value.

Any exposure assessment must consider the dissemination of the impact's magnitude, whether it is measured in financial terms or through evaluation of its effects on humans and the environment.

For risks that occur frequently, such as health insurance for a large population or the risk associated with a vehicle fleet, historical data can be used to predict future losses. However, it is important to include trend variables in the model to ensure accurate forecasting. Moreover, the anticipated yearly expense might serve as a suitable foundation for a budgetary analysis.

When dealing with extraordinary situations, the decisions about RM are mostly influenced by the seriousness and extent of the potential effects. In such cases, there may even be consideration of completely stopping or avoiding an activity that is judged too dangerous. It is crucial to ascertain the stakeholders' willingness to accept risks under such circumstances. In summary, it is important not to multiply the parameters. The assessment of exposure is done using a three-dimensional vector (F, S, and σ), where F represents the frequency, S represents the severity, and σ represents the standard deviation or a measure of volatility. Are the social and economic implications deemed acceptable at a specific degree of confidence?

Certain writers are promoting the examination of the most unfavourable outcome. Financial firms have established the concept of 'value at risk', whereas non-financial entities have defined 'cash flow at risk'. These measurements quantify the level of stress that a system or organisation can withstand without suffering irreversible harm or impairment. Contemporary writers now categorise it under the quantile-based methods for prediction (QBRM) and contend that it is inherently faulty and lacks a cohesive representation as a risk metric. Let us defer the issue to the experts in financial RM (FRM) and actuarial science. It is essential for RM experts to keep up with the rapid advancements in this industry.

To evaluate the seriousness of a situation, it is necessary to construct a hypothetical scenario that considers the worst possible outcome, in accordance with Murphy's Law (which states that anything that can go wrong, will go wrong). From an organisational perspective, it is crucial to acknowledge both the bad and beneficial effects. The worst-case scenario must include the issue of stakeholders' confidence and the damage to reputation.

When conducting risk assessment, it is important to be cautious because certain consequences, such as the long-term impact on the environment, cannot be easily quantified in monetary terms. These consequences may not always be considered in the financial model of the company, even when taking into account the long-term perspective of creating value for the shareholders. Additional purposes must be considered, whether they are genuine missions or just limits that each board of directors must address. These objectives encompass sustainable development, aid to individuals in distress, and so on. Expanding the evaluation tools to incorporate more characteristics beyond the three stated is likely essential. However, this might potentially contribute to the ongoing expansion of cindynics.

One more recommendation: although not everything can be measured in terms of money, whatever that can be measured should be done so meticulously and diligently, even if it is merely to minimise the remaining ambiguity.

Of Risk Centres and How to Use Them for Risk Assessment?

The proposed approach for assessing risks, known as the 'risk centre' method or diagnostic method, is based on a concept that views an organisation as a dynamic blend of five resource classes: Human, Technical, Information, Partners, and Financial.

The essence of the approach is to divide the 'complex system' into several sub-systems as necessary to ensure that the smaller components are easily understandable and used by humans. Next, the sub-system is examined as a composite of identical resources.

The identification of sub-systems inside an organisation aligns with the previously discussed system safety methodology. The cessation should occur once the threshold of a 'elementary sub-system' or 'micro firm' is attained. The cell remains alive and is overseen by a manager who is conscious of the tasks it must do, utilising the required resources from the five categories. Subsequently, we are able to detect, assess, and mitigate the risk associated with a single-celled entity, known as the risk centre, by utilising a mix of resources to achieve a specific objective aligned with the broader goals and missions of the business.

The risk centre manager should have a clear understanding of the limits of the risk centre and the external factors that affect it. They should possess a certain level of initiative to effectively manage their 'micro-enterprise' and navigate through the recognised dangers and opportunities. This individual is specifically identified as the 'risk-owner' in ERM presentations.

In a previous column, we have already provided a detailed explanation of the seven risk identification tools. However, once the risk centres have been identified, the primary tool to utilise is the questionnaire, or more precisely the interview. This interview will serve as the foundation for the workshop that will be organised with the management team. The purpose of this workshop is to understand and take ownership of the risks, as well as to establish priorities and determine necessary actions.

The interview should be conducted according to the main points listed in the box below:

OBJECTIVES

1. What are the missions of your department, service, *Business unit*, or profit centre?

RESOURCES

2. How are you organised?
3. Who is your staff, what are your buildings/workspace and equipment?
4. Where do you store your products, spare parts, raw materials, and information?
5. Where do your products, information go?
6. What are your communication channels?

STRATEGIC QUESTIONS

7. Assuming your building or office burns down tonight with all its contents, with no casualty to your personnel, how would you be operational tomorrow assuming your employees are ready to work?
8. Assuming, on the other hand, that you have suffered no damage, but your personnel are not present (*strike, pandemic, access closed*), how can you still manage to be operational?
9. In the event of a disruption in your logistics network, how could you maintain your centre's operations?
10. If your information system shuts down or in reduced operation how can you continue to operate?

HOW ARE YOU EQUIPPED TO MITIGATE THESE RISKS?

11. Immediately (pre-event mitigation)
    - prevention/protection
    - contractual risk sharing
12. When the hazard strikes (post-event mitigation)
    - - 'Business continuity planning'
    - - 'Crisis management & redeployment planning'

- **Question 1**: Aims to understand the activity of the risk centre and test the manager's grasp of his missions and position within the organisation.
- **Questions 2–6**: Aim to identify the resources currently used by the centre, including the 'free resources' and the interaction with other actors, within and beyond the organisation.
- **Questions 7–10**: Aim to destabilise the manager so that he can accept the possibility of changes and envision what he would have to do in the case of an emergency. Through the absence of his staff, on one hand, and the loss of all of his equipment on the other, he is led to select which among his resources are 'vital' for the continuation of his operation. Furthermore, through the wish list of what to do now, and what to do in the case of a disruption, he initiates the process of scenario identification that will help the staff workshop to lead to a robust mitigation plan at his level, i.e. to the definition of business continuity planning, the quantification of the need for 'exceptional financial resources' to implement it and 'sentinel event' that should prompt top management attention.
- **Questions 11 and 12**: Aim to develop a preliminary business continuity plan (BCP), the conditions for its successful implementation as well as early detection of the development that may lead to a crisis through media attention and public implication in the consequences of the 'undesirable event'. Those situations might develop into crises that are likely to require headquarters' input and assistance. Early warning may make all the difference between an aborted crisis and full-blown havoc!

Risk Map or Risk Matrix: What For?

The desired deliverable of the diagnosis exercise is a list of exposures, as exhaustive as possible, and a prioritisation by criticality. It is customary to assess a priority based on 'long-term economic impact' measured by the two variables: *frequency and severity*.

The risk matrix, which many consultants still insist on calling a 'risk-map', is materialised by a two-axis table, on one axis the probability of the event taking place (frequency) and on the other the potential impact (usually in monetary terms). This matrix does not have the stability over time of a physical geography map: it is merely a transitory help to decision-makers, whose decisions will immediately alter the risk profile of the organisation, not to mention the evolution in the external and internal context. However, this function is an information tool for managers, and executives must provide them some insight into the risk; therefore, the classes of risks thus described must be in measures that make sense to them in the light of the decision to be made:

- On the probability axis, for example: once a week, once a month, once a year, once a decade, possibly once a century, once a millennium; and
- On the impact axis: for low or middle severities, a reference to the impact on annual profit should be enlightening (less than 1 per thousand, 1%, 10%, etc.), and for catastrophic risks, a reference to the companies' net worth may prove more appropriate (20%, 50%, and possibly 1000%, or 10 times, etc.)

Combining frequency and severity provides the long-term weight of the risk, but judgement must be exercised, especially where improbable catastrophic events are concerned. At this stage, the traditional green, yellow, and red zones are designed on the acceptability of risk level dictated by deciders', or stakeholders', risk appetite. If an event whose potential impact is 1 per thousand of the profit would only happen once a year, it can be ignored. If the same event could occur once a week, the situation will call for treatment. On the other hand, a millennial flood, even potentially catastrophic, may be left untreated.

A key to efficient RM is an in-depth understanding of all the exposures to which an organisation is confronted, their characteristics, and root causes to infer their potential economic impact. The risk matrix provides an appropriate tool for classifying the risks.

Risk Matrix, a Permanent Process

However, more than the provisional output, the risk matrix, essential in the diagnosis exercise, is a permanent process that facilitates each risk owner's takeover of his risks. The approach that we reproduce here is a mirror of any project management exercise and will engage all operational managers in their risk-management mission. It is a three-stage process:

- *Collecting data* – All the elements pertinent to the management of risks must be collected and analysed in light of their potential impact on the organisation's strategic objectives. Therefore, constituting and keeping updated the risk data bank is at the heart of the RM culture and the tool for it is a RM information system (RMIS) which is now often a component of the organisation's information technology (IT) system. The databank is also enhanced through direct interviews with the risk centres' manager to uncover local potential threats and opportunities that could not be seen from documents, and the data collected are entered into an organisation-wide business analytics system.
- *Self-evaluation workshop* – Based on the elements in the RMIS and the subsequent interview of the manager, a meeting of the team in charge of the risk centre (operational unit) should be organized. During the meeting, each member participates in the risk assessment process and is asked to provide an assessment for each of the exposures. The difficulty in this type of exercise is

to obtain a consensus with each team member initially expressing his/her opinion, notwithstanding hierarchy. This is where the 'voting pads' become handy. Each member is equipped with one and a computer program will provide a consolidated visualisation of all the answers. The graph is supposed to provide a starting point for a discussion where both assessment and possible treatment can be openly discussed to reach a fruitful consensus.

- *Feedback loop* – At the end of the self-evaluation workshop, all exposures which are deemed strategic, i.e. those that impact the timely achievement of the organisation's strategic goals and missions, must be a key factor in developing the BCPs for the group. However, they may need to be passed on to a higher level in the hierarchy for a broader perspective on their global impact on the organisation, including external stakeholders. It is at this stage in the assessment process that a cindynic analysis may prove indispensable to extend the root-cause analysis beyond mechanical failure and focus on the social, cultural, and human components of the system.

Defining the situation at risk in terms of space, actors' networks (i.e. stakeholders) and time will require a good understanding of the ins and outs of the organisation as well as an outsider's 'eye' to avoid too much of a 'business as usual' approach. The final report to be consolidated in a bottom-up movement will be only the starting point of the next iteration when the executive team and/or the risk committee of the board has reviewed the results and made the necessary arbitrage to initiate the iterative improvement movement.

Why Does It Make Sense to Invest in Business Analytics?

During the last decade, RM has become a system to gather, process, and communicate information as we have previously stressed, as evidenced by ISO 31000:2018. At each step of the process, from the diagnosis or risk assessment to the audit of the program, there is a constant need for communication (to obtain the necessary information) to manage information (gather and explain) and communicate again (to present the results and draw practical consequences). This is why installing a RMIS, as a module of the business analytics system, i.e. a set of hardware and software to gather and treat all relevant data for making and implementing decisions, is an essential tool to efficiently manage risks in any organisation. The main attributes of business analytics are listed below:

Assistance to Decision-Making

The decisions made with and all along the RM process are based on systems that link efficiently data and people (staff, partners, etc.). The following are illustrations of what RMIS/BIS (information system) can provide:

- Exposures identification, analysis, and assessment: Collecting data on production sites, properties, and equipment, loss histories, values, and localisation of assets, etc.

- Investigation of the risk treatment options: Review past claims, including values and cash flows at risk to integrate trends in the investigation of the potential impacts of control and financial measures under consideration to mitigate risks, etc.
- Development and approval of the RM programs: Using investigation tools and models to quantify the measures matrix and thus selecting those bringing the maximum expected value (*enhancing opportunities and/or curbing threats*).
- Implementation of the RM programmes: Bring risk owners up to speed with their targets and ways to reach them, whatever happens. Provide insurance underwriters with quality information to come up with best cover conditions and provide data needed for an efficient management of retention programs.
- Audit of the RM programmes: Producing timely and accurate reports for top management to monitor organisation-wide RM efforts (activity standards) and achievements (result standards), thus enabling them to decide on necessary corrections if and when needed.

Reducing Uncertainties

One of the most difficult challenges for any RM professional is to narrow down the range of possible outcomes in any decision-making circumstance, i.e. limit the uncertainties at a level that the 'stakeholders can live with'. However, there remains the daunting question of defining and measuring uncertainty. One definition could be: 'The doubt concerning the capacity to forecast future events'. In financial terms, most models take the standard deviation of the probability distribution of potential outcomes as a measure of the risk/uncertainty. Improving the quality of information is transferred in a reduced standard deviation, and avenues of possible futures are carved out of 'the cloud of the unknown'. Enhancing the decision processes within the organisation is probably the main contribution of an efficient RMIS.

Improving Management Efficiency

Further to improve the decision process, business analytics impacts all aspects of RM. Among others, it improves productivity and plays a key role in the swift and efficient implementation of risk treatment programmes in the following:

- Collecting data on individual large claims or a series of smaller claims, on exposures and insurance covers for swift and equitable compensation, especially in the case of multiple or basket covers.
- Select appropriate information to help management with a clear picture of risk-financing solutions, specifically insurance cover, and ensure that proper insurance certificates are issued.
- Keep track of the transactions, processes, and settlements reached in the case of retention programmes, print relevant letters, and reassess reserve levels.

- Document proper information for future reference, like notes on claims history and historical covers, including trial-proof evidence, should it be needed.
- Keep a written track of important events, plan 'flags' to ensure the development of a file, close claim files in due course, etc.

Enhancing Communication

Analysis and reporting functions can be used to inform both staff and management on the progress of RM within the organisation, the major trends, and individual department contributions to RM. The RM information should be loaded on the information system capabilities of the organisation (business analytics) to facilitate interaction and edit clear and synthetic documents to illustrate the impact of RM on all the activities of the organisation to share with all stakeholders.

As an illustration, let us consider Intranet and internal e-mail capabilities, which are more and more common for organisations, even of medium size, to have developed to inform their entire staff. It is an excellent vehicle to keep supervisors and field managers informed on the evolution of their loss history in a timely fashion so that they can swiftly respond if a situation is deteriorating, as in the case of workers' compensation or fleet accidents where information can be updated in less than 48 hours.

The visibility of RM is greatly improved when operations receive accurate information on risks together with other management information. This puts RM on an equal footing with other sources of controllable costs within the organisation, and managers can take it as seriously as other disciplines.

As a base for ERM, business analytics plays a key role in instilling a risk-management culture throughout the organisation and within its main partners.

As an illustration, let us consider a decentralised structure, in which each entity may have developed over time its ways of managing risks and tending to claims from third parties. In some cases, it may be warranted because of differences in local and industrial cultural differences; in most cases, it will project an image of incoherent and uncoordinated management, and an overall lack of professionalism reflecting badly on the corporate image and reputation.

Integrating into business analytics all claims and risk information that is collected and processed will provide a tool to ensure proper and coordinated claims management policies, especially those involving third parties. Furthermore, the global picture thus produced will allow headquarters to make policy decisions and measure the anticipated impact of its decision on future claims costs.

Appendix 2: ERM and Complexity[1]

> Fools ignore complexity. Pragmatists suffer it. Some can avoid it. Geniuses remove it.
>
> Alan Perlis[2]

The pace of change and the growing global interactions between organisations worldwide have resulted in an increasingly complex web, creating significant risk management challenges for organisations. Therefore, the context in which they operate is becoming less predictable, and their leaders must learn to read through the complexity in the internal and external context.

As organisations grow larger and more intricate, an array of functions gets performed in them. For example, an aircraft manufacturer firm could have aircraft designers, outsourced parts to several suppliers and sub-contractors, a workforce that assembles the aircraft, people in a human resources division that look out for employees, administrative and finance employees that aim to make the operation sustainable, and sales force and intermediaries (financial) that negotiate the contracts with airlines and/or leasing companies, etc.

Increased complexity of an organisation's systems – products, processes, technologies, organisational structures, legal contracts, and so on – can create vulnerabilities. Complementary strategies will be needed to help mitigate the risk. Some well-known events in the recent past illustrate the issue, here are three:

- ***Ericsson***: In March 2000, a fire struck a semiconductor plant in New Mexico, leaving Ericsson Inc. short of millions of chips that the Swedish telecom giant was counting on to launch a new mobile phone product. As a result, Ericsson was ultimately driven from the market (it would later re-enter through a joint

[1]Adapted from Putting organisational complexity in its place. *Mc Kinsey Quarterly*, May 2010.

[2]American Scientist (1922–1990). Read more at: https://www.brainyquote.com/quotes/alan_perlis_177188

Enterprise Risk Management in Today's World, Part A: Enterprise-Wide Risk Management and Strategy, 175–188
Copyright © 2024 by Jean-Paul Louisot and Simon Grima
Published under exclusive licence by Emerald Publishing Limited
doi:10.1108/978-1-83797-406-120241017

venture with Sony Corp.) while its rival Nokia Corp. flourished. Ericsson failed to recognise the New Mexico plant as a bottleneck in a complex, interconnected global supply chain. Ericsson is not the only company to suffer a catastrophe due, in part, to the complexity of its systems.[3]

- ***Barings Bank***: In February 1995, Barings Bank, Britain's oldest merchant bank (it had financed the Napoleonic wars, the Louisiana Purchase, and the Erie Canal) went from strength and prestige to bankruptcy over days. The failure was caused by the actions of a single trader – Nick Leeson – who was based in a small office in Singapore. Soon after Leeson's appointment as general manager of Barings Securities Singapore, he used a secret account to hide losses he sustained by engaging in the unauthorised trading of futures and options. The complexity of the Barings systems enabled Leeson to fool others into thinking that he was making money when in fact he was losing millions. But after the January 1995, Kobe, Japan, earthquake had rocked the Asian financial markets, Leeson's accumulated losses – some $1.4 billion – became too enormous to hide, eventually leading to Barings' collapse.[4]

In the past, companies have tried to manage risks by focusing on threats outside the organisation: competition, shifts in the strategic landscape, natural disasters, or geopolitical events. They are generally less adept at detecting internal vulnerabilities that make breakdowns not just likely but, in many cases, inevitable. Vulnerabilities enter organisations and other human-designed systems as they grow more complex. Indeed, some systems are so complex that they defy a thorough understanding.

In such a complex social arrangement, where many groups of people contribute in varied ways, managers have become central as they coordinate thousands of diverse contributions into a single product or service. Therefore, managers at all levels (strategic, tactical, and operational) aim for internal consistency while trying to make their organisations relevant to the external context too. Thus, managing requires some level of understanding of what is happening, and a sense of direction; short of that, managers could easily lose their stakeholders' trust and confidence leading their firms into a state of competitive deficit; when it comes to the internal context, misreading the forces at play would prevent the manager from combining the diverse contributions.

Thus, managers at all levels operate in complexity, which is usually difficult to understand and monitor due to volatility. However, they must make sense of their complex environments to be efficient in their missions. Experience proves that they usually go through an 'interpretative process aimed at the understanding

---

[3]Ericsson. *The problem with mobile phones*. https://www.ericsson.com/en/about-us/history/changing-the-world/big-bang/the-problem-with-mobile-phones

[4]Others, F. B. A. (2024, February 20). Bankruptcy of Barings Bank (1995). Description, Nick Leeson, & facts. Encyclopedia Britannica. https://www.britannica.com/event/bankruptcy-of-Barings-Bank

of reality'.[5] In other words, managers engage in a learning process to figure out what is going on and to know what to do next. However, their learning is rarely perfect, facing at least three broad challenges due to complexity:

- First, to cope with such complexity, managers develop schemas that simplify their environments and provide some guidance on how to act in them. Nonetheless, given human beings' bounded rationality, a challenge arises from simplistic mental models that could restrict attention and bias managers;
- Second, as managers try to make sense of their complex environments, they look for information that could aid them. However, managers tend to be bombarded by sometimes bogus ideas and theories.

To understand how to manage complexity, executives need to consider it on two levels:

- ***Institutional complexity:*** a consequence of the number of nodes and interactions within an organisation (as well as outside it, in the case of networked businesses). This kind of complexity stems from strategic choices, the external context (such as the regulatory climate), and major choices about organisational and operating systems. It grows as an organisation adds units or increases the number or diversity of the interactions among them – for instance, by moving into a new geography, serving a new customer, or opening a new manufacturing location.
- ***Individual complexity***: the way employees and managers experience and deal with complexity.

Although the two levels are closely related, the distinction between them is important. Most companies focus exclusively on institutional complexity, often a legitimate target. But when the proposed solution involves, say, eliminating a product area or exiting a new market, it could destroy value. A better response is to focus on identifying and reducing the degree of individual complexity by making detailed organisational and operating-model choices, including clarifying roles, refining key processes, and developing appropriate skills and capabilities among the employees and managers beset by complexity. Concentrating on it from this perspective creates room to increase institutional complexity and thus to seek value in fresh strategic challenges.

Despite widespread agreement that organisational complexity makes it hard to get things done, few executives have a realistic understanding of how complexity affects their companies. When pressed, many leaders cite the *institutional* manifestations of complexity they experience: the number of countries the company operates in, for instance, or the number of brands or people they manage. In contrast, relatively few executives take into account the forms of *individual* complexity that the vast majority of their employees face – for example, poor processes, confusing role definitions, or unclear accountabilities.

[5]Dr Kurt Richardson. Managing complex organisations: Complexity thinking and the science and art of management, 30 June 2008, practitioner.

Recognising Complexity in Risk Management: The Challenge of the Improbable[6]

Are there significant limitations in the ability of the prevailing paradigm to take into account observed facts recognised? Is there a credible alternative? Is there a shift in the safety management paradigm to be expected? Can a different social organisation and risk management consensus be built around it? The prevailing safety management paradigm generates 'robust yet brittle' systems; unable to handle disturbances outside the range of contingencies they have been designed for; a paradigm shift is needed; a change in the accepted vision of uncertainty. Humankind lives with it and has evolved, developing cognitive and social skills to handle the associated unpredictability. A better understanding of these abilities is needed to engineer resilience in all systems.

Limitations of the Current Paradigm

A safety paradigm reveals its limits in three ways: (i) the safety objectives announced in its name finally prove unfulfilled in large proportions; (ii) accidents deemed impossible under this paradigm do occur; (iii) this paradigm fails to reassure the civil society.

Since the Fukushima Daiïchi accident,[7] these three paths have been wide open in the world of nuclear safety. Factually observed safety levels did not match with the announced objectives: the observed frequency of an uncontained core meltdown in the Western technology world is about twice the target one. Despite frequent suspicions that Tepco has been negligent, Tepco has reasonably used the available scientific knowledge, methodology, and expertise to predict the magnitude of potential tsunamis off the coast of Fukushima. The accident does not reveal a poor implementation of an effective paradigm but rather a reasonable application of a paradigm of limited effectiveness.

In other domains, like aviation, or offshore oil operations, several major recent accidents also recently illustrated this vulnerability in case of 'surprises' triggered by unexpected, unthought of events, or simply rare events (black swans). The usual response to this kind of exposure is to assert to have learned the lesson and then the scenario is added to the current threat list, so as not to be fooled next time. In other words, the common response is to commit to doing more of what has been done already: anticipating threats and responses and extending the domain of predetermination.

The Total Predetermination Fallacy

However, the real challenge is to the safety paradigm itself, i.e. the idea that safety can be based on the anticipation that all threats and all expected (safe) responses

---

[6]Chapter same title by Jean Pariès in *The illusion of risk control* (pp. 41–55). Springer, August 2017.

[7]Fukushima Daiichi Accident – World Nuclear Association. (n.d.). https://world-nuclear.org/information-library/safety-and-security/safety-of-plants/fukushima-daiichi-accident.aspx

leave no room for the unexpected. This safety paradigm dates from the 1950s and from efforts made in the post-war period to better control systems reliability and contingencies within the framework of the development of strategic nuclear forces, aerospace industry, and nuclear electricity. The 'enemy' was the emergence of unexpected behaviour, including technical failures, and 'human error'. Methods for a systematic anticipation of hazards, failures, and their effects (fault trees, Failure Modes and Effects Analysis (FMEA), etc.) were developed, as well as methods for a post-event analysis of unexpected events (root-cause analysis, fault tree). And while it was realised soon that human operators' behaviours were difficult to incorporate into predictive models; the limitations appeared also of an attempt to approach them like technical equipment by assigning them a calculable reliability coefficient (e.g. Technique for Human Error Rate Prediction (THERP) has long been in vogue and continues today).

In the 1980s, 'soft' social sciences were introduced in safety thinking to help better understand the role of individuals, teams, organisations, and cultures concerning accidents. But while the focus slowly shifted from technical to human failures, and then from front-line operators' failures to latent organisational defects, the core 'safety model' has remained unchanged. Deviations from the expected are used to describe risk nowadays and are considered the source of incidents and accidents; hence, a modern Grail is defined as a perfect world, where nothing goes wrong.

Increasing Complexity Creates Challenges for Risk Management[8]

A research project has been developed to uncover the causes and impacts of complexity in large companies across a range of industry sectors and countries. This paper, published by KPMG, found that managing complexity is a critical issue facing businesses, with more than 94% of senior decision-makers agreeing that managing complexity is essential for their organisation success. The leading causes of complexity identified in the study include:

- Regulation and government oversight;
- Information management;
- Speed of innovation; and
- Volatility of complexity.

With the causes of complexity having shifted over the last two years, business leaders face an ever-increasing difficult task of identifying risks arising from complexity and curbing them to acceptable levels. In such a volatile context, management will soon discover that the underlying driver of complexity has quickly evolved, triggering new risks. Increased risks to manage produced by complexity emerged as the greatest challenge in both mature and developing economies; more than 80% of executives stated that complexity creates more risks to be managed by their organisation.

---

[8]KPMG commissioned Lighthouse Global to a study, the results of which were published in January 2011.

While increasing challenges, complexity is also a source of new opportunities. At least 7 of 10 executives stated that complexity establishes the opportunity for:

- Gaining competitive advantages;
- Creating new and better strategies;
- Expanding into new markets; and
- Making their organisation more efficient.

To respond to the impact of complexity, businesses have made various efforts to adapt to the changes, with mixed results. These efforts include improving information management, changing the configuration of the organisation, investing in new geographies, and developing and hiring the new skills needed.

Complexity generates new challenges to organisations; one of the most serious is managing emerging risks due to constant innovation, complicated regulation, increased government oversight, overflow of information, and volatility. In addition to threats, opportunities await to be unearthed. Leaders must develop an understanding of causes and impacts of complexity to prepare efficient responses in the organisation's strategy to manage threats and opportunities caused by complexity.

Reduce – and Redirect – Complexity

Once senior managers have a clear picture of where complexity hampers effectiveness, they can begin to remove any complexity that doesn't add value and channel what's left to people who can handle it. Of course, managers must be mindful that not all complexity is equally manageable, and proceed accordingly (*see table here below complexity taxonomy*).

Complexity Taxonomy
Compliance complexity: it results from industry regulations and interventions by non-governmental organisations (NGOs). It is not typically manageable by companies.
Inherent complexity: intrinsic to the business and can only be jettisoned by exiting a portion of the business.
Designed complexity: results from choices about where the business operates, what it sells, to whom, and how. Companies can remove it, but this could mean simplifying valuable wrinkles in their business model.
Unnecessary complexity: arises from growing misalignment between the needs of the organisation and the processes supporting it. Once identified, it is easily managed.

Project Complexity and Risk Management[9]

Dealing effectively with risks in complex projects is difficult and requires management interventions that go beyond simple analytical approaches. This is one finding of a major field study into risk management practices and business processes of 35 major product developments in 17 high-technology companies. Almost one-half of the disturbances that occur are not being detected before they impact project performance. Yet, the risk-impact model presented in this article shows that risk does not affect all projects equally but depends on the effectiveness of collective managerial actions dealing with specific contingencies. The results of this study discuss why some organisations are more successful in detecting risks early in a project life cycle and in decoupling risk factors from work processes before they impact project performance.

The field data suggest that effective project risk management involves an intricately linked set of variables, related to work process, organisational environment, and people. Some of the best success scenarios point to the critical importance of recognising and dealing with risks early in their development. This requires broad involvement and collaboration across all participants in the project team and its environment and sophisticated methods for assessing feasibilities and usability early and frequently during the project life cycle. Specific managerial actions, organisational conditions, and work processes are suggested for fostering a project environment most conducive to effective cross-functional communication and collaboration among all stakeholders, a condition important to early risk detection and effective risk management in a complex project.

The Cost of Complexity[10]

The cost of complexity is borne by all, whether in the form of reduced profits in a business, diminished efficiency in the public sector, or excessive cost imposed on consumers, who must pay more for products produced through unnecessarily complex processes. The cost of complexity can be difficult to identify, however, as it defies measurement both in terms of direct costs and outcomes. More often than not it simply becomes a source of friction that slows everything down and takes a silent toll. Missed opportunities, reduced consumer satisfaction, slower growth, and lost investment are among the most common results of unnecessary complexity.

Examples of such complexity abound, whether in the form of multiple layers of required approvals in government, excessive and overlapping layers of production in businesses, and even on an individual level, such as numerous stops

---

[9]See Hans Thamhain. (2013, February 27). *Managing risks in complex projects*. Wiley. https://doi.org/10.1002/pmj.21325

[10]See the article same title by Dante Disparte and Daniel Wagner published in *Risk Management* magazine, 12 December 2016.

at security checkpoints at airports. All of mankind asked themselves why things need to be so complicated, and how much money and resources must be wasted in the process of maintaining 'normal' operating conditions. Justifying such inefficiencies through the status quo argument of 'that's the way it's always been done' demonstrates capitulation while negating just how much the world has changed.

Holding on status quo and avoiding decisions have become the outcome of most committees; research has shown that, on average, five people are involved in a decision-making process, particularly those that require consensus about change or procurement. The friction created by such unnecessary complexity is akin to that generated by corruption – both exact a tremendous price for individuals, businesses, and society; yet with so many people guilty of being accessories to complexity and friction, men and women are collectively de-incentivised to devote the energy and resources required to change for more efficient systems.

Some forms of lending and insurance that are intended to strengthen trade and investment flows end up contributing to what often become the most complex and time-consuming transactions in financial markets. For example, finance transaction projects typically add unnecessary 'drag' to what should be a streamlined process. As a result, a significant percentage of global trade and investment skew to larger firms that can afford to throw an army of lawyers, analysts, and advisors at a transaction, adding many months and millions to the process. The average project finance transaction can take more than a year to complete; involve dozens of underwriters, lenders, lawyers, and consultants; and require endless phone calls, meetings, and document revisions – all sources of friction that greatly contribute to inflated prices, high opportunity costs, and unnecessary complexity.

Time, effort, and cost required accommodating all these parties putting their thumbprint on agreements, and ensuring that every conceivable contingency is accounted for can be an insidious source of friction. While intending to 'de-risk' a deal, it ends up costing consumers much more than they would otherwise need to pay because of sunk costs, while scaring away would-be trade or investment partners in the process. If a *single* representative from each organisation were simply assigned to each task, and a hard deadline was attached to the process (along with a monetary penalty for failing to comply), the time required to reach financial closure could surely be reduced by months, saving millions.

Another area where friction and complexity exact a heavy toll on economic growth is in business-to-business (B2B) sales. On one end, legions of sales professionals armed with the latest sales tactics promote their products and services. Being prodded by a pervasive penalty-driven management culture, sales incentives are most often geared towards maximising short-term results, ignoring long-term risks, and deemphasising the development of solutions that genuinely add value to buyers. On the demand side of the equation is the 'valley of decision avoidance,' where those five decision-making purchase committee members are reluctant to drive change, despite implied economic and other advantages. While in the end, transactions are completed in this environment, the time, economic drag, and complexity added to the business cycle are detrimental to economic growth and the velocity of trade and investment, which has the pernicious effect of dampening hiring, generating inventory and eroding general economic confidence.

Companies that take months to enact a purchase decision in their home markets slow down the growth of the economy. Red tape, bureaucracy, and procrastination are for developed economies the plague that corruption, bribery, and fraud are for too many developing and emerging markets. However, procrastination can be overcome with nimbler decision-making, efficient processes, and a will to overcome risk aversion.

Since staff lacks incentives to implement fundamental reforms that would change organisational structures to unclog the insidious obstacles to efficiency, change must be fostered from the bottom up. The vast size, geographic spread, and multiple organisational layers of giant 'pace-setter' firms constitute often sources of complexity and friction. These giant firms tend to fall prey to avoidable risks resulting in strategic disruption; they are weakened by new business models emerging to exploit their lack of agility.

Similarly, unduly burdensome regulations meant to control risk accelerate the process of increasing complexity, often inducing tax optimisation opportunities that divert the global economy's natural flows of capital, taxes, and data. The first step of getting away from complexity and friction requires acknowledging adverse effects and the relationship between these forces. It opens the way to simplicity and reduces friction on the path to economic growth.

Complexity Learning Process

However, to establish a robust diagnostic of complexity, managers need to learn to 'read complexity' within and without their organisation and keep the 'complexity radar' operational at all times. The main constraint of the managerial learning process for complexity stems from the conditions under which it is carried out. Managers need to understand how to combine internal contributions to achieve external relevance of their organisations; neither of these two missions is easy; both internal and external contexts are nested in complex systems, constantly adapting. The complexity of internal or external context is generated by a large number of subsystems and components that interact in a non-simple way that can be explained only when using fuzzy logic.

Complex adaptive systems (CASs), such as organisations and their context, are characterised by the interaction of myriads of interdependent components, both mechanical and human. These are nonlinear systems in the sense that the whole is not the mere sum of the parts, but a dynamic if fluid combination. Furthermore, in CASs, feedback processes are essential, and thus, the behaviour of an agent becomes the factor that influences the behaviour of other agents, which at the same time comes back to influence again the original agent. Thus, sometimes CASs, because of their internal feedback loops, amplify signals that propagate throughout and could escalate in the occurrence of infrequent and radical events.

Fuzzy Logic

A system of logic in which a statement can be true, false, or any of a continuum of values in between.

A branch of logic designed to allow degrees of imprecision in reasoning and knowledge, typified by terms such as 'very', 'quite possibly', and 'unlikely', to be represented in such a way that the information can be processed by a computer.

A form of algebra employing a range of values from 'true' to 'false' that is used in making decisions with imprecise data. The outcome of an operation is assigned a value between 0 and 1 corresponding to its degree of truth. Fuzzy logic is used, for example, in artificial intelligence systems.

Now, because of the intricacies of the networks that are formed, understanding cause and effect relationships in CASs can become confusing or even impossible, even more so as most systems are like clouds with no definite frontier. Finally, among many other types of features that distinguish a CAS, it is important to distinguish the capacity of these systems to adjust to their contexts and potentially adapt to them provided the leadership can read the trends.

The key to managerial insight is to understand variables in play and the relationships between them (*see table above – fuzzy logic*). However, as organisations and their external environments are complex systems, then it should be clear that, under such conditions, managers have a hard time grasping them. Furthermore, contexts in which managers operate are constantly evolving, and a manager's grip on the context and organisation's complexity might prove only a temporary accomplishment. Therefore, complexity and change combine to create uncertainty. Complexity, change, and uncertainty become the bedrock upon which lie most managerial learning challenges; i.e. they are deeply rooted in risk management.

The Challenges of Complexity Learning

Three managerial learning challenges are emerging from the complexity that managers are confronted with. It could be the case that managers' incapacity to cope with these three broad challenges emerges overall from the overconfidence that has characterised managerial learning so far. Thus, there is a need for professionals to start working on promoting a new approach to management learning, which differs greatly from the previous ones: a careful-based learning ideal, which would entail the quality of carefulness, critical thinking, and a deep learning style, underpinned by the dispositions to learn and negative capability. Now, a careful-based learning ideal could be instrumental in improving managers' performance when confronting these challenges.

Nevertheless, all actors must keep in mind that, in the end, human psychology might not be capable or prepared to understand fully the complexity of this 'Brownian world'. Therefore, the first step of careful-based learning is to be cautious about ambition, accepting that complexity sometimes lies far beyond human capacities and that even if carefulness could help managers cope with it more effectively, this can never be the perfect tool. In the end, imperfect and cognitively bounded human beings might see their talents enhanced by artificial intelligence facilitated by business analytics.

Ways to Meet the Challenges of Complexity Learning

Current trends and pressures for change in managerial responsibilities must be monitored carefully, including social media. The management role must be examined from the perspective of direction-setting, decision-making, and strategic planning; the organising role covers structure and design, communications and information technology, human resource management, and the management of change and innovation; the leadership role covers the basics of organisational behaviour, group and team dynamics, motivation and leadership styles; and the controlling or performance management function introducing operations and value chain management.

Therefore, managers must learn to:

1. Critically analyse environmental pressures on management historically and contemporarily and the responsiveness of the managerial function to environmental shifts.
2. Demonstrate coherent and advanced knowledge of managerial functions of planning, organising, leading, and controlling across the organisation in diverse and complex environments.
3. Critically analyse managerial roles and functions at different organisational levels and in different types of organisations.
4. Communicate proficiently in professional practice to a variety of audiences and function as an effective member or leader of a diverse team.

As already mentioned, there are inherent limits to human intervention in a complex system like the economy but humans have difficulty in grasping their limitations; this is true of business leaders operating in today's rapidly changing and unpredictable global environment. Forests, oceans, or ant colonies are CASs, in which local behaviours and events can cascade and reshape the entire system. Businesses are also CASs; therefore, they are neither fully controllable nor predictable; traditional approaches to management, based on the premise of predictability, fall short when addressing current business challenges.

For long-term success, business leaders cannot rely only on a traditional 'mechanical' management approach, seeking to reach a company's desired outcomes through engineering processes and control of its various components' behaviour. They must also use a 'biological' approach acknowledging that business issues are uncertain and complex and must be addressed indirectly. The thinking process must move from traditional physics to quantum physics and make good use of fuzzy logic and artificial intelligence.

Complexity cannot be avoided in organisations, but the solution is not an unending search for leanness. Instead, executives should try to discover where complexity matters and how to build the right processes, skills, and culture to manage it. Embracing complexity only at the strategic level but also tactical and operational levels may create a competitive advantage. Companies acting on complexity create more value than their rivals and are more resilient in a constantly evolving context; especially in a time of rupture turning into opportunities when turned into 'creative ruptures'.

Therefore, whenever executives consciously funnel complexity into new locations or 'design in' new elements that create added complexity for added value creation, they must ensure that local staff is ready to embrace this complexity. In such situations, companies often uncover a need for improved key capabilities in human resources (HR) and other functional areas.

Whenever companies tackle complexity, they will find some individuals who seem less troubled by it than others. This is not surprising as people are different: some freeze like deer in headlights in the face of ambiguity, uncertainty, complex roles, and unclear accountabilities; others can get their work done regardless. Companies need to assess individual strengths and weaknesses to identify staff who can respond intelligently to complexity. Although some people can deal with complexity naturally, others can be trained to develop the ability to tolerate ambiguity and actively manage complexity. Such skills will enable employees to create networks within organisations, build relationships and help overcome poor processes, bridge organisational silos, or manage whatever value-creating pockets of complexity their companies decide to maintain.

Coping with Complexity, Uncertainty and Ambiguity in Risk Governance: A Synthesis[11]

Risk governance covers both the institutional structure and the policy process that guides and restrains the collective activities of a group, society, or international community to regulate, reduce, or control risk problems.

The contemporary handling of collectively relevant risk problems has shifted from traditional state-centric approaches with hierarchically organised governmental agencies as the dominant locus of power to multi-level governance systems, in which the political authority for handling risk problems is distributed to separately set-up public bodies. These bodies are characterised by overlapping jurisdictions that do not match the traditional hierarchical order and multi-actor alliances including traditional governmental branches, executive, legislative, and judiciary branches. Socially relevant actors from civil society, most notably industry, science, and NGOs are also concerned with risk. This results in an increasingly

[11]Article same title by Renn, O., Klinke, A., & van Asselt, M. (2011). *Ambio, 40*(2), PMC3357789. Courtesy of Springer.

multilayered and diversified socio-political landscape in which a multitude of actors; their perceptions and evaluations mix a diversity of knowledge and evidence claims, value commitments, and political interests. They clash and combine to influence processes of risk analysis, decision-making, and risk management.

Institutional diversity can offer considerable benefits when complex, uncertain, and ambiguous risk problems need to be addressed because:

- First, risk problems with different scopes can be managed at different levels;
- Second, an inherent degree of overlap and redundancy makes non-hierarchical adaptive and integrative risk governance systems more resilient and therefore less vulnerable; and
- Third, a larger number of actors facilitate experimentation and learning.

Disadvantages are the possible transformation of risk in commodity; the fragmentation of the risk governance process; costly collective risk decision-making; the potential loss of democratic accountability and paralysis by analysis, i.e. the inability to make decisions due to unresolved cognitive and normative conflicts and lack of accountability with regard to multiple responsibilities and duties.

Thus, understanding the dynamics, structures, and functionality of risk governance processes requires a general and comprehensive understanding of procedural mechanisms and structural configurations.

The classic model of the risk management process comprises three components: risk assessment, management, and communication. It proved to be too narrowly focused on private or public regulatory bodies as to be capable of covering the variety of actors and processes in governing risk.

Some authors point out complex problems such as those of the Baltic Sea that need a more sophisticated and, in particular, iterative approach to risk management. Others emphasise the need for a multi-level governance system, which is capable of integrating top-down and bottom-up approaches. Others highlighted the importance of the evaluation of risk as a separate phase in the risk governance process while some illustrated the crucial function of framing for gaining a better understanding of the media discourse about risk. All these analyses and case studies underline the need to enrich the classic risk governance model by adding two additional stages dealing with risk characterisation/evaluation and pre-assessment (or framing). These stages will be explained later in the paper.

Furthermore, risk governance calls for the involvement of experts, stakeholders, and the public as a core feature for communication and deliberation. Relying on expanded inclusion in the risk governance process of stakeholders was a recurring theme when it came to climate change.

Risk governance highlights the importance of uncertain,[12] complex, and/or ambiguous risks. The assessment and management routines in place do not do justice to the nature of such risks. The consequences of this maltreatment range

---

[12]Others, F. B. A. (2024, February 20). Bankruptcy of Barings Bank (1995). Description, Nick Leeson, & facts. Encyclopedia Britannica. https://www.britannica.com/event/bankruptcy-of-Barings-Bank

from social amplification or irresponsible attenuation of the risk, sustained controversy, deadlocks, legitimacy problems, unintelligible decision-making, trade conflicts, border conflicts, expensive re-bound measures, and lock-ins. To summarise, it is urgent to develop better conceptual and operational approaches to understand and characterise, let alone manage non-simple risks.

> Simplicity is hard to build, easy to use, and hard to charge for. Complexity is easy to build, hard to use, and easy to charge for.'
>
> Chris Sacca[13]

[13]American Businessman. Read more at: https://www.brainyquote.com/quotes/chris_sacca_838291?src=t_complexity

Appendix 3: Managing Cognitive Risk

> The brain is a magnificent monster. Its billions of nerve cells – called neurons – lie in a tangled web that displays cognitive powers far exceeding all the silicon machines we have built to imitate it. (William A. Wellman[1])

Frameworks for enterprise risk management (ERM)[2] (such as COSO ERM, ISO 31000, and the NIST Cyber-Security Guide or ISO 27000 Series standards) have one thing in common: each of the traditional risk management frameworks is based on guidelines to establish a rudimentary basis for the development of risk management programmes. Along the way, the term 'guidance' was confusing and replaced with 'standard(s) of risk practice', and in many cases, particularly for early adopters, a risk management programme is assumed to be mature while the path to maturity can be long.

The challenge facing traditional risk management frameworks is that the 'E' in the ERM refers to comprehensive and integrated management but does not apply well as the world transitions to Industry 4.0 and hybrid models of commercial and military operations. Technology has extended the company's boundaries to the cloud and a variety of third-party and tertiary providers that do not maintain the same standards as stand-alone organisations. Moreover, and more importantly, none of the traditional risk frameworks seem to take into account the scientific rigour found in perspective theory, decision science, behavioural science, cognitive science, or the more limited sciences of human factors analysis.

From a cognitive science perspective, existing gaps in traditional risk management frameworks expose organisations to higher risks while increasing

[1]William Wellman, born William Augustus Wellman (1896–1975), was an American film director best known for the movies *Wings* (1927), *A Star Is Born* (1937), and *The Strange Incident* (1943).
[2]For the introduction, https://papers.ssrn.com/sol3/papers.cfm?abstract_id=3952818.

Enterprise Risk Management in Today's World, Part A: Enterprise-Wide Risk Management and Strategy, 189–203
Copyright © 2024 by Jean-Paul Louisot and Simon Grima
Published under exclusive licence by Emerald Publishing Limited
doi:10.1108/978-1-83797-406-120241018

technological complexity, higher rates of cyber-threats, and threats and advances in artificial intelligence, creating an inflection point in corporate governance in general. No doubt we could review this assertion in the light of the contributions of the Cindynics, especially with the use of the hyperspace of danger developed 30 years ago by Georges-Yves Kervern, however, remains the need for additional rigour in traditional risk guidelines or general revisions to the concept of risk management practice in corporate governance.

It is only recently that behavioural economics has begun to be gradually accepted by traditional economists as a rigorous discipline that can serve as an alternative perspective on decision-making. However, widespread acceptance and increasing adoption of economic behavioural theories and concepts, as well as advances in computer firepower, provide opportunities to apply practical applications to improve risk management practices.

Cognitive risks are factors of subconscious and unconscious influence on human decision-making: heuristics and biases. To understand the scope of cognitive risk, one needs to examine organisational failure, and the science that explains why decision-makers systematically make judgement errors and repeat the same mistakes. It's about taking a multidisciplinary, pedestrian walk through behavioural science with a light touch, using stories to explain why decision-makers constantly make cognitive mistakes that not only increase risk but also at the same time fail to recognise their errors.

This science has deep roots in organisational behaviour, psychology, human factors, cognitive sciences, and behavioural sciences, all influenced by classical philosophers and activated by advanced analytics and artificial intelligence. Humans persist with limited rationality, but as the speed of information, data, money, and life in general accelerates, they will need to develop the right tools not only to keep pace but to survive and thrive.

In light of all these factors that complicate risk, a fundamental solution is proposed: a cognitive risk framework for ERM and cyber-security. There are five pillars in a cognitive risk framework with five maturity levels, but there is no universally prescribed maturity level. It's more of a journey by different paths. Each organisation must follow its path, but the goal is the same: to minimise errors that could have been avoided. The aim is to explain why risks are difficult to discuss and why decision-makers systematically ignore the aggregation of these hidden risks in collective decision-making within an organisation.

The cognitive risk framework was designed to explore the two most complex risks facing organisations: uncertainty and decision-making in uncertainty. The first pillar is cognitive governance, which is a structured approach to institutionalise rational decision-making across the enterprise. Each pillar is complementary and builds on the next in a succession of continuous learning. There is no end point because the pillars evolve with technology. Risk management in an organisation relies on a team effort to gather risk information based on an efficient framework for sound decision-making. Need for designers of risk solutions made possible by the right technology and nurtured by collaboration.

> Humans are not machines. They analyze the information based on their experience, knowledge, and cognitive bias. All this makes their perception, their unique point of view. (Naved Abdali[3])

A Contextual Model of a Cognitive Risk Management Framework Within ERM Is Required[4]

> Cognitive psychology tells us that the unaided human mind is vulnerable to many errors and illusions due to its dependence on its memory for vivid anecdotes rather than systematic statistics. (Steven Pinker[5])

A contextual model of a cognitive risk management framework for ERM was first published on 4 January 2017, revised on 26 March. The general acceptance and increasing adoption of economic behavioural theories and concepts, as well as advances in computer firepower, provide opportunities to apply practical applications to improve risk management practice. The objective here is to develop a contextual model of a cognitive risk management framework for ERM defines the limits and opportunities to improve risk management within an organisation by combining behavioural science with a more rigorous analytical approach to risk management.

The author's thesis is that managers and staff are subject to natural limits in Bayesian probability predictions as well as errors in judgement due in part to insufficient experience or data to draw reliable and consistent conclusions with a high degree of confidence. In this context, a cognitive risk framework helps to recognise these limitations in judgement.

The Cognitive Risk Management Framework for Cyber-Security and the five pillars of the framework were proposed as guides for the development of an advanced ERM framework to address complex and asymmetrical risks such as cyber-risks. 'One of the key tasks of the organisation is to first identify where the knowledge is that can provide the various types of factual premises that decisions require' – Herbert Simon Context: In a 1998 review of Amos Tversky's contributions to behavioural economics (Laibson and Zeckhauser) discussed how Tversky systematically exposed the theoretical flaws of rationality by individual actors in pursuit of perfect optimality. Tversky and Kahneman's *Judgment Under Uncertainty: Heuristics and Biases* (1974) *and Prospect Theory* (1979) demonstrated

---

[3]Naved Abdali CPA (Canada), author of INVESTING – Hopes, Hypes, and Heartbreaks Manager, financial auditor at the Tangerine Bank.

[4]See https://www.researchgate.net/publication/340176017_A_Contextual_Model_of_a_Cognitive_Risk_Framework_for_Enterprise_Risk_Management.

[5]Steven Pinker, born in Montreal (Canada), is a psycholinguist and cognitive psychologist Canadian-American successful author of popular books.

that there are errors in actual decisions. «Proponents of rational choice assume that predicting these errors is difficult or, in the more orthodox conception of rationality, impossible».

Tversky's work rejects this vision of decision-making. Tversky and his colleagues show that economic rationality is systematically violated and that decision-making errors are both widespread and predictable. This now indisputable point has been established by two central working bodies: Tversky and Kahneman's papers on heuristics and prejudice, and their papers on framing theory and perspective. Much of Tversky and Kahneman's contributions are less known to the general public and are misinterpreted as a purely theoretical treatment by some risk professionals. As researchers, Tversky and Kahneman were well versed in mathematics, which helped to highlight systemic errors in complex probability judgements and the use of heuristics in an inappropriate context.

As revolutionary as behavioural science has been in the economic theory of questioning, Tversky and Kahneman's work focuses on a narrow set of heuristics: representativeness, availability, and anchoring as universal errors. The authors used these three fundamental heuristics generally to describe how decision-makers substitute mental shortcuts for probabilistic judgements; this leads to biased inferences and a lack of rigour in decision-making in uncertainty. Cognitive Risk Framework: Over the past 30 years, Prospect Theory's data analysis expertise and computational firepower have made significant progress in addressing the low Bayesian probabilities recognised by Tversky and Kahneman.

In addition, the automotive industry and Apple Inc., among others, have successfully integrated behavioural science into product design to reduce risk, anticipate human errors, and improve user experience by adding value to financial results. This paper assumes that these early examples of progress indicate untapped potential if applied constructively. There are distractions, and even Tversky and Kahneman have admitted inherent weaknesses that are not easy to solve.

For example, observers doubt that laboratory results do not reproduce real situations; that arbitrary frames do not reflect reality as well as a lack of predictive mathematical accuracy. Since Laibson and Zeckhauser's (1998) critique of Tversky's contributions to economics, many cognition researches have evolved to include big data, computational neuroscience, cognitive computing, cognitive security, intelligent computing, and the rapid progress of early machine learning and artificial intelligence.

A cognitive risk framework is proposed to take advantage of the rapid advancement of these technologies in risk management, but technology alone is not a panacea. Many of these technologies are evolving, but further progress will continue at various stages. This will require risk professionals to start thinking about how to formalise the steps to integrate these tools into an ERM programme in combination with other human elements. The Cognitive Risk Framework envisions these new technologies, as promising as they are, as a pillar of a robust and comprehensive framework for managing increasingly complex threats, such as cyber- and enterprise risks. The five pillars include cognitive governance, design of intentional controls, active intelligence and defence, cognitive security and the human element, and decision support – situational awareness.

A cognitive risk framework does not replace other risk frameworks such as COSO ERM, ISO 31000, or NIST for managing a range of risks in the enterprise. Traditional risk management frameworks focus primarily on administering policies, procedures, organising resources, and auditing the implementation of risk management processes. The missing elements in traditional risk frameworks are twofold:

1. Traditional risk management frameworks largely ignore the science of risk analysis;
2. The traditional risk management framework considers only tangential human factors, resulting in gaps in the leading cause of cyber-risk vulnerability and decision-making failure in uncertainty.

A cognitive risk framework is presented to build on the progress made to date in risk management practice and provide a path to demonstrably improve business risk using advanced analytics to inform decision-making in ways only now possible. One of the basic principles of perspective theory is the recognition of errors in decision-making arising from small sample sizes or poor data quality. Tversky and Kahneman noted several observations where even highly qualified researchers routinely made inference errors derived from poor sampling techniques.

While many recognise the importance of data, organisations must anticipate that an interdisciplinary team of experts is needed to update a cognitive risk framework. The data will either become the engine of a cognitive risk framework or its Achilles heel and could be the least valued investment in accelerating a cognition-based risk programme. Much has been said about big data and the promise to collect and analyse data pools to improve policy decisions by industry, government, and non-governmental organisations (NGOs), but that promise is still not being kept. The limitations of big data stem from the lack of universal data structures and agree on data categorisation standards that enable organisations to leverage data regardless of country, language, industry, or purpose.

A quote attributed to Albert Einstein still resonates: 'Everything that matters cannot be counted and everything that can be counted does not matter'. This suggests that values play an equally important role in analysis. The challenge is to agree on values that resonate universally (Kunreuther & Slovic, 1996).

A cognitive risk framework provides for much more diverse competencies than currently exist in information technology (IT) risk management and security. Data are only one consideration in developing a strong cognitive risk framework. Other considerations will include the development of a structure and processes that facilitate practitioner adoption across multiple industries and organisations of different sizes.

Although it is expected that a cognitive risk management framework can be successfully implemented in large and small organisations (small- and medium-sized enterprises [SMEs]), risk management professionals may decide to adopt a modified version of the five pillars or develop solutions to address specific risks such as cyber-security as a stand-alone programme solution. Cognitive governance is the first pillar of a cognitive risk framework as an organisational principle of ERM. The other four pillars serve as drivers of cognitive governance that is envisioned as a set of tools, technologies, and practices developed around human factors that complement the administrative functions of traditional risk management frameworks.

A more robust development of the cognitive risk framework has been published that details the steps and actions an organisation can take to implement cognition in risk management programmes (see below). The mistake in traditional risk management frameworks is that there are no guidelines to give every person in an organisation the tools, practices, and capacities to manage the various risks faced by different levels of all organisations. Organisations use sanctions or incentives for collaborators to comply with the mixed results from the boardroom to the workshop.

Traditional risk management frameworks are designed as hierarchical command and control processes that are too rigid to respond to rapidly evolving systemic events, such as cyber-security and pandemics, which are asymmetrical and require new decision-making approaches under uncertain conditions. Cognitive governance is focused on empowering everyone within organisations with better tools, data, and competencies to manage risk at every level of the organisation.

Evidence of the failure of the rigid response of command and control is evident in the spread of the pandemic that the world has experienced recently. Too many decisions, we see that people have learned to innovate and improvise using the tools at their disposal to find solutions to manage risks as new information arrives. This interaction of improvisation and new information inputs is at the heart of a cognitive risk framework.

The goal is to eliminate bottlenecks that exist intrinsically in the hierarchy by creating a culture of innovation at all levels of the organisation to solve problems and share learning, creating an autonomous culture that creates real-time resilience that is not possible in a top-down structure. The next steps in a cognitive risk framework will explore each of these concepts in detail and provide guidance to create a culture of cognition that allows the organisation to build resilience, become more sensitive to emerging risks, and improve situational awareness.

> The first meaning of 'cognitive' for us is that the observations of others are made phenomenologically: that is, trying to take the role of the other, to see things from his conscious point of view. (Lawrence Kohlberg[6])

The Contextual Model of a Cognitive Risk Management Framework with Five Pillars[7]

> Cognitive dissonance, denial, and cowardice that spare us painful truths and prevent us from acting in defence of innocent victims

---

[6]Lawrence Kohlberg (1927–1987) was an American psychologist who taught at Chicago University and Harvard.

[7]See https://dl.acm.org/doi/abs/10.1080/07366981.2016.1257219 and https://www.corporatecomplianceinsights.com/cognitive-governance-risk-framework/.

> while allowing 'beloved' individuals to continue their heinous behaviour must be thrown from the bottom of our souls. (Mira Sorvino[8])

This part is a summary since the model, especially the five pillars, is described in detail in the articles cited in the bibliography. The cognitive risk framework is adapted to cyber-security to address two narrative arcs in cyber-warfare: the rise of the «hacker» as an industry and the «paradox of cyber-security», namely why the billions spent on cyber-security do not deal with semantic cyber-attacks.

Semantic cyber-attacks, also known as social engineering, manipulate the perception and interpretation of human users of computer-generated data to obtain non-public confidential data. The cyber-battlefield has gone from an attack on material goods to a much softer target: the human mind. If human behaviour is the new and last «weak link» of cyber-security armour, the problem is to build cognitive defences at the intersection of human–machine interactions.

The answer is yes, but the change needed requires a new way of thinking about security, data governance, and strategy. The concepts mentioned in the Capital Framework Review Committee (CFRC) Cyber-Security Cognitive Risk Framework are drawn from a wide range of research on multidisciplinary topics. Cognitive risk management is a sister discipline to a parallel scientific corpus called Cognitive Informatics Security or CogSec. It is also important to note that as the creator of the Financial Compliance and Reporting Committee (FCRC), the principles, and practices prescribed here are borrowed from the security of cognitive computing, machine learning, artificial intelligence, and artificial intelligence and behavioural and cognitive sciences, among a few that are still evolving.

The Cognitive Risk Framework for Cyber-Security is built around five pillars: Intentional Control Design, Cognitive Computing Security, Cognitive Risk Governance, Cyber Intelligence Security and Active Defence Strategies, and Legal Considerations of 'Best Efforts' in Cyberspace.

Cognitive governance is a radical change from traditional risk management. Research and professional practice over more than a decade suggests that risk management is undergoing a profound renewal. By analysing how physicists, engineers, actuaries, healthcare professionals, researchers, and Nobel laureates solve complex problems, professionals have found new ways to think about risks and the tools needed to reduce them. However, it must be kept in mind that there is no one-size-fits-all solution that can be applied generically to manage risk. This should not be a surprise given the economic and commercial failures that are repeated repeatedly, but the question remained unanswered: Is there a common thread leading to failure?

The most surprising failure, often cited in all risk disciplines, is human behaviour and error! In particular, human behaviour is cited as the greatest vulnerability of cyber-security, but it is also the main cause of fraud as well as operational and organisational failure. In contrast, traditional risk management frameworks are designed to ensure the effectiveness of financial and operational controls in

[8]Mira Sorvino, born in Tenafly (New Jersey), is an American actress and producer.

alignment with organisational strategy. The difference between the two is the emphasis on design around the human element. A cognitive risk framework does not compete with traditional risk frameworks; it complements the baseline work already in place.

Atul Gawande[9] called these failures in the ineptitude of performance, while psychologists Daniel Kahneman and Amos Tversky describe them as heuristics in concert with Herbert Simon, who captured the magnitude of the problem in bounded rationality. Each of these observations provides insight into how to help mitigate our limitations, but there is resistance to adapt even when the costs of these failures increase. The falsity of homo economicus applies equally to risk management, but the question remained: what to do?

The transition from 20th-century processes to digital transformation requires new frameworks, tools, and, more importantly, new thinking about risks. Technology and data support better risk-taking, but understanding human error creates a multiplier effect. If technology and data are the levers for better performance, reducing human error is the multiplier; the answer is harder than it seems!

Dr Gawande explains it well: 'You can do better. You don't have to be a genius. You have to be diligent. It takes moral clarity. It takes ingenuity. Most importantly, it takes a willingness to try'.

The aforementioned cognitive risk framework was created to begin exploring the answers to these basic questions and provide a pathway for more complex risk methodologies. Cognitive governance is an unconventional approach to oversight by senior managers and risk professionals. Cognitive governance includes five disciplines:

- Risk governance separates risk management and risk assessment tasks;
- Risk perception aims to understand the different views and perceptions of risk that hinder risk governance;
- Human element design addresses cognitive load, situational awareness, and human–machine interactions;
- Intelligence and modelling focus on business performance, efficiency, security, and risk; and
- Capital structure relates to adjusted returns on capital and capital exposures due to oblique legal and contractual obligations.

Cognitive governance is designed to expose the blind spots and inefficiencies that exist in all organisations that view risk management as a distinct distinction from strategy. An overly simplified example of cognitive governance used by J.P. Morgan involved the development of a machine learning algorithm, COIN (contractual intelligence), to do in seconds what took 360,000 hours each year for lawyers and loan officers.

On the other hand, most organisations lack the resources to invest in artificial intelligence but can still benefit from a focus on cognitive governance through the

[9]Atul Gawande is an American surgeon, writer, and researcher in public health.

simplification process. Simplification is a discovery process to uncover the risks that lie hidden in complexity.

Instead of starting with an answer, like traditional risk frameworks, a cognitive risk framework focuses on asking better, yet unanswered, questions. To fully explain cognitive governance, we need to break down the five principles of cognitive governance and demonstrate how the rest of the pillars are guided and informed by its principles.

> Many cognitive psychologists see the brain as a computer. But each brain is absolutely individual, both in its development and in the way it meets the world. (Gerald Edelman[10])

Cognitive Risk Detection, Cognitive Ability, and Risk Aversion[11]

> The challenge of cognitive science is to link our consensual reality to our internal reality, but the challenge of physics is to link our consensual reality to our external reality. (Max Tegmark[12])

In today's technology landscape, access to data and media is ubiquitous and instantaneous and can spread like wildfire. More than ever, brand perception is critical and can change very quickly. What if it was possible to receive an early warning about third-party behaviour that could compromise the supply system or information about threats that could harm the brand's reputation? It's about analysing how cognitive risk detection capabilities give an overview of all this.

- **Stay ahead of emerging events**
  To address urgent issues and critical threats, an organisation needs the ability to collect and analyse large amounts of external data. This is exactly what cognitive risk detection offers. It allows:

  - Interpret signals more effectively – both threats and opportunities;
  - Understand the potential impact on the organisation;
  - Improve the quality of information by integrating internal organisation data as required; and
  - Make informed decisions for the organisation.

---

[10]Gerald Maurice Edelman (1929–2014) was an American biologist.

[11]See https://www2.deloitte.com/us/en/pages/risk/solutions/cognitive-risk-sensing.html and https://www.cambridge.org/core/journals/judgment-and-decision-making/article/cognitive-ability-and-risk-aversion-a-systematic-review-and-meta-analysis/7FE14959 6B97B7B3F6C56E045A9DBE2D.

[12]Max Tegmark is a Swedish-born cosmologist at the Massachusetts Institute of Technology, a quote from Our Mathematical Universe: My Quest for the Ultimate Nature of Reality.

Cognitive risk detection can help an organisation analyse available data around the world to better anticipate emerging events and obtain the information needed to forecast risks.

- **Cognitive risk field detection**
  In practice, the detection of cognitive risk follows three axes:

  → *Quantification and prioritisation of risks for a consumer products company*
  How could a reputation incident affect the brand of a multinational consumer products company? To achieve this, our risk detection platform provided information about the company's products, services, marketing campaigns, and operations. This has allowed the organisation to become more agile and proactive in prioritising related emerging risks. A framework has also been created to financially quantify the impact of sales on reputation risk in various high-impact scenarios.
  → *Third-party risk management for a life sciences company*
  A life sciences multinational was looking for more detailed risk information from its third parties and suppliers. Deloitte Risk & Financial Advisory selected thousands of suppliers. It now provides real-time continuous monitoring of third-party risk to help the company proactively identify entity-specific risk events.
  → *Detect the global external environment for a catering company*
  For a global retail/food service company, getting information on emerging product safety, potential supply chain disruptions and regulatory risk is a top priority. To support operational excellence, cognitive risk detection is used worldwide to monitor external factors that could impact the supply, delivery, and consumption of the company's products.

One question remains about the choice of managers and leaders: are very intelligent people less risk averse? Over the past two decades, researchers have argued that there is a negative relationship between cognitive ability and risk aversion. Although many studies confirm this, the link between cognitive ability and risk aversion has not been consistently observed.

In conclusion, the current meta-analysis provides strong evidence of a significant but weak negative relationship between cognitive ability and risk aversion in the area of earnings. However, no significant relationship was found in the mixed domain or loss domain, suggesting that the relationship is domain specific. Importantly, there were no significant gender differences in earnings and losses. Furthermore, none of the moderator variables studied in this study consistently influenced the relationship between cognitive ability and risk aversion in all three domains. Future research should aim to better understand the relationship between cognitive ability and risk aversion using more reliable measures to elicit risk preferences.

> We need to recognize our own behavioural errors. To be honest, you are not likely to become a cognitive Zen master anytime soon.

> But a little illumination could prevent you from making common placement mistakes. (Barry Ritholtz[13])

Fuzzy Logic Cognitive Maps in Systems Risk Analysis[14]

> The human brain functions as a binary computer and can only analyze zeros and zeros based on exact information (or black and white). Our heart is more like a chemical computer that uses fuzzy logic to analyze information that cannot be easily defined by zeros or zeros. (Naveen Jain[15])

The modern world relies on sophisticated human systems and new technologies to make decisions in the face of uncertainty. As a result, decision-makers attempt to control the risks that arise from the complexity of these systems when making decisions. Risk exposure is inevitable in areas such as management, engineering, medicine, etc.

Decision-makers use techniques to assess potential risks as part of the risk assessment and to analyse the causes and effects associated with them. Therefore, a variety of qualitative and quantitative techniques have been developed and applied in various sciences and industries. However, the complexity of a technique to analyse the relationships between risks and risk factors, the time of analysis, the level of robustness, and the reliability of risk analysis techniques are potential characteristics to be considered.

Meanwhile, fuzzy cognitive maps can simultaneously analyse risk-based factors in a system, taking into account the causal relationships between them. An Risk Transfer Committee (RTC) can therefore be used as an effective decision-making tool in systems risk analysis and management. Time can be saved by using Credit Conversion Factor (CCF) methods, especially in modelling complex systems when many variables interact, and there are restrictions with expert interactions. RTCs assist decision-makers considering cognitive mechanisms that influence risk management decision-making and provide corrective and preventive actions to improve system performance.

Other characteristics of the CCF method are to:

- model complex systems with limited and missing data or in the case of high costs for data collection;
- display what can happen in the system due to causal relationships and their initial states; and

---

[13]Barry Ritholtz is an American author, newspaper columnist, blogger, equity analyst, IT director and co-founder of Ritholtz Wealth Management, and guest commentator on Bloomberg Television.

[14]See file:///d:/Users/LOUISOT/Downloads/s40747-020-00228-2.pdf.

[15]Naveen Jain is an Indian-American business executive, entrepreneur, founder, and former CEO of InfoSpace.

- reduce reliance on expert opinions over the majority of decision-making techniques.

Therefore, in the field of system risk analysis, the current and future states of a system can be analysed and predicted using fuzzy logic as well as other analyses and scenario execution techniques. In other words, the application of the CCF method allows decision-makers to monitor the future state of the system through the technique of creating scenarios and using learning algorithms as well as analysing its current state. Moreover, this method allows decision-makers to identify preventive or corrective measures to control the negative effects of risks.

Thus, the identification of the characteristics of the CCF and how to implement this method in the treatment of various problems in the field of risk analysis such as decision-making, modelling, and forecasting can demonstrate how useful a tool this method is.

In recent decades, several researchers, in particular Papageorgiou, Salmeron, Groumpos, and Stylios, and their research groups have developed CCF and learning algorithms with different applications. Their attempts have led many research groups to develop and apply RTCs in various fields. The main synthesis articles on RTCs are described below.

One of the first synthesis articles on Marginal Cost of Funds (MCF) was carried out by Stach et al. is a study of algorithms designed to improve the accuracy of causal relationship weights and map structure. In other words, the main objective of this study was to study MCF learning algorithms and classify them into two categories, including Hebbian Learning Rule-Based Methods and Genetic Algorithm (GA), which is one of the population-based algorithms. In the following, Papageorgiou examined research that represented and developed learning algorithms related to RTCs. They classified them into three population-based groups, Hebbian, and hybrid algorithms. Papageorgiou reviewed research on FCM's trends and applications over a decade. They attempted to describe the growing trend of FCM's applications to improve its applicability in various areas. In addition, Papageorgiou and Salmeron studied studies with applications of FCM in different fields over a decade.

Historical data and expert opinions can be used to draw fuzzy cognitive maps (CCF). In a computed CCF, time series data are used as input, and a neural network is used to approximate the weights of a map. This opinion is categorised into automated and semi-automated groups. The semi-automated category is often used to draw a map. Within this category, certain inputs are required to derive an RTC that arises from the knowledge and experience of an expert in the related field.

As a result, concepts and causal relationships between them can be drawn. In the automated category, the numerical vectors are converted into fuzzy sets, which are introduced by Zadeh, and the degree of similarity between the vectors and the type of relationship (direct and inverse) between them is determined using fuzzy logic. To determine the weight of relationships based on the similarity between vectors related to the two concepts studied, the relationships presented in the research of Schneider et al. are used, in which, the way of approaching direct and inverse relations was distinguished from each other.

The type of automated drawing is based solely on historical data and does not require human inference. Since RTCs can model a variety of simple and complex systems with an infinite number of concepts and links, they have become a useful tool in modelling; therefore, a variety of RTCs has been developed. After drawing the MCFs, the accurate estimation of the map weights is a very important problem. Expert opinions are the basis of most RTCs. Human knowledge is an important tool in the process of designing different types of maps, but in some situations, there is no expert opinion or the opinions expressed are subjective and imprecise. In addition, there could be many more variables and components. Therefore, it is necessary to present a mechanism to address these issues.

Learning algorithms can be supervised or unsupervised; these algorithms have different training patterns, in supervised algorithms, labelled patterns are used, and in unsupervised algorithms, unlabelled patterns are used. Learning algorithms are divided into four categories: hybrid algorithms based on Hebbian, population-based algorithms, and other algorithms. Each category has its characteristics and consists of certain algorithms.

Finally, based on the development of cognitive sciences, CCF has been developed and used in various scientific fields, particularly over the last decade. One of the main applications of RTCs is in the risk-included systems. Therefore, this study focused on RTC applications in the risk area based on the concepts of failure, accident, incident, hazard, risk, error, and defect. From the review of studies of different risk-based concepts using RTCs, it appears that this method is a useful tool for solving complex risk-based problems in a wide range of areas.

Most of the CCF applications in systems risk analysis have been performed to solve these problems in the fields of engineering, medicine, and management sciences. RTCs can help researchers analyse and prioritise risk-based concepts in the form of decision-making, modelling, analysis, prediction, systematic learning, classification, and a combination of these concepts. According to the results of this study, decision-making is the most used application, when decision-makers are faced with a risk-based problem.

In short, by simultaneously examining past research and the applicability of the CCF method to real-world problems, it can be said that future studies will focus on both engineering and medical fields, as well as management issues. Specifically, because of the importance of analysing potential risks in the industry sector and evaluating medical failures, these areas will be of interest to more researchers. On the other hand, most of the issues raised in these areas have a decision-making character in which economic or political decision-makers attempt to provide preventive actions by simulating and analysing the system to reduce the imposed cost of certain risks and failures.

To do this, it is proposed to take into account uncertainty in the definition of concepts and the causal relationships between them and to maintain this uncertainty until reaching the final result of the model through the development of learning algorithms in the fuzzy logic approach.

> Elementary schools do things well in the first place - they are multidisciplinary and use fuzzy logic, and you do and do things.

> The same goes for doctoral studies. You enter as a question mark and leave as a question mark. (Ken Robinson[16])

Where Does Risk Management Go in the Age of Cognitive Science and Cindynics?[17]

> Intolerance of uncertainty and ignorance stems not only from pride, but from a universal human desire to find meanings and patterns everywhere. The mind hates the void. (John Elster[18])

As a result of successive financial frauds, Sarbanes-Oxley, in 2002, required 'independent auditors' of public companies to report to an audit committee that generally includes at least one 'financial expert'. Nevertheless, the audit committee alone cannot anticipate or respond to all the risks faced by a contemporary organisation. 'It seems clear that today the Crown corporation too often fails to identify and manage the risks it faces' (Ramirez & Simkins, 2008), which historically leads to a lack of confidence in corporate risk management functions.

In a critical study of enterprise-wide corporate governance and risk management, researchers at Loyola University Chicago, School of Law (Ramirez & Simkins, 2008), identify barriers to effective board governance and, specifically, address systemic gaps in the current legal framework that do not facilitate effective risk management across the organisation. 'Historically, risk management in U.S. companies has not inspired confidence. Human resource management also poses risks for businesses'.

Global and integrated ERM emerged in the 1990s and has continued to grow in importance, although it has not yet been systematically adopted. Too often, business risk management continues to be carried out in silos and fragmented between the various components of an organisation. The COSO (sponsoring organisations committee)[19] is widely recognised for defining the MERA. COSO ERM even in its 2017 version is intentionally broad with a foundation built on internal controls over financial reporting and strategic risks.

Other organisations, such as the Casualty Actuarial Society (CAS),[20] provide a narrow definition of ERM that encompasses processes that result in increased value creation for stakeholders. These two divergent views represent a lack of consensus on the Technical Risk Assessment (TRA) as well as the fact that there is no

---

[16]Ken Robinson is a British author, speaker, and education expert known for his contributions to the development of creativity and innovation.

[17]For the conclusion, see https://papers.ssrn.com/sol3/papers.cfm?abstract_id=3952818.

[18]Jon Elster, a Norwegian philosopher and sociologist, his work focuses on analytical Marxism and rational choice theory, a quote from Explaining Social Behavior: More Nuts and Bolts for the Social Sciences.

[19]COSO. (n.d.). https://www.coso.org/.

[20]Casualty Actuarial Society. (2023, September 1). Casualty actuarial society. https://www.casact.org/.

single approach that consistently addresses risk profiles across industry types or business models. Neither of these TRA definitions has sufficiently advanced the practice of risk.

Finally, the COSO ERM updated its risk management framework guidelines in 2017, removing the familiar COSO cube and replacing it with principle-based guidelines. ISO 31000 revised its guidelines in 2018, which included risk assessment techniques updated in 31010:2019. In 2018, the NIST Cyber-Security Framework (CSF) was updated to reflect new findings in field security practice. This study did not examine the ISO and NIST standards. The COSO ERM guidelines were progressive and did not reflect the necessary conceptual upgrades. It remains to be seen whether 15 years is sufficient to assess whether COSO ERM, ISO 31000, and NIST as well as other compliance and risk verification programmes have proven effective in practice.

While the hybrid phase of Industry 4.0, the fourth industrial revolution, continues to emerge, researchers and risk professionals must begin to adopt more advanced risk management methods that encompass a multidisciplinary approach to risk that should include virtual risks, human risk factors, scientific methods of risk analysis, and cyber-security. Indeed, the human element in risk management is now clearly identified as the bottleneck in progress in practice.

The baby boom generation of risk professionals has not been required to acquire the skills of modern risk professionals in science, the military, or any other discipline where risk has a significant impact. However, the operational risks, human error, and technological complexity of cyber-security require a more rigorous approach to training and applying risk management. The COVID-19 pandemic illustrates the vulnerability of cognitive ability to manage asymmetric risks. Machine learning algorithms, devices connected to the Internet of Things, and increased fragility in an Internet-based economy will expose the lack of preparedness that has been hidden by a lack of transparency in bad risk practices.

The hyperspace of danger model developed in 1984 by George-Yves Kervern[21] remains almost 40 years later a carrier of openings for the systematic consideration of socio-cultural and human factors; however, it remains too little implemented in the field despite its appearance as an appendix to ISO 31010. However, the combination of the identification of stakeholder networks and deficits in the framework proposed by ISO 31000 should provide answers to the shortcomings of standards and models identified by cognitive sciences. A development on the contribution of cindynics is attached in the appendix will allow the reader to appreciate its contribution to the development of a new global and integrated risk management.

> Because, after all, how do we know that two and two make four? Or that the force of gravity works? Or that the past is immutable? If the past and the outside world exist only in the mind, and the mind itself is controllable – what then? (Orwell, 1984, p. 80)[22]

---

[21]See Appendix 4.

[22]Orwell, G. (2021). 1984 – George Orwell. Harrap's.

Appendix 4: Brief Overview of the Cindynics

During the 1990s, the first studies using the iceberg concept to define the cost of risk were published as part of the:

- General Electric (GE) in the United States' Six Sigma programme, to calculate the total cost of additional work to address manufacturing quality deficiencies (the Six Sigma method addresses the entire Iceberg); and
- 'Safety and Health Executive' of London, for calculating the total cost of accidents at work.

The ability to estimate a total cost for accidents or disasters is an essential element to justify the allocation of resources, particularly financial, for prevention, protection, risk engineering, and more generally risk management. Is this an important factor in determining the budgets to be allocated to prevent or contain future pandemics or other natural or technological disasters? For the health sector, it is also a way to raise public awareness of its role in creating a safer society and to improve the perception of risk in the public domain, even in France the problem of white plans.

Any strategic process begins with describing the organisation's situation in context. The situation emerges from a list of networks of stakeholders involved in sustainable development. While the description must be holistic, different models propose such an approach including what is known as cindynics.

Some trace the first step in cindynics[1] to the earthquake in Lisbon. Science starts where beliefs fade. The earthquake in Lisbon in 1755 was the source of one of the most famous battle between Voltaire and Jean-Jacques Rousseau. The main result was the affirmation that mankind was to refuse fate. This is reflected in Bernstein[2] comment 'Risk is not a fate but a choice'.

---

[1]Cindynics was forged from the Greek Word Kindunos which means hazard, is the science of danger.

[2]Bernstein, P. L. (1996). *Against the gods: The remarkable story of risk.* John Wiley & Sons.

Enterprise Risk Management in Today's World, Part A:
Enterprise-Wide Risk Management and Strategy, 205–215
Copyright © 2024 by Jean-Paul Louisot and Simon Grima
Published under exclusive licence by Emerald Publishing Limited
doi:10.1108/978-1-83797-406-120241019

In a way, the Lisbon episode may well be the first public manifestation of what is essential in managing risks: a clear refusal of passively accepting 'fate', a definite will to actively forge the future through domesticating probabilities, thus reducing the field of uncertainty.

However, since the financial crisis of 2008, black swans or fat tails represent a major challenge to all professionals in charge of the management of an organisation. The traditional approaches to identifying and quantifying uncertainties based on probability or trend analysis are at a loss in a world that changes fast and may be subject to unexpected, and sometimes unsuspected ruptures.

These 'dangerous or hazardous' situations can develop into opportunities or threats depending on how the leadership can anticipate them and exploit them for the benefit of their organisation and its growth in a resilient society. Human factors are a key factor in the anticipation and development of such situations.

Although decision-makers must learn to decide under uncertainty, it is far from sufficient to prepare for the black swans. Furthermore, system safety approaches that consider the human component as a physical element fall short of taking into account the fact that humans are part of a complex system that they influence and try to change to their benefit, even through observation.

In such a volatile situation, the concepts developed as early as the late 1980s could prove very valuable if properly used and translated into practical tools, whereas they may appear at first as too conceptual for experience. The concepts of 'cindynic situation' and 'hyperspace of danger' allow for the identification of divergences between groups of stakeholders in a given situation and thus allow anticipating 'major uncertainties' and working on them to reduce their likelihood and/or their negative consequences (threats) while enhancing the positive consequences (opportunities).

This scientific approach to perils and hazards was initiated in December 1987 when a conference was called at the UNESCO Palace. Many industrial sectors were in a state of shock after major catastrophes like Chernobyl, Bhopal, and Challenger. They offered an open field for experience and feedback loops. Since then, the cindynics have continued to grow through teaching in many universities in France and abroad. The focal point is a conference organised every other year. Many efforts have been concentrated on axiology and attempts at objective measures. Before his death in December 2008, G.-Y. Kervern reviewed the presentation that follows (see Bibliography) in the light of the most recent developments in cindynics through the various conferences, until September 2008. I tried to continue on the same path, hence the paragraphs on pandemics.

1. Basic Concepts

The first one is the concept of 'cindynic situation' that requires a formal definition. This in turn can be understood only in the light of what constitutes a peril and hazards study. According to the modern theory of description, a hazardous situation can be defined only if the field of the 'hazard study' is identified by:

- Limits in time (life span);
- Limits in space (boundaries);

- Limits the actors' networks involved; and
- The perspective of the observer studying the system.

At this stage of the development of the sciences of hazard, the perspective can follow five main dimensions:

- *First dimension – memory, history – statistics (a space of statistics)*

It consists of all the information contained in the data banks of the large institutions' feedback from experience (electricity of France power plants, AIR France flights incidents, forest fires monitored by the Sophia Antipolis Center of the Ecole des Mines de Paris, claims data gathered by insurers and reinsurers).

- *Second dimension – representations and models drawn from the facts – epistemic (a space of models)*

It is the scientific body of knowledge that allows anticipating possible effects using physical, chemical principles, material resistance, propagation, contagion, explosion, and geo-cindynic principles (inundation, volcanic eruptions, earthquakes, landslides, tornadoes, and hurricanes, for example).

- *Third dimension – goals and objectives – teological (a space of goals)*

It requires a precise definition by all the actors and networks involved in the cindynic situation of their reasons for living, acting, and working.

In truth, this is an arduous and tiresome task to express why humans act as they act and what motivates humankind. However, it is only too easy to identify an organisation that 'went overboard' only because it lacked a defined target. For example, there are two common objectives for risk-management 'survival' and 'continuity of customer (public) service'. These two objectives lead to fundamentally different cindynic attitudes. The organisation, or its environment, will have to harmonise these conflicting goals. It is what we call a 'social transaction', which is hopefully democratically solved.

- *Fourth dimension – norms, laws, rules, standards, deontology, compulsory or voluntary, controls, etc. – deontological (a space of rules)*

It is all the normative set that makes life possible in a given society. For example, the need for a road code was felt as soon as there were enough automobiles to make it impossible to rely on the courtesy of each driver: the code is compulsory and makes driving on the road reasonably safe and predictable. The rules for behaving in society, like how to use a knife or a fork when eating, are aimed at reducing the risk of injuring one's neighbour as well as a way to identify social origins.

On the other hand, there are situations in which the rules are not yet clarified. For example, skiers on the same track may be of widely different expertise thus endangering each other. In addition, some use equipment not necessarily compatible with the safety of others (cross-country sky and mono-ski, etc.). How to conduct a serious analysis of accidents in skiing domains? Should experience-drawn codes be enforced? But can rules be defined if objectives are not defined beforehand? Should we promote personal safety or freedom of experimentation?

- *Fifth dimension – value systems – axiological (a space of values)*

It is the set of fundamental objectives and values shared by a group of individuals or other collective actors (stakeholders) involved in a cindynic situation. As an illustration, when our ancestors declared that 'the motherland is in danger', during World War 2, for example; the word motherland, or 'patria' (hence the word patriot), meant the shared heritage that, after scrutiny, can be best summarised in the fundamental values shared. The integrity of this set of values may lead the population to accept heavy sacrifices. When the media use the word apocalyptic or catastrophic, they often mean a situation in which our value system is at stake.

These five dimensions or spaces can be represented on a five-axis diagram, and the resulting diagram is a representation of the 'hyperspace of danger' (Fig. A4).

In combining these five dimensions, these five spaces, one can identify some traditional fields of study and thinking.

- Combining facts (statistics) and models gives the feedback loop crucial to most large corporations' risk managers.
- Combining objectives, norms, and values leads to practical ethics. Social workers have identified in this domain, authority functions. These functions are funded on values that board the objectives and define norms that they enforce hereafter. If there is no source of authority to enforce the norms, daily minor breaches will lead to major breaches and soon the earth will return to a primitive jungle.

This new extended framework provides a broader picture that allows visualising the limitations of the actions too often conducted with a narrow scope. Any hazard study can be efficient only if complete, i.e. extended to all the actors and networks involved in the situation. Then, the analysis must cover all of the five dimensions identified above.

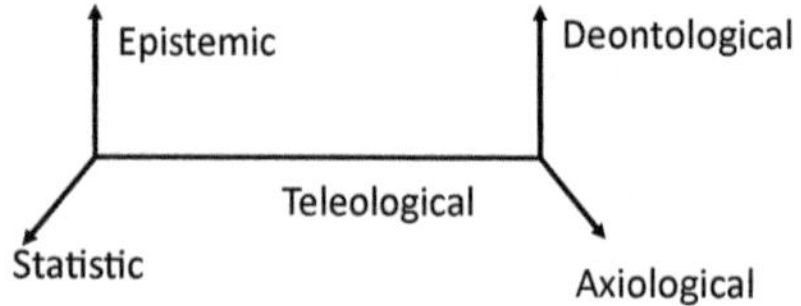

Fig. A4. The Hyperspace of Danger.

2. Dysfunctions

The first stage of a diagnostic to be established as described above consists in identifying the networks and their state in the five dimensions or spaces of the cindynic model. The next step will be to recognise the incoherencies or dissonances between two or several networks of actors involved in a given situation. These dissonances must be analysed from the point of view of each of the actors. It is therefore necessary to analyse dissonances in each dimension and between the dimensions.

In this framework, the risk control instrument we call prevention is aimed at reducing the level of hazard in any situation. In a social environment, for example, some actors may feel that an 'explosion is bound to occur'. This is what will be called the cindynic potential.

The potential is increasing with the dissonances existing between the various networks in the five spaces. A prevention campaign will apply to the dissonances, an attempt at reducing them without trying to homogenise all five dimensions for all the actors. A less ambitious goal will be to try to install in each dimension between all the actors' networks a 'minimum plate-form' for a common life. In other words, it is essential to find:

- Figures, facts, or data, accepted by the various actors as a statistical truth,
- Some models, as a common body of knowledge;
- Objectives that can be shared by the various actors;
- Norms, rules, or deontological principles that all may accept to abide by; and
- Values, to which all may adhere, like solidarity, no exclusion, transparency, and truthfulness.

The starting point is to establish a list of points of agreement and points of disagreement. Agreeing on what divides is essential. The definition of these minimum plate-forms is the result of lengthy negotiations between the various actors' networks and most often one particular network that acts as a catalyst or mediator. It is the coordinator of the prevention campaign for the entire situation.

The 'defiance' between two networks, face to face, has been defined as a function of the dissonances between these two networks following the five dimensions. Establishing trust and confidence, i.e. a trusting relationship, will require reducing the dissonances through negotiations, which will be the chore of the prevention campaign. This process can be illustrated by three examples:

- *Family systemic therapy*: Dr Catherine Guitton[3] focalised her approach to dissonances between networks:
  → The family seeking therapeutic help; and
  → The family reunited with the addition of two therapists.

[3]Dr Catherine Guitton, Psychiatrist, Hôpital Psychiatrique Paul Guiraud, Villejuif (France).

When healing is reached on the patient pointed to by the family, the result was obtained thanks to a work on the dissonances rather than a direct process on the patients themselves.

- *Adolescents and violence*: Dr M. Monroy's[4] research demonstrates that violence typically found in the 15–24 age group is related to a tear, a disparity along the five dimensions. This system can be divided into two subsystems between which a tremendous tension builds up.
  - → The traditional family with its set of facts, models, goals, norms, and values;
  - → An antagonistic unit conceived by the adolescent, opposed, often diametrically and violently, to the 'family tradition'.

These dissonances can lead the adolescent to a process of negotiation and aggression with violent phases in which he will play his trump card, his own life. From this may stem aggressions, accidents, and even, sometimes, fatal solutions of this process of scission, specific to adolescence.

- *The case of the sects*: It is in this process of scission that the success of some sects in attracting an adolescent following may be found. Their ability to conceal from the adolescents their potential dangers comes from the fact they sell them a ready-made 'turn-key' hyperspace. The kit, involving all five dimensions, is provided when the adolescent is ripe. As a social dissident, the adolescent needs personal equipment in all five dimensions.

Violence in the sects stems from the fact that the kit thus provided is sacred. The sacredness prevents any questioning of the kit. Any escape is a threat to the sacredness of the kit. Therefore, it must be repressed through violence, including brainwashing and/or physical abuse or destruction, as fit any totalitarian regime that has become master in large-scale violence.

In a book on the major psychological risk (see Bibliography) where the danger genesis in the family is analysed according to the cindynic framework, Dr M. Monroy tries to grasp all the situations involved by numbering all the actors involved in most of these situations.

- Network I: Family;
- Network II: Friends and peers;
- Network III: Schooling and professional environment;
- Network IV: Other risk takers or stakeholders (bike riders, drug users, delinquents);
- Network V: Other networks embodying political and civilian society (sources of norms, rules, and values);
- Network VI: Social workers and therapists.

---

[4]Dr Michel Monroy La société défensive (French Edition), PUF, Paris (15 Feb 2003).

This list of standard networks allows spotting the dissonances between them that build the cindynic potential of the situation. In the case of exposures confronting an organisation, an analysis of the actors' networks according to the five dimensions facilitates the identification of the deficits specific to the situation. For example, the distances between what is and what should be provided an insight into what changes a prevention campaign should bring about. These deficits should be identified through a systemic approach to hazardous situations. It can be:

- Total **lack** of a dimension or even several (no data available).
- Inadequate content of a dimension (an objective such as `let us have fun').
- Degeneration, most often a disorder, of a dimension (Mafia model in Russia).
- **Blocking** in a plan combining two dimensions:
  - **Blocking** of feedback from experience (dimensions statistics and models).
  - Ethical **Blocking** of authority functions ensures that rules are respected in the social game (dimensions norms and values).
- Disarticulated hyperspace in the five dimensions creates isolation and an absence of cohesiveness between the dimensions (fiefdoms **dividing** a corporation).

These deficits always appear in reports by commissions established to inquire about catastrophes. It is striking to realise how all these reports' conclusions narrow down to a few recurring explanations.

How do these situations change? Situations with their dissonances and their deficits 'explode' naturally unless they change slowly under the leadership of a prevention campaign manager.

In the first case, non-intentional actors of change are involved. The catastrophic events taking place bring about a violent and sudden revision of the content of the five dimensions among the networks involved in the 'accident'. Usually, all five dimensions are modified, revised facts, new models, new goals, implicit or explicit, new rules, and new values.

In the second case, which all organisations should prefer, the transformer chooses to act as such. He is the coordinator of the negotiation process that involves all the various actors in the situation. Deficits and dissonances are reduced through 'negotiation' and 'mediation'. The cindynic potential is diminished so that it is lower than the trigger point (critical point) inherent to the situation.

3. General Principles and Axioms

Exchanges between different industrial sectors, cindynic conferences, and the research on complexity by Le Moigne[5] (University of Aix en Provence, derived

[5]Jean-Louis Le Moigne is a French specialist in systemic and constructivist epistemology.

from the Nobel Prize Herbert A. Simon[6]) have developed some general principles. The cindynic axioms explain the emergence of dissonances and deficits.

- *Cyndinyc Axiom 1 – Relativity*: The perception of danger varies according to each actor's situation (see cognitive risk). Therefore, there is no 'objective' measure of danger. This principle is the basis for the concept of situation.
- *Cindynic Axiom 2 – Convention*: The measures of risk (traditionally measured by the vector Frequency – Severity) depend on convention between actors.
- *Cindynic Axiom 3 – Goals dependency*: Goals are directly impacting the assessment of risks. The actors in the networks may have conflicting perceived objectives. It is essential to try to define and prioritise the goals of the various actors or stakeholders involved in the situation (insufficient clarification of goals is a current pitfall in complex systems).
- *Cindynic Axiom 4 – Ambiguity*: It states that there is always a lack of clarity in the five dimensions. It is a major task of prevention to reduce these ambiguities.
- *Cindynic Axiom 5 – Ambiguity reduction*: It states that accidents and catastrophes are accompanied by brutal transformations in the five dimensions. The reduction of the ambiguity (or contradictions) of the content of the five dimensions will happen when they are excessive. This reduction can be involuntary and brutal, resulting in an accident, or voluntary and progressive achieved through a prevention process.

The theories by Lorenz on chaos and Prigogine on bifurcations offer an essential contribution at this stage. It should be noted that this principle is in agreement with a broad definition of the field of risk management. It applies to any event generated or accompanied by a rupture in parameters and constraints essential to the management of the organisation.

- *Cindynic Axiom 6 – Crisis*: It states that a crisis results from a tear in the social cloth. This means a dysfunction in the networks of actors involved in a given situation. Crisis management consists of an emergency reconstitution of the networks. It should be noted that this principle is in agreement with the definition of a crisis as included here above and the principle of crisis management stated.
- *Cindynic Axiom 7 – Ago-antagonistic conflict*: It states that any therapy is inherently dangerous. Human actions and medications are accompanied by inherent dangers. There is always a curing aspect, reducing danger (cindynolitic), and an aggravating factor, creating new danger (cindynogenetic).

---

[6]Herbert Alexander Simon (June 15, 1916 – February 9, 2001) was among the founding fathers of several of today's important scientific domains, including artificial intelligence, information processing, decision-making, problem-solving, attention economics, organization theory, complex systems, and computer simulation of scientific discovery. He coined the terms bounded rationality and satisfying and was the first to analyze the architecture of complexity and to propose a preferential attachment mechanism to explain power law distributions (source: Wikipedia).

The main benefit of applying these principles is to reduce the time lost in fruitless unending discussions on:

- How accurate are the quantitative evaluations of catastrophes – Quantitative measures result from conventions, scales, or units of measures (Axiom 2), and
- Negative effects of proposed prevention measures – In any action, positive and negative impacts are intertwined (Axiom 7).

4. Perspectives

In a cindynic approach, hazards can be characterised by:

- Various actors' networks facing hazardous situations;
- The way they approach the whole situation;
- The structuring of these approaches following the five dimensions (statistics, models, objectives, norms, and values);
- The identification of 'dissonances' between the various actors' networks; and
- The deficits that impact the dimensions.

Dissonances and deficits follow a limited number of 'cindynic principles' that can be broadly applied. They also offer fruitful insights into measures to control exposures that impact the roots of the situation rather than, as is too often the case, and reducing only the superficial effects.

For nearly four decades now, the approach has been applied with success to technical hazards, Acts of God, and, more recently, psychological hazards in the family as in the city. It can surely be successfully extended to situations of violence (workplace, schools, neighbourhoods, etc.). In some situations, it will be necessary to revisit the seven principles to facilitate their use in some specific situations.

The objective is clear: Situations that could generate violence should be detected as early as possible, they should then be analysed thoroughly, and their criticality reduced and, if possible, eliminated.

Cindynics offer a scientific approach to understanding, acting, and improving. Thus, they offer an entirely new perspective to risk management professionals; they dramatically enlarge the scope of their action in line with the trend towards holistic or strategic risk management while providing an enriched set of tools for a rational action at the roots of danger.

5. Applying the Cindynic Approach to the COVID-19 Pandemic

Dr Hansen,[7] an expert in disaster medicine and a specialist in cindynics, explained the contribution of the cindynic approach to the 2019 coronavirus crisis from the beginning of the pandemic.

[7]See Coronavirus - Les apports de la cindynique, « science du danger » - https://www.esanum.fr/today/posts/coronavirus-les-apports-de-la-cindynique-science-du-danger

> Very little is known about the characteristics of this virus (tropism, virulence, contagiousness) and its short, medium? and long-term clinical consequences. Yet policy-makers must make strategic decisions to ensure the best possible balance between protecting the health of the population and preserving socio-economic activity. However, it is its characteristics that make it possible to model the behaviour of a given species of coronavirus.

At that time, the 900 confirmed cases of infection with 2019-nCoV (as of 25 January 2020) were mostly located in China in the city of Wuhan. Isolated cases were found in other Chinese cities and a dozen countries (Thailand, Singapore, Japan, the Republic of Korea, Vietnam, Taiwan, the United States, Mexico, France, etc.).

At this point, modelling of the virus' behaviour had not been shared. It seems that the reproductive rate or transmission rate (RT) – the number of secondary cases generated from a contagious individual – had not yet been determined with certainty. Later, the value of RT was found to be greater than 1, and in this case, each contaminated person is likely to contaminate several people. Otherwise, the epidemic will run out. This RT value varies over time, depending on the measures taken by the authorities or the immune status of the affected population. Influenza varies from 4 to 5 depending on the episodes.

Nor had the COVID-19 tropism been perfectly defined. What animal species are contaminated with humans? What organs are affected? What are the target cells? To answer this question, immunohistochemical markings of post-mortem samples on animals and deceased victims present on the Huanan South China Seafood Market were studied, but in mid-2022, no definitive conclusion was published.

The question of lethality is still not precisely determined. It seems that it is currently between 2% and 3% of symptomatic cases. However, the decline is not enough to be sure that this statistic is reliable. Finally, in January 2020, there were no cases of human-to-human contamination from 'imported' cases, so no autonomous secondary focus outside China. What will happen in the future?

In such a context, cindynics provide the art of asking the right questions. Cindynics study the evolution of situations to appreciate their propensity to move towards a more or less dangerous area. They do not simply calculate a probability or the supposed gravity of a situation, but they evaluate the character of the situation as 'terable' (which pierces, perforates). For this, they invite decision-makers, public or private, to evaluate their decisions through the five axes of questions related to the hyperspace of danger:

- **Data**: what facts do decision-makers want to share?
- **Models**: how do these decision-makers think their plan can be organised and work? What representations do they have of the stakes of this plan, and what representations do they want to transmit to their partners?
- **Rules**: what do the decision-makers of an action plan choose to impose?

- **Purposes**: what are the information/instructions/recommendations/instructions they provide?
- **Values**: what do they do it for? What guides the choice?

In the case of the pandemic, Dr Hansen suggested a list of the basic elements to be taken into consideration, the relevance of which is later seen:

- What will be the tolerance threshold of the French population to this epidemic, even if its overall mortality is finally three times less? (Knowing that she considers it 'normal' that influenza causes about 65,600 emergency room visits, 11,000 hospitalisations, 1,900 resuscitation admissions, and 290 deaths each year.)
- From how many cases of severe respiratory distress caused by the pandemic, will the management of the 5,700 resuscitation beds become a problem?
- At what rate will hospitals be unable to cope with the usual influx of patients?

Glossary (Essential Concepts in Risk Management)

- **Risk**[1] – Effect of uncertainty on objectives

Note 1: An effect is a deviation from the expected. It can be positive, negative, or both. Risk addresses both opportunities and threats.

Note 2: Objectives can have different aspects and categories and can be applied at different levels.

Note 3: Risk is usually expressed in terms of risk sources, potential events, their consequences, and their likelihood.

- **Stakeholder/interested party** – A person or organisation that can affect, be affected by, or perceive themselves to be affected by a decision or activity.
- **Risk source** – Element which alone or in combination has the potential to give rise to risk (3.1).
- **Event** – Occurrence or change of a particular set of circumstances.

Note 1: An event can be one or more occurrences and can have several causes and several consequences.

Note 2: An event can also be something that is expected which does not happen, or something that is not expected which does happen.

Note 3: An event can be a risk source.

- **Consequence** – Outcome of an event (3.5) affecting objectives

Note 1: A consequence can be certain or uncertain and can have positive or negative direct or indirect effects on objectives.

Note 2: Consequences can be expressed qualitatively or quantitatively.

Note 3: Initial consequences can escalate through cascading and cumulative effects.

---

[1]ISO 31000:2009 definition.

- **Likelihood** – Chance of something happening

Note 1: In risk management terminology, the word 'likelihood' is used to refer to the chance of something happening, whether defined, measured, or determined objectively or subjectively, qualitatively or quantitatively, and described using general terms or mathematically (such as a probability or a frequency over a given time span).

- **Control/treatment** – Measure that maintains and/or modifies risk

Note 1: Controls include but are not limited to any process, policy, device, practice, or other conditions and/or actions that maintain and/or modify risk.

Note 2: Controls may not always exert the intended or assumed modifying effect.

- **Risk management framework** – Its development encompasses integrating, designing, implementing, evaluating, and improving risk management across the organisation.
- **Risk management process** – It involves the systematic application of policies, procedures, and practices to the activities of communicating and consulting, establishing the context, and assessing, treating, monitoring, reviewing, recording, and reporting risk.

The preceding terms are derived from ISO31000:2018 standard.

- **Exposure**: *A*n exposure is defined by three elements, i.e. the financial consequences of a peril striking a given resource of the organisation, i.e.:

  - Object of risk;
  - Peril;
  - Consequences on objectives (financial and other consequences).

- **Risk management**: Risk management is a continuous process of making and carrying out decisions that will reduce to an acceptable level the impact or uncertainties of the exposures bearing on an entity.
- **Risk governance**: Governance refers to the actions, processes, traditions, and institutions by which authority is exercised and decisions are taken and implemented. Risk governance applies the principles of good governance to the identification, assessment, management, and communication of risks (*see International Risk Governance Council*).
- **Chief risk officer (CRO):** A chief risk officer is an executive responsible for identifying, analysing, and mitigating internal and external events that could threaten a company.

The chief risk officer works to ensure that the company is compliant with government regulations, such as Sarbanes-Oxley, and reviews factors that could negatively affect a company's activities.

CROs typically have post-graduate education with over 20 years of experience in accounting, economics, legal, or actuarial backgrounds. They are also referred to as chief risk management officers (CRMOs) (*see Investopedia*).

- **Loss prevention**: Reduce frequency/probability/likelihood through actions on the causes of risk.
- **Loss reduction:** Reduce severity/consequences/impact through actions on the consequences of risk.
- **Contractual risk transfer(for risk control):** A situation is deemed 'too risky' for an activity to be engaged in considering know-how, financial strength, and overall level of resources and transfer the activity to a partner, upstream, sub-contractor or supplier, or downstream, customer or partner.
- **Contractual transfer (for risk financing):** The transfer is aimed only at the financial impact of the exposure. The third party will not bear the legal responsibility of the exposure, but only all or part of its financial consequences should a loss occur falling within the scope of the contract, like in an insurance contract.

Bibliography

Bakhtavar, E., Valipour, M., Yousefi, S. et al. (2021). Fuzzy cognitive maps in systems risk analysis: a comprehensive review. *Complex & Intelligent Systems*, 7, 621 -637.

Barton, L. (1991). A case study in crisis management: The Perrier recall. *Industrial Management & Data Systems*, *91*(7), 6–8. https://doi.org/10.1108/02635579110007077

Bernstein, P. L. (1996). *Against the Gods. The remarkable story of risk.* John Wiley & Sons.

Bland, D. E. (2000). *Treasury risk.* Witherby & Co.

Bø, E., Hovi, I. B., & Pinchasik, D. R. (2023). COVID-19 disruptions and Norwegian food and pharmaceutical supply chains: Insights into supply chain risk management, resilience, and reliability. *Sustainable Futures*, *5*, 100102. https://doi.org/10.1016/j.sftr.2022.100102

Bone, J. (2019). *Cognitive governance: The first pillar of a cognitive risk framework – An alternative approach to cybersecurity and enterprise risk management.* https://www.corporatecomplianceinsights.com/cognitive-governance-risk-framework/

Bone, J. (2020). *A contextual model of a cognitive risk framework for enterprise risk management.* https://www.researchgate.net/publication/340176017_A_Contextual_Model_of_a_Cognitive_Risk_Framework_for_Enterprise_Risk_Management

Bone, J. (2021).*The biggest gap in ERM practice: The human element and the science of risk.* https://papers.ssrn.com/sol3/papers.cfm?abstract_id=3952818

Bradshaw, W. A. (1998) *Learning about risk. Choices, connections and competencies.* The Canadian Institute of Chartered Accountants.

Brown, A. (1980). *Cuthbert Heath: The maker of modern Lloyds.* David & Charles. ISBN 9780715379424.

Condamin, L., Loiusot, J.-P., & Naïm, P. (2006, December). *Risk quantification.* Wiley.

Daley, S. (2000, January 2). Huge storm damage in France. *The New York Times.* https://www.nytimes.com/2000/01/02/weekinreview/dec-26-jan-1-huge-storm-damage-in-france.html

Damghani, K. K., Taghavifard, M. T., & Moghaddam, T. (2009). *Decision making under uncertain and risky situations.* Tehran University.

Deliotte. (2019). *Cognitive risk sensing – Get the intelligence you need, when it matters most.* https://www2.deloitte.com/us/en/pages/risk/solutions/cognitive-risk-sensing.html

Donaldson, T., & Dunfee, T. W. (1999). *Ties that binds (a social contracts approach to business ethics).* Harvard Business School Press.

Dylan, E. (2012). *Risk intelligence.* Simon & Chuster, Inc.

Elms, D. (1998). *Owning the future. Integrated risk management in practice.* Center for Advanced Engineering – University of Canterbury Christchurch.

Garbolino, E., Chéry, J.P., Guarnieri, F. (2019). The Systemic Approach: Concepts, Method and Tools. In F. Guarnieri, E. Garbolino (Eds.), *Safety Dynamics. Advanced Sciences and Technologies for Security Applications* (pp. 1–30). Springer.

Harrington, S. E., & Niehaus, G. R. (1999). *Risk management and insurance* (8th ed.). Irwin & McGraw-Hill.

Holdeman, E. (2021, March 27). *A decade of disasters, 2000-2009.* GovTech. https://www.govtech.com/recovery/a-decade-of-disasters-2000-2009.html

Hosni, H. (2016). *Mathematical fuzzy logic in reasoning and decision making under uncertainty.* Dipartimento di Filosofia, Universita Degli Studi di Milano. http://www.filosofia.unimi.it/~hosni/

How to implement and sustain organisational change. (2018). McKinsey & Company. Home McKinsey Implementation. Podcast July 2018.

Kauffman, S. A. (1991). Anti-chaos and adaptation. *Scientific American*, *265*(2), 78–84.

Kervern, G.-Y. (1993a). FOCUS: Studying risks: The science of cindynics. *Business Ethics: A European Review*, *2*(3), 140–142. https://doi.org/10.1111/j.1467-8608.1993.tb00034.x

Kervern, G.-Y. (1993b). *La culture réseau (ethique et ecologie de l'entreprise)*. Editions ESKA.

Kervern, G.-Y. (1994). *Latest advances in cindynics*. Economica.

Kervern, G.-Y. (1995). *Éléments fondamentaux des cindyniques*. Economica.

Kervern, G.-Y. (2022). *Le mauvais génie face à la science du risque: Les Cindyniques*. [The evil genius in front of the risk science: The Cindynics.]

Kervern, G.-Y., & Boulenger, P. (2008). *Cindyniques concepts et mode d'emploi*. Economica.

Kervern, G.-Y., & Rubise, P. (1991). *L'archipel du danger. Introduction aux cindyniques*. Economica.

Klewes, J., & Wreschniok, R. (Eds.) (2009, November). *Reputation capital* (pp. 115–178). Springer Pleon. Three articles: Managing reputational risk – A cindynic approach; Managing reputational risk – Case studies; Managing reputational risk – From theory to practice.

Kunreuther, H., & Slovic, P. (1996). Science, Values, and Risk. Annals of the *American Academy of Political and Social Science, 545,* 116–125. https://doi.org/10.1177/000271629654500101

Lilleholt, L. (2023). *Cognitive ability and risk aversion: A systematic review and meta-analysis*. Published online by Cambridge University Press, January 1, 2023. https://www.cambridge.org/core/journals/judgment-and-decision-making/article/cognitive-ability-and-risk-aversion-a-systematic-review-and-meta-analysis/7FE149596B97B7B3F6C56E045A9DBE2D

Louisot, J.-P. (2014). *100 Questions pour comprendre la gestion des risques* (2nd ed.). AFNOR.

Louisot, J.-P., & Ketcham, C. (Eds.). (2009, September). *Enterprise-wide risk management: Developing and implementing*. IIA Malvern.

Louisot, J.-P., & Ketcham, C. (2014). *Enterprise risk management: Issues & cases*. Wiley.

Mandela, N. (1995). *Long walk to freedom: The autobiography of Nelson Mandela.* Abacus.

Ramirez, S., & Simkins, B. (2008). Enterprise-Wide Risk Management and Corporate Governance. *Business, Law, Economics - Loyola University of Chicago Law Journal.* https://www.semanticscholar.org/paper/Enterprise-Wide-Risk-Management-and-Corporate-Simkins-Ramirez/3b870fbab0f9e0e0641fcd3ce1a63531652c27e0

Sophie, G.-G., & Louisot, J.-P. (2014). *Diagnostic des risques* (2nd ed.). AFNOR.

The five pillars of a cognitive risk framework: Part II. https://dl.acm.org/doi/abs/10.1080/07366981.2016.1257219

Walker, B., Holling, C. S., Carpenter, S. R., & Kinzig, A. (2004). Resilience, adaptability, and transformability in social-ecological systems. *Ecology and Society*, *9*(2), 5.

Woods, D. D., & Wreathall, J. (2008). Stress-strain plots as a basis for assessing system resilience. *Resilience Engineering: Remaining Sensitive to the Possibility of Failure*, *1*, 145–161.

Wybo, J. (1998). *Introduction aux cindyniques*. ESKA.

Further Reading

The following documents have not been quoted in the text but are relevant for professionals embarking in a cognitive risk-management journey:

A cognitive risk framework for the 4th industrial revolution – Introducing the human element to risk management. https://www.corporatecomplianceinsights.com/a-cognitive-risk-framework-for-the-4th-industrial-revolution/

Berthet, V. *The impact of cognitive biases on professionals' decision-making: A review of four occupational areas.* https://www.frontiersin.org/articles/10.3389/fpsyg.2021.802439/full

Bone, J. *Five reasons a cognitive risk framework is superior to COSO's ERM framework.* https://grcindex.medium.com/five-reasons-a-cognitive-risk-framework-is-superior-to-cosos-erm-framework-46142942bb26

Bone, J. *Why COSO's internal control framework can't give you confidence.* https://grcindex.medium.com/why-cosos-internal-control-framework-can-t-give-you-confidence-645a3fd1001d

de-Juan-Ripoll, C., Giglioli, I. A. C., Llanes-Jurado, J., Marín-Morales, J., & Alcañiz, M. *Why do we take risks? Perception of the situation and risk proneness predict domain-specific risk taking.* https://www.frontiersin.org/articles/10.3389/fpsyg.2021.562381/full

Fuzzy cognitive maps in systems risk analysis: A comprehensive review. https://link.springer.com/article/10.1007/s40747-020-00228-2

Petrov, A., Thomas, J. Balduino, R., Allard, M., & Joshi, A. *Cognitive risk management – Business applications of NLP technology.* https://towardsdatascience.com/cognitive-risk-management-7c7bcfe84219

The biggest gap in ERM practice: The human element and the science of risk. https://papers.ssrn.com/sol3/papers.cfm?abstract_id=3952818

Index

www.ingramcontent.com/pod-product-compliance
Lightning Source LLC
Jackson TN
JSHW011917131224
75386JS00004B/230

* 9 7 8 1 8 3 7 9 7 4 0 7 8 *